LAS VEGAS HOME BOOK

"YOU USE A GLASS MIRROR TO SEE YOUR FACE; YOU USE WORKS OF ART TO SEE YOUR SOUL."

George Bernard Shaw

LAS VEGAS HOME BOOK

A COMPREHENSIVE HANDS-ON SOURCEBOOK TO BUILDING, REMODELING, DECORATING, FURNISHING AND LANDSCAPING A LUXURY HOME IN THE LAS VEGAS VALLEY

Photo courtesy of **Christopher Homes**
Photo by **Greg Cava Photography**

PUBLISHED BY

THE
ASHLEY
GROUP

Chicago New York Los Angeles

Las Vegas Philadelphia Atlanta Detroit

Arizona Southeast Florida Washington D.C. Colorado

San Francisco North Carolina Dallas/Fort Worth

San Diego Houston Boston Seattle

Kansas City Orange County Ohio Connecticut/Westchester County

LAS VEGAS HOME BOOK

Published By
The Ashley Group
7140 Industrial Road Suite 1000
Las Vegas, NV 89118
702-614-4960 fax 702-263-6596

Cahners

Cahners Business Information
A Division of Reed Elsevier Inc

ISBN 1-58862-036-0

Las Vegas HOME BOOK
Publisher *Shauna Lutz*
Editor-in-Chief *Dana Felmly*
Managing Editor *Laurence P. Maloney*
Senior Editor *James Scalzitti*
Assistant Editor *Alison M. Ishihara*
Writer *Carol White*
Office Manager *Angela Burton*
Regional Office Manager *Janet Durbin*
Account Executives *Starla Hagler, Sheree Jensen*
Group Production Director *Susan Lokaj*
Production Directors *Paul Ojeda, Catherine Wajer*
Production Manager *Kristen Axelson*
New Business Manager *Margaret S. Guzek*
Creative Director *Bill Weaver*
Senior Art Director *LN Vaillancourt*
Graphic Designers *W. Keel, Kelli Aylward*
Ad Service Coordinators *Sean Kealey*
Prepress *Cahners Prepress*
Printed in Hong Kong by *Dai Nippon Printing Co.*

THE ASHLEY GROUP
Group Publisher *Paul A. Casper*
Director of Publications *N. David Shiba*
Regional Director *Jeffrey R. Lewis*
Group Controller *Patricia Lavigne*
Group Administration *Nicole Port, Kimberly Spizzirri*

CAHNERS BUSINESS INFORMATION
President, Global Construction and Retail Division *David Israel*
Chief Financial Officer *John Poulin*
Executive Vice President *Ronald C. Andriani*
Vice President, Finance *David Lench*

Front Cover *Loerwald Construction, Photo by Jeffrey Green*
Back Cover *Sydni Jay Associates, Photo by Jeffrey Green*

Note

The premier edition of the **Las Vegas Home Book** was created like most other successful products and brands are - out of need. **The Home Book** concept was originally conceived by Paul Casper, currently Group Publisher of The Ashley Group. Paul, a resident of Chicago's North Shore, at one time was planning the renovation of his home. However, he quickly discovered problems locating credible professionals to help his dream become a reality. Well, Paul's dream did become a reality - it just happens to be a different dream now! Instead of Paul simply finishing his new home, he saw the need by consumers nationwide to have a complete home resource guide at their disposal. Thus, he created the distinct **Home Book** to fulfill consumers' needs for reliable and accessible home improvement information.

After three successful years, the **Home Book** drew the attention of Cahners Business Information. In April 1999, Cahners purchased it, and since then, the **Home Book** network has grown rapidly. By the end of 2001, there were Home Books in 14 markets nationwide. In addition to Las Vegas and Chicago, Home Books are available in Washington D.C., Detroit, South Florida, Colorado, Dallas/Fort Worth, Los Angeles, Atlanta, San Diego, Philadelphia, Arizona, New York and North Carolina. Within the next year, Home Books will be published in Houston, Seattle, Boston and Kansas City, among other cities.

Public demand for quality home improvement services continues to increase. The Ashley Group recognizes this trend, which is why we exact the same amount of dedication and hard work from ourselves that we expect from our **Home Book** advertisers. We hope our hard work rewards you with the quality craftsmanship you deserve, turning your dream house into a reality.

Congratulations on purchasing a **Home Book**.. Now reward yourself by kicking back and delving through its pages. We hope you enjoy the inspiring ideas within.

Dana Felmly *Editor-in-Chief*

Why
You Should
Use This
Book

Why You'll Want to Use the Las Vegas Home Book

At times, in this high-speed information-driven culture, we can easily become lost and disoriented. Where we find information, how we find it, and how credible this information is, has become critical to consumers everywhere.

The *Las Vegas Home Book* recognizes and addresses these concerns, and provides ease of use and comfort to consumers looking to build, renovate or enhance their home. As a consumer, the anxiety of searching for trustworthy, experienced housing professionals can be overwhelming.

Relief is in Sight

The *Las Vegas Home Book* puts an end to this stress. It offers you, the reader, a comprehensive, hands-on guide to building, remodeling, decorating, furnishing and landscaping a home in Las Vegas, and the surrounding areas. The book also offers readers convenience and comfort.

Convenience

The **Las Vegas Home Book** compiles the area's top home service providers with easy-to-read listings by trade. It also dissuades readers' fears of unreliable service providers by featuring many of the finest professionals available, specialists who rank among the top 10 of their respective fields in Philadelphia. Their outstanding work has netted them many awards in their fields. The other listings are recommendations made by these advertisers.

The goal of the **Las Vegas Home Book** creators is to provide a high quality product that goes well beyond the scope of mere Yellow Pages. Its focus is to provide consumers with credible, reliable, and experienced professionals, accompanied by photographic examples of their work.

This crucial resource was unavailable to the founders of the **Las Vegas Home Book** when they were working on their own home improvement projects. This lack of information spurred them on to create the book, and to assist other consumers in finding the proper professionals that suit their specific needs. Now, thanks to the team's entrepreneurial spirit, you have the **Las Vegas Home Book** at your fingertips, to guide you on your home enhancement journey.

Comfort

Embrace this book, enjoy it and relish it, because at one time it didn't exist; but now, someone has done your homework for you. Instead of running all over town, you'll find in these pages:

* More than 700 listings of professionals, specializing in 40 different trades.

* Instructional information for choosing and working with architects, contractors, landscapers and interior designers.

13

* More than 1,000 photos inspiring innovative interior and exterior modeling ideas.

* A compilation of the area's top home enhancement service providers with easy-to-read listings by trade.

Excitement...**The Las Vegas Home Book** can turn your dream into a reality!

Shanna Lutz

Las Vegas Home Book

About the Front Cover:
Enhanced with authentic touches, this imposing Tuscan home was custom-built by Loerwald Construction.

Contents

Continued

71

229

107

111

75

26

Las Vegas Home Book

About the Back Cover:
Impressive and sumptuous, this
Las Vegas interior was designed
by Sydni Jay Associates.

Contents

98

92

23

35

537

49

How To Use

TABLE OF CONTENTS

Start here for an at-a-glance guide to the 12 tabbed categories and numerous subcategories. The book is organized for quick, easy access to the information you want, when you want it. The Table of Contents provides an introduction to the comprehensive selection of information.

DESIGN UPDATE

Read what top home industry professionals think are the most exciting new styles, future trends and best ideas in their fields as we continue into the millennium. See even more inspiring photos of some of the Las Vegas Valley's most beautiful, up-to-date luxury homes and landscapes. It's a visual feast, full of great ideas.

TIMELINES

An innovative reference tool, TimeLines gives you an at-a-glance chance to see the step-by-step progression of a home project. The projects include the building of a custom home, the remodeling of a luxury home kitchen and bath, a multi-phase landscaping project, and the interior design of several rooms. The TimeLines appear as eight-page gatefolds with glossy pictures, clearly laid-out timelines and easy-to-read paragraphs.

"HOW-TO" ARTICLES

Each tabbed section begins with a locally researched article on how to achieve the best possible result in your home building, remodeling, decorating or landscape project. These pages help take the fear and trepidation out of the process. You'll receive the kind of information you need to communicate effectively with professionals and to be prepared for the nature of the process. Each article is a step-by-step guide, aiding you in finding the materials you need in the order you'll need them.

HOT DISTRICTS

An easy guide to a day of shopping in three of our city's hottest districts —West Las Vegas, Central Las Vegas and East Central Las Vegas. Use the Hot District maps and information to plan weekend shopping sprees to some of the liveliest centers for furniture, fabrics, accessories, art, antiques and more.

This Book

DIVIDER TABS

Use the sturdy tabs to go directly to the section of the book you're interested in. A table of contents for each section's subcategories is printed on the front of each tab. Quick, easy, convenient.

LISTINGS

Culled from current, comprehensive data and qualified through careful local research, the listings are a valuable resource as you assemble the team of experts and top quality suppliers for your home project. We have included references to their ad pages throughout the book.

FEATURES!

From Interior Design Spotlight to New in the Showroom, we've devoted attention to specific areas within the various sections. We've also gone in-depth, with feature articles in the Architects and Home Builders sections.

COST ESTIMATES

If you're wondering what costs you may incur while undertaking a home project, check out our sample cost estimates. From architecture to arts and antiques, we describe a project in each chapter and give a sample cost break down for each.

BEAUTIFUL VISUALS

The most beautiful, inspiring and comprehensive collections of homes and materials of distinction in the Las Vegas Valley. On these pages, our advertisers present exceptional examples of their finest work. Use these visuals for ideas as well as resources.

INDEXES

This extensive cross reference system allows easy access to the information on the pages of the book. You can check by alphabetical order or individual profession.

19

The
A
Grou

THE ASHLEY GROUP

The Ashley Group is the largest provider of home
quality designing, building, and decorating information and
For more on the many products of **The Ashley**
Cahners Business Information (www.cahners.com)
U.S. provider of business information to 16
manufacturing and retail. Cahners' rich content portfolio

RESOURCE COLLECTION

visual resource images and strives to provide the highest
resources available to upscale consumers and professionals.
Group, visit our website at <u>www.theashleygroup.com</u>.
a member of the Reed Elsevier plc group, is a leading
vertical markets, including entertainment,
encompasses more than 140 Websites as well as *Variety*,
market-leading business-to-business magazines.

Design

What are the hot ideas and attitudes that are shaping home
Read Design Update, where top local professionals t

BALANCING ACT
City Center Gallery: "With the new millennium in
full swing, we have witnessed a refreshing trend in
the art of balancing classic and contemporary design.
The meshing of these two styles creates a familiar
appeal while upholding a unique originality, resulting
in a style that can take you into the new century."

Update

eriors and landscapes in the Las Vegas Valley?
at's happening now and what's coming in the future.

NATURAL FINISHES

Ideal Supply Company: "Natural finishes have never been more popular. This is especially evident in the increased use of copper, nickel, bronze and wrought iron faucetry finishes. Currently popular is a unique pairing of wrought iron with a natural granite look."

ELEGANT UPGRADES

Cabinet West Distributors: "Current trends in cabinetry are moving toward affordable, one-of-a-kind offerings. Once, high-end glazed, rustic, distressed or antiqued finishes were only available at a premium price. Today's rich, lighter hues, when accented by glaze, give semi-custom lines and products a unique and elegant look. Fluted columns and hand-carved moldings are now also appearing on cabinetry as standard upgrade features."

SHADOW PLAY

A.K.A. Designs: "Today's residential windows are being dressed in increasingly creative ways. A popular trend is the use of custom metal windowscapes. This imaginative solution for difficult-to-dress window openings offers homeowners a bonus in the beautifully designed shadow it creates."

🅐 PERFECT COMPLEMENTS

Cottura:
"As a complement to today's Mediterranean, Southwest and Country décors, Renaissance-inspired Italian ceramic dinnerware, art and accessories continue in popularity. People are also setting eclectic tables by creatively mixing and matching complementary dinnerware designs."

HOMES IN HARMONY

Rio Décor Design & Fine Art: "The desire for healthy and harmonious living spaces has increased the popularity of Feng Shui, the ancient Chinese philosophy of balance in life. In interior design, Feng Shui is expressed by placing furnishings and art work in such a way that energy flows through the space in a manner that is smooth, free and harmonious. "

🅐

OUTDOOR ROOMS

Quality Masonry: "Today, stone and brick are everywhere. You can see its beauty in many cozy garden courtyards. The increasing number of outdoor rooms found in new homes confirm its popularity. Durable and maintenance-free, stone remains in style."

UNCONVENTIONAL FLOORING

rEvolution: "The new generation of homebuyers want flexible elements in their homes which are unique and easy to maintain. For homeowners who wish to marry innovation and function, unconventional flooring options are in demand. One such creative concept is painted concrete flooring, which can range in style from colorful and athletic to sleek and tranquil."

SENSUAL MOODS

Daniels West Interiors: "Today's homeowners want their rooms to have ambiance. To create a mood, they're adding color and special accessories. Even the smallest items, like scented candles, a sculptured candle holder, or floral or sensual fabric are being used to give environments a perfect alter ego."

Photo by **Audrey Dempsey**

FAUX FINISHES

Original Finishes: "The latest improvement in wall glazing is a new technique that highlights the darker tones in a paint application to lend character and glamour to walls and ceilings. This glaze, which can be applied to smooth or textured walls, is most dramatic when used with mid-tones and darker colors."

HOME WORKOUT

Pacific Fitness: "Most people hate to work out. But staying healthy and fit is not a chore when there is a personalized gym in the home. Today, fitness rooms are popular. They can be simple but modern, and many feature a variety of pieces, from treadmills to elliptical machines. Fitness rooms can also be accented with mirrored walls, a dry sauna or a racquetball court."

🅐

IMPROVED VISION

Abbotts Audio and Video:
"The latest marvel of TV technology - High Definition Television - has become more popular. HDTV offers an incredibly crisp image and a more panoramic screen size, thus allowing viewers to see more of what the director meant for them to see."

🅐 MARVELOUS MARBLE

Elite Tile:
"As more large, European styled homes are built, people are appreciating the feeling and class that an opulent marble floor can engender. With a wide variety of tone, color and pattern, each floor becomes a unique experience in itself. By using the stone's innate range of light to dark, each marble floor can be customized to accent any motif. Stone flooring conveys a sense of permanence, imperial power and stability."

29

Photo by **CHAWLA Associates**

WATER THERAPY

Tranquility Ponds: "In the Las Vegas area, the division between the inside and outside of the home is easily and delightfully blurred. As a result, water gardens have grown in popularity. Busy homeowners say they enjoy the soothing sound of a gentle waterfall at the end of a hectic day. They also enjoy the calming sight of birds bathing or fish playfully swimming by."

❹ UNEXPECTED GLASS

Glassic Art: "Glass has become an innovative product for areas never before considered. It is breathtaking in its new applications for traditional entry-ways, waterfalls and almost anything in the bathroom."

IMPROVED VIEWS

Sunbelt Windows and Doors: "Those who demand excellence in their homes are discovering a world of distinctive and technologically advanced windows and doors. As design elements, they can be fashioned to complement the most elegant and innovative architecture. As functional components, windows and doors can be used to control energy efficiency, illuminate interiors and create breathtaking views."

ARCHITECTURAL ELEMENTS RENAISSANCE

Realm of Design, Inc.: "There's a new renaissance in the world of architectural elements. This latest trend focuses on adapting the best in architectural design and finishes. Adding features such as columns and moldings to an entry way or fireplace surround can make a statement, convey a mood or create a sense of drama."

ELEGANT KITCHENS

Custom Cabinet Factory of New York: "Today's sophisticated homeowners desire sophisticated kitchens. Design may integrate commercial appliances with mahogany cabinetry adorned with tasteful moldings, ebony accents and stainless steel handles. Elegant, yet functional, today's kitchens are a dream for the cook and a pleasure when entertaining friends."

OUTDOOR LIVING

Dayton Masonry: "Outdoor living is popular with residents of the Las Vegas Valley. With some of the best weather in the United States, homeowners are focusing on making their outdoor living space as functional and appealing as the inside of their homes. We're seeing more patios, fireplaces, barbecues and waterfalls created to blend effortlessly into the outdoor surroundings. Built with natural materials like stone and brick, these special outdoor spaces create a harmony between natural and built environments that can have a positive effect on one's spiritual and psychological health."

STONE ART

Granite World, Ltd.: "The continuing use of natural stone in new residences proves that whether a home celebrates Old World charm or a more contemporary style, the beauty and elegance of marble and granite endure."

ART AS INTERIOR DESIGN

Art At Your Door/Gallery II: "Las Vegas is turning into a major metropolitan area, and art is finding a prominent place in this city. The art scene in Las Vegas is growing and art buyers are becoming more sophisticated year after year. As a result, art is becoming an integral part of every room and an expression of homeowners' individual tastes in designing their homes."

FASHIONABLE WINDOWS

Blinds By Debbie: "Technological advances and refinements in style have elevated window treatments to an art form that superbly blends the practical with the aesthetically pleasing."

HOT FINISHES

Phoenix and Company: "As interior design trends change, so do the types of wall finishes, ceiling treatments and decorative applications. Right now, we're fashioning faux finish walls and decorative ceilings for the area's many Mediterranean-styled homes. As the look of the Orient gains in popularity, we're also seeing more lacquered walls, sometimes enhanced with metallic touches."

 BACK TO THE PAST

Specialized Development:
"The latest trend in homebuilding is the Old World look. Santa Barbara Mediterranean is very popular, with many homes featuring knotty-alder distressed doors, round barrel tiled roofs, and smooth sand hand-finishes on the exterior walls. Popular, too, are hand-textured, faux-finished interior walls and oil-rubbed bronze hardware."

THE COSMOPOLITAN LOOK

Herbert Gordon Press Design Associates: "For years, the 'Desert Look' was common in the Las Vegas Valley area. Now, luxury homeowners desire interior design which features exciting trends from around the world. These trends involve colors and combinations that invoke attitudes for their spaces and unique functions for their rooms. In Las Vegas' luxury high-rise and sprawling custom homes, a more cosmopolitan feel is in!"

OUTSIDE IN

The Plantworks: "In the world of artificial, people are looking for more natural, botanically correct floral arrangements, greenery and accents. Custom-built trees are larger, with natural woods and larger canopies."

● COOLING IT

Glassy Business: "With the increasing popularity of more and larger windows, as well as atriums and skylights, homeowners are becoming aware of negative side effects: heat build-up, high energy costs and rapidly fading carpets and fabrics. Instead of replacing the glass to solve these problems, more people are using solar window film."

B

35

Photo by **Graetzer Communications**

WALL UPHOLSTERY

House of Draperies:
"From brocade covered walls or a silk tented ceiling in a powder room, to fullly upholstered walls in the ever popular media room, wall upholstery is one of the hottest trends in Las Vegas. The use of textiles as a wall covering evokes a sense of warmth and richness unsurpassed by any other medium."

Photo by Lynn Gato

❷ THE PERSONAL TOUCH

Superior Moulding of Nevada:
"Today's knowledgeable homeowners are paying more attention to detail. Instead of accepting plain trim in their homes, Southern Nevadans are asking for decorative crown and base molding."

A NEW TRADITION

Panache Interior Design: "Old World elegance and traditional savoir-faire are quickly outshining the garish neon lights of The Strip. An increasingly sophisticated clientele now drives designers to the pinnacle of perfection. Because the new Las Vegas customer insists on luxurious comfort and longevity of style, local resources and creativity are flourishing."

❷

ACCENT ENHANCEMENTS

Lladró: "Eclectic decor is the current home furnishing trend, and it is a style that lends itself well to a home filled with objects of charm and intricacy. Examples of this are expressive sculptures living in harmony with traditional vases and decorative accents that reflect the interests and passions of the homeowner."

CHANGING ROLES

Larry Tindall Residential Designers: "As a place for community, privacy, ceremony and outdoor living, today's homes reflect multiple roles and lifestyles. Designers are evolving constantly to reflect the current values and needs of homeowners. Today these values include practicality, security, affordability and environmental responsibility, along with the enduring needs for comfort."

LIGHTING THE NIGHT

Outdoor Lighting Perspectives of Las Vegas: "Due to the birth of new, stylish and more durable outdoor lighting products and systems, today's homeowners are able to enjoy the Las Vegas Valley outdoors long into the night. As well as enhancing a home's landscaped area, these systems also offer increased security."

PARTNERING FOR SUCCESS

Summer Land Construction: "Today's more sophisticated homebuyers are realizing the importance of the partnering process when remodeling or building a new home. They are learning that the design process does not stop when the blueprints are completed, but continues on as plans are refined with subtle finishes and accents. As a result, they are committing to partner with both the contractor and the interior designer, and it has produced wonderful results."

ELEGANCE AND VERSATILITY

Bang & Olufsen: "Today, customers want high-quality picture and digital surround sound. They want a complete cinema experience that blends with their décor. Price is no longer the determining factor, rather the concern is how the system fits with one's own lifestyle. Compromise is not in the vocabulary of these customers. Home theater has the versatility to deliver the impact of a cinema experience for event viewing, and the compact elegance for daily viewing. Some systems allow users to control everything from lights to a two piece projector with the touch of a button."

GREENING THE DESERT
Southern Highlands Estates: "In dramatic contrast to the natural desert surroundings, today's homeowners are treating their senses to the magnificent sight of pine groves and the beauty of spreading shade trees. They're inhaling the aroma of freshly planted flowers, listening to the murmur of lazy streams, and delighting in the view of tumbling waterfalls spilling into large ponds."

KITCHENS IN DISGUISE

Loerwald Construction: "Homeowners desire more elaborate detailing and elegant molding, for more striking cabinetry in today's kitchens. As a result, today's kitchens look as if they are filled with fine furniture."

42

STAIRS FOR STYLE

Nevada Stairs, Inc.: "More homeowners are appreciating the importance of beautifully designed stairs. Whether circular or straight, or renaissance or contemporary, a sweeping, grand staircase can be the focal point of the entryway. Much more than an important and functional part of the home, today's staircases are dramatic, permanent pieces of furniture and leave a lasting first impression."

THE TECH LIFE

Absolute Audio-Video: "Due to continuing technological advances, people want their home to be a magical environment of sight and sound, one that reflects their lifestyle and that can be accessed with the touch of a finger. More people are asking for dedicated theater rooms in their residences, as well as home automation and security systems."

EYE ON DESIGN

Stanley & Associates: "Since interior design tends to be driven by architecture, the Tuscan style is still in vogue. At the same time, the clean and simple lines of contemporary interiors continue to be the preference of many."

DIFFERENT DREAMS

Hunt's Woodwork and Designs, Inc.: "As new residents arrive here on a daily basis, the Las Vegas market is becoming an eclectic and varied mix of styles, tastes and designs. As a result, creating 'out of the box' has become the norm, and we find ourselves designing in styles that come from all over the country and the world."

GREEN PERFECTION

Southwest Greens: "The popularity of golf has made the backyard putting green one of the fastest growing outdoor home improvements. Popular, too, are high-tech synthetic golf greens."

Photo by **Art Nadler**

FURNITURE WITH DRAMA

Mortise & Tenon: "Today's grand living areas with stone floors and high, vaulted ceilings require equally dramatic furniture. Sectional sofas with generous proportions, overstuffed down cushions and sumptuous fabrics add an element of style and fit the scale of these large rooms."

NATURAL SELECTION

Jon J. Jannotta Architects-Planners, Inc.

"There is a bond between man and nature that is as old as time itself. Lately, that feeling has been expressed in an increasing desire to marry architecture with nature in perfect harmony. As a result, today's homes blend the outside with the inside through larger, panoramic windows. In addition, the designs of many homes also echo the surrounding environment."

A

ELEGANT TABLEWARE

Noritake Factory Store:
"The fine art of setting a beautiful table is as popular as ever. Lovely crystal and accent pieces add an elegant touch to any table."

RETURN TO ELEGANCE

Milton Homer:
"We are seeing a return to elegance with supple and luxurious fabrics and an extensive use of elaborate trims and fringes. Even updated styles have a plush and comfortable appeal, which can create a versatile environment for both relaxing and entertaining."

21ST CENTURY KITCHENS

Golan Cabinets: "The 21st century kitchen is best described as 'everything old is new again.' This is demonstrated by the reintroduction of several different glazes used in the finishing process. What makes these glazes work is the wide selection of sleek, warm colors, which blend effortlessly with everything from contemporary to traditional to ultra-modern."

OLD WORLD CRAFT

Zo'Calos: "In the Las Vegas Valley area, outdoor entertaining is a popular pastime. Not surprisingly, iron outdoor furniture remains in vogue. Today, however, consumers are discovering that mass-produced products are inferior substitutes for the lasting, durable quality and intricate detail provided by the talents of Old World craftsmen. As a result, more homeowners are demanding custom hand-crafted iron products."

48

LIVING INSIDE OUT

Ozzie Kraft Enterprises, Inc.: "Today, the trend is to utilize outdoor poolscapes as extensions to interior living spaces. Homeowners are also incorporating new amenities, such as waterfalls, firepits, sophisticated sound systems and outdoor kitchens."

ENVIRONMENTAL ENHANCEMENT

D. A. Seppala Co.: "Today, many people are realizing that the walls of a room can set a mood. The beauty created by applying translucent glazes, rubbed finishes, decorative accents and even murals can change flat walls into uplifting environmental enhancements."

A CREATIVE MIX

Arizona Tile: "There has been an explosion in creativity when it comes to mixing natural stones. Designers are softening the polished surface of granite by integrating tumbled travertine, slate, honed granite or limestone. Ceramic tiles, as well, are being created with the look of stone. Mixed and carved stone listelles are being used to add focal emphasis in field tile to create a tactile and visual excitement."

KITCHEN COLORS

Pinnacle Distribution Concepts: "Today's homeowners want the surfaces in their kitchens and baths to be just as stylish and elegant as the other rooms in their homes. As a result, color trends are evolving, and manufacturers of solid surfaces have created an expanded palette of hues to meet the demands of the consumer. Some of the most popular shades include blues and neutral colors such as cool and warm gray, clay, taupe and pale brown."

DESIGNING WITH WATER

Sundance Pools & Spas, Inc.: "Whether the overall pool plan is fanciful or elegantly simple, today's home-owners insist that it be beautifully executed and make an artistic statement. They want a design-driven outdoor environment that includes enhance-ments, such as artistic pools and water features."

50

OUTDOOR INDOOR LIVING

John C. Mackey, Residential Designer: "The desert house continues to bring the outdoors in with large sliding glass doors, continuous flooring and waterscapes. Traditional indoor activities are drawn outdoors with built in barbecue kitchens in patio areas by the pool, sitting areas with fireplaces, entertainment centers and spas."

UPDATED
PERIOD STYLE

Interior Motives: "Updated versions of period styles are making their mark in the bath area. The Tuscan or Italian Country style, characterized by antiqued and glazed finishes, is extremely popular for creating this lush retreat."

NATURAL
SELECTION

Rio Designs: "Homeowners want a comfortable, yet elegant home. They want to shelter their objects of affection from invasion, yet they also want to feel the freshness and serenity of nature outdoors. Today, the true elements of the outside are being brought inside. This is achieved with beautiful, rich textures and colors drawn from nature, as well as the use of stone and lustrous woods serving as neutral and natural backgrounds."

GAMES ARE BACK

Billiard World: "The family room is quickly gaining in popularity, and more families are choosing to design their homes with a separate family game room. Along with a place to play cards or a board game, today's game rooms feature pool tables, blackjack bars, casino tables and more."

OUTSIDE YOUR DOOR

S & S Landscape Design & Construction: "More than ever before, the custom home is about living well and having a place to enjoy more than any other. In the Las Vegas area, that includes the out-of-doors, as outdoor spaces have become an extension of indoor living spaces in an environment of sunny weather and beautiful landscapes."

WEATHER BEATERS

Accent Awning Company: "The awning industry has advanced dramatically in the past 10 years. Today's homeowners may use motorized, fully automated retractable awnings, sunscreens or security shutters to cool hot spots or the entire house. To control exterior sun, there is a trend toward fully automated sun and wind sensors. These control systems will automatically extend an awning when it is sunny, retract it when it is cloudy or dark, and also offer the safety of rolling the awning during high winds."

DESERT DÉCOR

M. F. Keller Development: "In the Las Vegas Valley area, the Southwest look is gaining in popularity. Today's homeowners want a smooth wall texture that mimics adobe-style homes for both exterior and interior walls. Inside, floors boast imported Mexican Saltino tile, and walls display the brown, green or beige of Nevada's natural desert landscape. Popular, too, is cabinetry in colors such as forest green, cranberry red and turquoise blue."

55

CABINET ART

Kiss Cabinet, Inc.: "Old World styling is at its peak, and attention to details is a must. Wood-carvings and hand-carved crown moldings adorn cabinetry. And inside these cabinets, new interior components have been developed to deliver the state-of-the-art cabinet of your dreams."

HOME AS A REFUGE

Jan Stevens Design: "Today home life is a refuge with the challenges of the day left outside the door. People want their space to be comfortable, not stiff, inviting, not delicate. Most importantly, they want it to be a shelter for the soul. As a result, they have chosen to use worry-free fabrics and finishes that welcome family and friends with open arms. Simply said, "Home is not work in many ways."

BIGGER BEDS

Custom Bed Source, Inc.: "Today's spacious master bedroom can dwarf a standard king-size bed. As a result, customers are choosing beds in ultra king and super ultra king sizes to accommodate a larger, more open floor plan."

CUSTOM STYLE

De Atelier Design Group: "Color is all the rage, so have fun with it! In this powder room, color, elegance and surprise are co-mingled with functional art. The base of the pedestal sink is designed to speak for itself and when it is lit, it becomes a true sculpture. The color-coordinating mirror and shelves equally enhance this room."

LARGER LOTS

Philip Morgan Company: "These days, more people are imagining their dream homes on estate-size lots. A site of at least a half-acre can mean more privacy and design flexibility, with room for a separate pool, barbecue and entertainment area, or perhaps a possible guesthouse, workshop or studio."

Home Books

12 Tips
For Pursuing Quality

1. Assemble a Team of Professionals During Preliminaries.
Search out and value creativity.

2. Educate Yourself on What to Expect
But also be prepared to be flexible in the likely event of set-backs.

3. Realize the Value and Worth of Design.
It's the best value for your investment.

4. Be Involved in the Process.
It's more personally satisfying and yields the best results.

5. Bigger Isn't Better – Better is Better.
Look for what produces quality and you'll never look back.

6. Understand the Process.
Be aware of products, prices and schedules, to be a productive part of the creative team.

7. Present a Realistic Budget.
Creative, workable ideas can be explored.

8. Create the Right Environment.
Mutual respect, trust and communication get the job done.

9. There Are No Immediate Miracles.
Time is a necessary component in the quest for quality.

10. Have Faith in Yourself.
Discover your own taste and style.

11. Plan for the Future.
Lifestyles and products aren't static.

12. Do Sweat the Details.
Establish the discipline to stay organized.

LAS VEGAS
HOME
BOOK

1740 Industrial Road., Las Vegas, NV 89118 702-614-4960 fax 702-263-6596

UPSCALE DECORATING VENUES

Hot Districts

Where the Unexpected Resides

Imagine meeting a leading furniture designer who listens to your dreams and instinctively understands just what you want, or entering an antique shop and finding an elegant one-of-a-kind piece that is the perfect focal point for your foyer. Whether you're building a new residence or redecorating a single room, the search for furnishings and decorative art objects that speak to your spirit can be a joyous experience and one filled with discovery.

Every town boasts elegant shops and "appointment only" showrooms that are "hot" — places only the insiders know. Sometimes located on a popular shopping street, often tucked away in an outlying area, they are beloved shopping venues that leading interior decorators and architects frequent…and treasure.

Whether you're looking for a furniture or glass craftsman to bring your vision to life, custom moldings for a new residence or an exquisite, imported treasure to lend focus to a well-appointed room, these "hot" shopping venues can spark your creativity and shorten your search immeasurably. The problem is knowing just where they are.

We created this special section to help you locate these unique and popular shopping meccas. To make it easier, they have been divided into local areas that include the address and telephone number of each store, even an easy-to-follow map.

In a book designed to inspire you and get your creative juices flowing, this is the place where you can start to make it all become real. Whether quaint or cutting-edge, elegant or funky, in these pages you'll find shops that are the leading lights in today's galaxy of elegance, art and interior design. Peruse this special section and enjoy. Then go out and discover something wonderful!

HOT DISTRICTS

West Las Vegas

Shopping in the Mountain's Shadow

Travel west on Sahara Avenue and point yourself in the direction of the popular Red Rock National Park. A rapidly growing area with lovely residences, the West Las Vegas area is also home to a number of delightful shopping venues. You might want to begin your shopping day with a bracing cappuccino or bite of lunch in a cafe along the way. When it's time to shop, you'll be pleasantly surprised. From luxurious furnishings and accessories to original fine art, custom-made furniture and billiard tables…everything a well dressed home could desire is right here.

Ⓐ Amen Wardy Homes
4230 S. Decatur Blvd.
702-734-1433
Mon.-Fri. 9 a.m.-5 p.m.
Sat. and Sun. by appointment
Come visit Amen Wardy Homes. It's the only destination for unique and luxurious home furnishings, exquisite accessories, beautiful table settings and imaginative one-of-a-kind gifts from all over the world.

Ⓑ Art At Your Door/Gallery II
8605 W. Sahara
702-256-7278
Mon.-Sat. 10 a.m.-6 p.m.
Art At Your Door/Gallery II is one of the largest fine art and custom framing galleries in Nevada. In our gallery you'll find one of the largest selections of fine art from internationally acclaimed artists. Our on-site custom framing department offers the best selection of frames and highest level of expertise.

Ⓒ Billiard World, Inc.
5411 W. Charleston Blvd.
702-259-6010
Mon.-Sat. 9 a.m.-6 p.m.
Sun. By appointment
Billiard World has everything you need for a fun family game room. Come visit; you'll find pool and Ping-Pong tables, as well as foosball, air hockey and shuffleboard games. We also offer a variety of game room furniture and lighting.

Ⓓ Magdalena's
8125 W. Sahara Ave. Ste. 160
702-228-3924
Mon.-Sat. 10 a.m.-4 p.m.
Sun. Noon-5 p.m.
We invite you to tour our showroom, view our lifestyle vignettes and formulate ideas for your personal furniture needs. You'll find our showroom dynamic and relaxing, often whimsical and upbeat. Our knowledgeable staff looks forward to making your dreams come true…item by item…room by room…project by project.

Magdalena's

Mortise & Tenon
4590 W. Sahara Ave.
702-880-4400
Tues.-Sat. 10 a.m.-7 p.m.
Sun. Noon-5 p.m.
Custom made, handcrafted furniture that
is livable, user-friendly and designed in
collaboration with the customer. We also
offer a unique collection of accessories
and original art.

❼ Nest Featherings
6425 W. Sahara Ave.
702-362-6707
Mon.-Sat. 10 a.m.-6 p.m.
At Nest Featherings you'll discover
furniture and accessories that are rich
in detail and grow more beautiful with
age. Come see our exceptional collection
of fresh designs for every room in
your home.

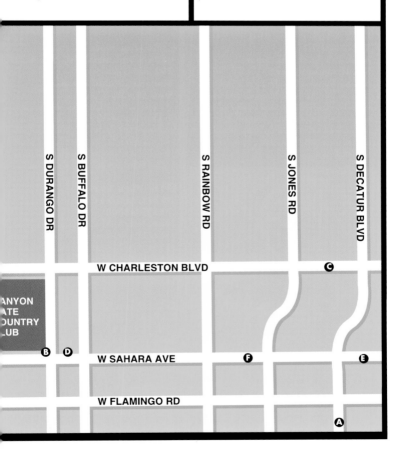

Central Las Vegas

Unassuming, Incredible!

Every town boasts showrooms in unassuming venues that interior designers and architects know and treasure. This is one of those areas. Whether you're looking for an exquisite piece of art, the latest exercise equipment, or furnishings and accessories that speak to your spirit, you'll find it all here. You'll find plenty of parking, as well.

Ⓐ Lighting Design Center
6415 Hinson St.
702-897-8866
Mon.-Fri. 9 a.m.-4:45 p.m.
Bring your interior designer or custom builder and enjoy our trade-only wholesale lighting design showroom. You'll discover the ideal environment to make lighting concepts become reality as well as a knowledgeable staff that is always ready to offer assistance.

Ⓑ Milton Homer
5455 S. Valley View Blvd.
702-798-0707
Mon.-Fri. 8:30 a.m.-5 p.m.
Sat. By appointment
Milton Homes offers the most sought-after styles in interior furnishings and accessory collections, whether casual or formal, contemporary or traditional. Our designers are uniquely qualified to help make your home all you dreamed it could be, from concept to completion.

Ⓒ Pacific Fitness Equipment
3850 W. Desert Inn Rd.
702-227-9850
Mon.-Fri. 10 a.m.-7 p.m.
Sat. 10 a.m.-6 p.m.
Sun. 11 a.m.-5 p.m.
Pacific Fitness' sales, design and service center offers the very best in gym-quality exercise equipment for the home. Specializing in treadmills and universal gyms, we provide the most variety and selection of any specialty fitness store in th Valley.

Ⓓ Showcase Slots
4305 S. Industrial Rd., Ste. B-110
702-740-5722
Mon.-Sat. 9 a.m.-5 p.m.
Sun. 10 a.m.-3 p.m.
We offer a wide variety of antique slots, modern casino slots and video poker machines for the home gameroom. All of our machines are beautifully and professionally reconditioned, and each comes with a full warranty and owners manual.

Ⓔ The Plant Works
3930 Graphics Center Dr.
702-795-3600
Mon.-Sat. 8:30 a.m.-5 p.m.
We offer a full line of quality silk flowers o stems or bushes, green bushes, custom-built trees, palms and designer accessorie We also have furniture, mirrors, pots and containers, and candles.

Ⓕ The Natural Touch
5480 S. Valley View
702-365-0197
Mon.-Fri. 8 a.m.-5 p.m.
The Natural Touch features a unique and eclectic mix of accessories and silk plants, flowers, trees and, in season, holiday déco from around the world. Our experienced designers will create permanent botanical to your requirements or you may choose from the many offerings in the store.

Zo'calos
Photo by **W & A Marketing**

Ɵ Widmen Galleries & Fine Art Printing
4795 Industrial Rd.
702-795-0003
Mon.-Fri. 10 a.m.-6 p.m.
Sat. 10 a.m.-5 p.m.
Sun. and evenings by appointment
Our new gallery overlooking the Strip features originals and limited edition Gicleé reproductions. We also showcase glass, stone, wood and metal sculpture. Our state-of-the-art printing facility is available for fine art and photo reproductions.

Ɵ Zo'Calos
7470 S. Industrial Rd., #104
702-269-6550
Mon.-Fri. 10 a.m.-6 p.m.
Sat. 10 a.m.-5 p.m.
Foremost makers of hand-forged iron furnishings, Zo'Calos offers custom, handcrafted outdoor and indoor furniture. Created by talented, Old World craftsmen, our pieces exhibit durable quality and intricate detail.

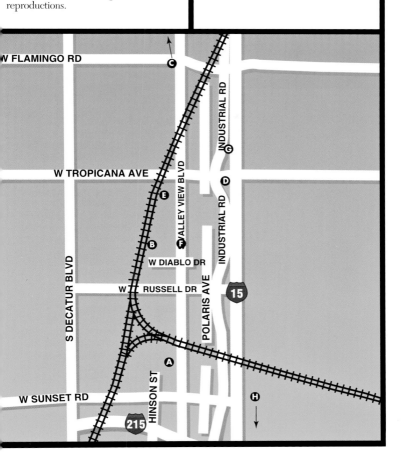

East Central Las Vegas

Shopping the World

A h, the Las Vegas Strip. Where else could you have lunch in Rome, sightsee in Paris and walk from ancient Egypt to New York all in one day? Here in the heart of town you'll find round-the-clock fun as well as wonderful shops and stores, filled with international treasures. You'll discover porcelain art from Spain, chandeliers from Venice, and china and crystal from all over the world. With a world of shopping at your fingertips, how could you resist!

Ⓐ Antiquities
3500 S. Las Vegas Blvd. Ste. E5
702-792-2274
Sun.-Thurs. 10 a.m.-11 p.m.
Fri. & Sat. 10 a.m.-Midnight
We have everything a well-dressed home theater could want. Like original, restored Coke machines, popcorn machines, and even antique gas pumps. Antiquities also offers a wide variety of Hollywood memorabilia, from original costumes and guitars, to neon signs and actual movie promotional photos.

Ⓑ Bang & Olufsen
3200 S. Las Vegas Blvd.
702-731-9200
Mon.-Fri. 10 a.m.-9 p.m.
Sat. 10 a.m.-7 p.m.
Sun. noon-6 p.m.
Bang & Olufsen specializes in high-end consumer electronics, custom home theater installations, light control and superb customer service, whenever and wherever our customers need it.

Ⓒ The Lladró Center
The Grand Canal Shoppes at the Venetian
3377 S. Las Vegas Blvd., Ste. 2245
702-414-3747
Sun.-Thurs. 10 a.m.-11 p.m.
Fri. & Sat. 10 a.m.-Midnight
Llardó has created a one-of-a-kind setting to showcase the world's most celebrated collection of art in fine porcelain. We have over 1,000 different styles to choose from—many of which can be inscribed with your own personal message. Come in and let our knowledgeable and courteous staff help you select the perfect sculpture for yourself or as a gift.

Ⓓ Noritake Factory Store
7400 S. Las Vegas Blvd., Ste. 246
702-897-7199
Mon.-Sat. 10 a.m.-9 p.m.
Sun. 10 a.m.-6 p.m.
We feature an extensive selection of first quality china and crystal giftware. Currently, we stock over 100 active patterns, which include place settings and all accessory pieces. We also offer bridal registry services as well as shipping within the continental United States.

Lladró Center

Cottura Ceramic Art Imports
3570 S. Las Vegas Blvd.
In Caesars Palace Hotel
Appian Way
702–892-9353
Mon.-Sun. 9 a.m.-11 p.m.
Cottura offers a large selection of hand-made, hand-painted Italian, Portuguese and Spanish ceramics. And that's just the beginning. Two floors of handmade

Florentine linens, Italian sterling silver flatware and Venetian glassware grace the tables throughout our store. Venetian, ceramic and hand-painted wooden chandeliers hang from the ceiling, illuminating the many Renaissance-inspired patterns from the villages of Umbria and Tuscany. Ours is a jewel of a shop.

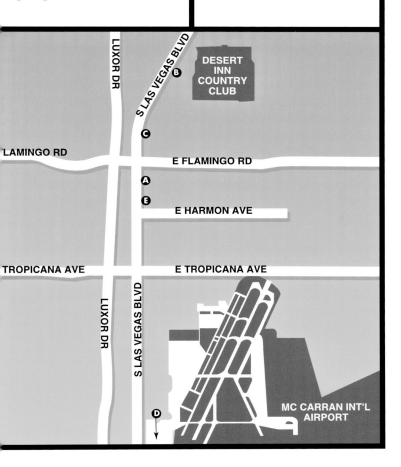

Finally...
Las Vegas' Own
Home & Design
Sourcebook

The **Las Vegas Home Book** is your final destination when searching for home remodeling, building and decorating resources. This comprehensive, hands-on sourcebook to building, remodeling, decorating, furnishing and landscaping a luxury home is required reading for the serious and discriminating homeowner. With more than 700 full-color, beautiful pages, the **Las Vegas Home Book** is the most complete and well-organized reference to the home industry. This hardcover volume covers all aspects of the process, includes listings of hundreds of industry professionals, and is accompanied by informative and valuable editorial discussing the most recent trends. Ordering your copy of the **Las Vegas Home Book** now can ensure that you have the blueprints to your dream home, in your hand, today.

O R D E R   F O R M

INTERIOR DESIGNERS

BUILDERS & REMODELERS

KITCHEN & BATH

BEAUTIFULLY DESIGNED EDITORIAL PAGES

COUNTERTOPS

ARCHITECTS

CUSTOM CABINETS

NEW IN THE SHOWROOM, HOME FURNISHINGS

Just a Sampling
of the Spectacular
pages in your
Home Book

Only If You Want the Very Best...

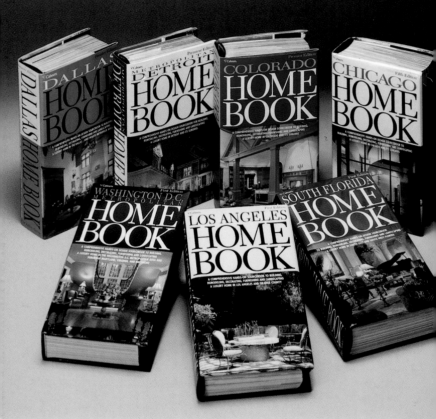

The
Ashley
Group

ARCHITECTS

Richard Luke
ARCHITECTS

"To me, a building— *if it is beautiful*—is the love of one man;

he's made it out of his love for *space and materials.* "

Martha Graham

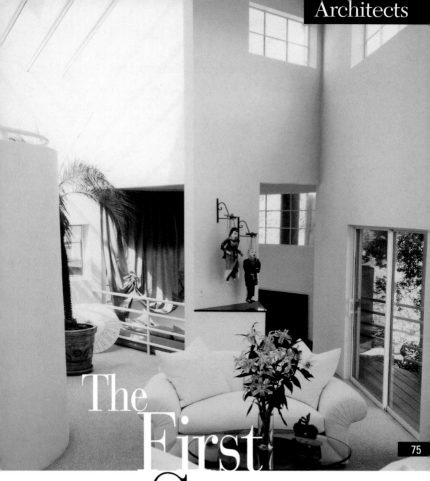

The First Step

An architect is the first step in realizing your vision for your new or remodeled home. This professional is not only skilled in the technical areas of space planning, engineering and drafting, but also happens to be an expert in materials, finishes, energy efficiency and even landscaping. An architect takes the time to learn how you live, what your needs are, and how you'd like to see your dreams come to fruition, all the while keeping your budget in mind. He or she can assemble seemingly disparate elements into a design that combines your needs and your desires, with grace, beauty and efficiency. We have the privilege of featuring the finest of these creative, technically proficient problem solvers to help you bring your ultimate home to life.

Photo courtesy of **Jon Jannotta, Architects-Planners, Inc.**

Architects

WHAT'S YOUR LIFESTYLE?

- Who lives in the house now?
- Who will live there in the future?
- Who visits and for how long?
- Do you like traditional, contemporary or eclectic design?
- Why are you moving or remodeling?
- What aspects of your current home need to be improved upon?
- Do you like functional, minimalist design, or embellishments and lots of style?
- Do you entertain formally or informally?
- How much time will you spend in the master bedroom? Is it spent reading, watching TV, working or exercising?
- What are the primary functions of the kitchen?
- Do you need a home office?
- Do you like lots of open space or little nooks and crannies?
- What kind of storage do you need?

BRINGING IDEAS TO LIFE

Whether you're building your dream home in the city, a second vacation home, or remodeling your home in the suburbs, it takes a team to design and build a high quality residential project. A team of an architect, builder, interior designer, kitchen and bath designer, and landscape architect/designer should be assembled very early in the process. When these five professionals have the opportunity to collaborate before ground is broken, you'll reap the rewards for years to come. Their blend of experience and ideas can give you insights into the fabulous possibilities of your home and site you never considered. Their association will surely save you time, money and eventually frustration.

THE ARCHITECT — MAKING THE DREAM REAL

Licensed architects provide three basic, easily defined tasks. First, they design, taking into account budget, site, owner's needs and existing house style. Second, they produce the necessary technical drawings and specifications to accomplish the desires of their clients, and explain to a contractor in adequate detail what work needs to be done. Lastly, architects participate in the construction process. This straightforward mission requires more than education.

It requires listening. The best architects have gained their status by giving their clients exactly what they want - even when those clients have difficulty articulating what that is. How? By creatively interpreting word pictures into real pictures. By eliciting the spirit of the project and following that spirit responsibly as they develop an unparalleled design.

It requires experience. Significant architects, such as those included in your Home Book, maintain a reputation for superiority because their buildings are stunningly conceived, properly designed and technically sound. If a unique, steeply pitched roof was custom-designed for you by a licensed architect with an established reputation, you can be confident that it is buildable.

Suggestions by an experienced architect can add value and interest to your new home or remodeling project. He or she may suggest you wire your home for the technology of the future, frame up an attic for future use as a second floor, or build your countertops at varying levels to accommodate people of different heights

This area is blessed with many talented architects. It's not uncommon for any number of them to be working on a luxury vacation retreat in another country or a unique second home in another state. Their vision and devotion to design set a standard of excellence for dynamic and uncompromising quality.

WORKING WITH AN ARCHITECT

The best relationships are characterized by close collaborative communication. The architect is the person you're relying on to take your ideas, elevate them to the highest level, and bring them to life in a custom design that's never been built before. So take your time in selecting the architect. It's not unusual for clients to spend two or three months interviewing prospective architects.

In preparation for the interview process, spend time fine-tuning your ideas. Put together an Idea Notebook (See the sidebar 'Compile an Idea Notebook'). Make a wish list that includes every absolute requirement and every fantasy you've ever wanted in a home. Visit builder's models to discover what 3,000 sq. ft. looks like in comparison to 6,000 sq. ft., how volume ceilings impact you or what loft living feels like. Look at established and new neighborhoods to get ideas about the relationship between landscaping and homes, and what level of landscaping you want.

GOOD COMMUNICATION SETS THE TONE

The first meeting is the time to communicate all of your desires for your new home or remodeling project, from the abstract to the concrete. You're creating something new, so be creative in imprinting your spirit and personality on the project. Be bold in expressing your ideas, even if they are not fully developed or seem unrealistic. Share your Idea Notebook and allow the architect to keep it as plans are being developed. Be prepared to talk about your lifestyle, because the architect will be trying to soak up as much information about you and your wishes as possible.

• Be frank about your budget. Although some clients are unrestricted by budgetary concerns, most must put some control on costs, and good architects expect and respect this. Great ideas can be achieved on a budget, and the architect will tell you what can be achieved for your budget.

• However, sticking to your budget requires tremendous self-discipline. If there's a luxury you really want, (a second laundry room, a built-in aquarium) it's probably just as practical to build it into your design from the outset, instead of paying for it in a change order once building has begun.

COMPILE AN IDEA NOTEBOOK

It's hard to put an idea into words, but so easy to show with a picture. Fill a good-sized notebook with plain white paper, tuck a roll of clear tape and a pair of scissors into the front flap, and you've got an Idea Notebook. Fill it with pictures, snapshots of homes you like, sketches of your own, little bits of paper that show a color you love, notes to yourself on your priorities and wishes. Circle the parts of the pictures and make spontaneous notes: "Love the finish on the cabinets," "Great rug," "Don't want windows this big." Show this to your architect, and other team members. Not only will it help keep ideas in the front of your mind, but will spark the creativity and increase understanding of the entire team.

ONE PERSON'S PROJECT ESTIMATE

Adding More Living Space

It's fun to imagine, but what might it actually cost to undertake a project described in this chapter? The example below describes a typical project and gives a general estimate of the costs involved.

Project Description

The addition of a 15 x 20 sq. ft. family room and the rehabilitation of the kitchen and powder room.

Architects' fees can be calculated in different ways. One way is to apply a percentage to all items that the architect designs, specifies and coordinates during construction. The following estimate is based on a percentage fee basis.

Family Room Addition
Traditionally detailed family room addition (300 sq. ft./$300 sq. ft.) $90,000
Exterior: brick and stone, classical frieze board, copper gutters and downspouts, cedar shingles or slate roofing.
Interior: 5/8-inch drywall with poplar base and crown moldings, herringbone clear oak flooring.
Entertainment cabinetry $10,000
Cherry rail-and-stile construction

Kitchen Rehab
Cabinetry, custom high-end $45,000
Appliances (built-in refrigerator, commercial grade equipment) $18,000
Stone countertops and backsplash $10,000
Plumbing, including fixtures $8,000
Electrical, including fixtures $6,000
Demolition and minimal construction $15,000
HVAC (heating, ventilating and air conditioning) $2,000

Powder Room Rehab
Cabinetry, custom high end $2,500
Stone countertops and tilework $5,000
Demolition and construction $3,000
Plumbing, including fixtures $7,000
Electrical, including fixtures $3,000

Sub Total **$224,500**
Contingency (10.00%) **$22,450**
Architectural fees (15.00%) **$33,675**

Total: **$280,625**

Note: Small additions cost more, on a square foot basis, than a large addition or a new house due to economies of scale.

Built-in refrigerator,
Commercial grade
equipment

Custom
high-end
cabinetry

stone
countertops
& backsplash

BUILT TO LAST

Custom home clients in the Las Vegas Valley are abandoning the quest for the big house in favor of designing a home of high quality, integrity and harmonious balance. When the emphasis is on using top quality materials and custom design to create a comfortable home, the result is truly built to last.

TOO BIG, TOO SMALL, JUST RIGHT?

If you're designing rooms with dimensions different from what you're used to, get out the tape measure. If you're downsizing, can you fit the furniture into this space? Is the new, larger size big enough – or too big? Ask your architect, builder, or interior designer if there's a similar project you can visit to get a good feel for size.

Ask lots of questions. Architects of luxury homes in the area are committed to providing their clients with information up front about the design process, the building process and their fees. These architects respect the sophistication and intelligence of their clientele, but do not necessarily expect them to have a high level of design experience or architectural expertise. Educating you is on their agenda.

• What is the breadth of services? Although this information is in your contract, it's important to know the level of services a firm will provide. There is no set standard and you need to be sure if an architect will provide the kind of services you want – from basic "no-frills" through "full service."

• Find out who you will be working with. Will you be working with one person or a team? Who will execute your drawings?

• Ask for references. Speak to past and current clients who built projects similar to yours. Ask for references from contractors with whom the architect works.

• Does the architect carry liability insurance?

• Ask to see examples of the architect's work – finished homes, job sites, and architectural plans. Does the work look and feel like what you want?

• Find out how many projects the architect has in progress. Will you get the attention you deserve?

• Decide if you like the architect. For successful collaboration, there must be a good personal connection. As you both suggest, reject, and refine ideas, a shared sense of humor and good communication will be what makes the process workable and enjoyable. Ask yourself, "Do I trust this person to deliver my dream and take care of business in the process?" If the answer is anything less than a strong and sure, "yes!" keep looking.

UNDERSTANDING ARCHITECTS' FEES AND CONTRACTS

Fees and fee structures vary greatly among architects, and comparing them can be confusing, even for the experienced client. Architects, like licensed professionals in other fields, are prohibited from setting fees as a group and agreeing on rates. They arrive at their fees based on:

(A) an hourly rate
(B) lump sum total
(C) percentage of construction cost
(D) dollars per square foot
(E) size of the job
(F) a combination of the above

The final quoted fee will include a set of services that may vary greatly from architect to architect. From a "no frills" to a "full service" bid, services are vastly different. For example, a no frills agreement budgets the architect's fee at two to seven percent of the construction cost; a full service contract budgets the architect's fee at 12 to 18 percent. Some firms include contractor's selection, bid procurement, field inspections, interior cabinetry, plumbing and lighting design, and punch list. Others don't.

One concrete basis for comparison is the architectural drawings. There can be a vast difference in the number of pages of drawings, the layers of drawings and the detail level of the specifications. Some include extra sketchbooks with drawings of all the construction details and in-depth written specs which call out every doorknob and fixture. Some offer impressive three-dimensional scale models to help you better visualize the end result, and computerized virtual walk throughs.

The benefit of a more detailed set of drawings is a more accurate, cost-effective construction bid. The more details noted in the drawings and text, the fewer contingencies a contractor will have to speculate on. The drawings are the sum total of what your contract with a builder is based upon. If a detail isn't included in the drawings, then it's not part of the project and you'll be billed extra for it.

Services should be clearly outlined in your contract. Many local architects use a standard American Institute of Architects (AIA) contract, in a long or short form. Some use a letter of agreement.

Have your attorney read the contract. Be clear that the level of service you desire is what the architect is prepared to deliver.

THE DESIGN PHASE

The architect will be in communication with you as your project progresses through the phases of schematic design, design development, preparation of construction documents, bidding and negotiating with a contractor, and contract administration (monitoring the construction). If any of these services will not be supplied, you should find out at your initial meeting.

The creativity belongs in the first phases. This is when you move walls, add windows, change your mind about the two-person whirlpool tub in favor of a shower surround, and see how far your budget will take you.

The time involved in the design process varies depending on the size of the project, your individual availability, and coordinating schedules.

WHY YOU SHOULD WORK WITH A TOP ARCHITECT

1. They are expert problem solvers. A talented architect can create solutions to your design problems, and solve the problems that stand in the way of achieving your dream.

2. They have creative ideas. You may see a two-story addition strictly in terms of its function – a great room with a master suite upstairs. An architect immediately applies a creative eye to the possibilities.

3. They provide a priceless product and service. A popular misconception about architects is that their fees make their services an extravagance. In reality, an architect's fee represents a small percentage of the overall building cost.

Architects

AMERICAN INSTITUTE OF ARCHITECTS

**AIA Las Vegas
Paul B. Sogg
Arch. Bldg.
4505 South
Maryland
Parkway, UNLV
Las Vegas,
NV 89154
Phone:
702 895 0936
Fax: 702 895 4417
www.aianevada.
org**

**AIA is a
professional
association
of licensed
architects,
with a strong
commitment to
educating and
serving the
general public.
It frequently
sponsors free
seminars called
"Working With an
Architect," which
feature local
architects
speaking on home
design and
building. AIA has
also produced
an educational
package including
a video entitled
"Investing in a
Dream" and a
brochure "You and
Your Architect."
It's available
at many local
libraries
throughout
the area.**

A good architect will encourage you to take as much time as you want in the first phases. It's not always easy to temper the euphoria that comes with starting to build a dream home, but the longer you live with the drawings, the happier you'll be. Spread the plans on a table and take an extra week or month to look at them.

Think practically. Consider what you don't like about your current home. If noise from the dishwasher bothers you at night, tell your architect you want a quiet bedroom, and a quiet dishwasher. Think about the nature of your future needs. Architects note that their clients are beginning to ask for "barrier-free" and ergonomic designs for more comfortable living as they age, or as their parents move in with them.

BUILDING BEGINS: BIDDING AND NEGOTIATION

If your contract includes it, your architect will bid your project to contractors he or she considers appropriate for your project, and any contractor you wish to consider. You may want to include a contractor to provide a "control" bid. If you wish to hire a specific contractor, you needn't go through the bidding process, unless you're simply curious about the range of responses you may receive. After the architect has analyzed the bids and the field is narrowed, you will want to meet the contractors to see if you're compatible, if you're able to communicate clearly, and if you sense a genuine interest in your project. These meetings can take place as a contractor walks through a home to be remodeled, or on a tour of a previously built project if you're building a new home.

If your plans come in over budget, the architect is responsible for bringing the costs down, except, of course, if the excess is caused by some item the architect had previously cautioned you would be prohibitive.

Not all people select an architect first. It's not uncommon for the builder to help in the selection of an architect, or for a builder to offer "design/build" services with architects on staff, just as an architectural firm may have interior designers on staff. ■

GEARING ARCHITECTURE ....**(702) 791-5561**
1700 East Desert Inn, Suite 404, Las Vegas   Fax: (702) 369-4668
See Ad on Page: 88
Principal/Owner: Scott R. Gearing
e-mail: gal@lv.rmci.net
Additional Information: Gearing Architecture has a solid reputation for tailoring each
project to accommodate the special needs and requirements of our clients.

JON J. JANNOTTA ARCHITECTS-PLANNERS, ...**(702) 221-8833**
3760 South Jones Boulevard, Las Vegas   Fax: (702) 221-8878
See Ad on Page: 86,87
Principal/Owner: Jon J. Jannotta

MARC LEMOINE ARCHITECTURE, LLC ....**(702) 646-0123**
8687 West Sahara Avenue, Las Vegas   Fax: (702) 646-0083
See Ad on Page: 84,85
Principal/Owner: Marc Lemoine
e-mail: marcarc@anv.net

RICHARD LUKE ARCHITECTS ....**(702) 838-8468**
9061 West Sahara Avenue, Suite 105, Las Vegas   Fax: (702) 838-8472
See Ad on Page: 72, 73, 90
Principal/Owner: Richard Luke
Website: www.richardluke.com   e-mail: richard@richardluke.com

THE MOFFITT PARTNERSHIP ....**(702) 878-4069**
4362 Bella Fiore, Las Vegas
See Ad on Page: 89
Principal/Owner: Gerald Moffitt
e-mail: gmofflv@aol.com
Additional Information: Since 1957 the Moffitt Partnership has practiced fine
architecture now limited to residences of quality.

MARC LEMOINE
ARCHITECTURE, LLC

8687 W. SAHARA AVE., SUITE 150
LAS VEGAS, NEVADA 89117
OFFICE   •   702-646-0123
FAX   •   702-646-0083
E-MAIL   •   marcarc@anv.net

Jon J. Jannotta

Architectural

Designer

of the 1998

Street of Dreams

Beach House

JON J. JANNOTTA
ARCHITECTS · PLANNERS, INC

Jon J. Jannotta Architects-Planners, Inc. is more than just another architectural firm, providing highly professional services in residential and commercial architecture as well as hotel and resort design, site planning, and community planning.

Mr. Jannottas' creative approach to design has earned him numerous awards in residential and commercial design.

3760 S. Jones Blvd. Las Vegas, NV 89103
P. (702)221-8833 • F. (702)221-8878

**Gearing
Architecture
LTD.**

1700
East
Desert Inn Road
Suite 404
Las Vegas
Nevada
89109
702.791.5567
FAX 702.369.4668

THE MOFFITT PARTNERSHIP

PAST AND PRESENT

ARCHITECTS FOR FINE RESIDENCES   702 878 4069

4362 BELLA FIORE, SUMMERLIN

Finally...
Las Vegas' Own
Home & Design
Sourcebook

The **Las Vegas Home Book** is your final destination when searching for home remodeling, building and decorating resources. This comprehensive, hands-on sourcebook to building, remodeling, decorating, furnishing, and landscaping a luxury home is required reading for the serious and discriminating homeowner. With more than 700 full-color, beautiful pages, the **Las Vegas Home Book** is the most complete and well-organized reference to the home industry. This hardcover volume covers all aspects of the process, includes listings of hundreds of industry professionals, and is accompanied by informative and valuable editorial discussing the most recent trends. Ordering your copy of the **Las Vegas Home Book** now can ensure that you have the blueprints to your dream home, in your hand, today.

Order your copy now!

LAS VEGAS
HOME
BOOK

Published by
The Ashley Group
1740 Industrial Rd.,Las Vegas, NV 89118
702-614-4960 fax 702-263-6596
E-mail: ashleybooksales@cahners.com

Sharing
THE DREAM

What would you like in your dream home? A lower-level bowling alley? A separate building to show off a beloved car collection? An aviary off the breakfast nook? It's easy to visualize the parts. It can be a bit harder to envision the whole.

Aglow with lights, this elegant residence awaits tonight's guests.

Photo courtesy of **Richard Luke Architects**
Photo by **Chawla Associates**

Archi

tects

This contemporary kitchen area featured specially selected lights and a unique architectural ceiling treatment.

Photo courtesy of **Scott Gearing Architecture**
Photo by **Christopher Hukill**

An architect can provide this vision by giving your dreams shape and putting them into three dimensions. But gifted architects can do even more than that. During the "dream phase" or conceptual period of a project, they can help you access the dynamics or soul of the house—the feeling and poetry that is unique to you and your family. And that can make the difference between a house you like and a home you love. But how do you most clearly communicate your personal dreams? Architects have many ways to help.

Many meet in a client's current home or walk the site of their new one. Others share pictures or ask clients to show them pictures of homes or rooms they like. And some give their clients a lifestyle questionnaire to fill out. But the one technique that all top architects agree upon is listening. As Jon Jannotta of Jon J. Jannotta Architects-Planners, Inc. said, "Listening attentively and asking the right questions is key."

Top architects encourage dialogue in many different ways. Richard Luke, President of Richard Luke Architects, asks clients to compile a scrapbook

Archi

Sleek and high tech, this kitchen and dining area is neatly tucked away beneath a skylight enhanced loft.

Photo courtesy of **Jon J. Jannotta Architects-Planners, Inc.**

and bring it to conceptual meetings. Scott Gearing, principal of Gearing Architecture, Ltd., believes in collaboration. "I tell client couples that the design process is a huge collaboration between many people but it starts with them—first, they have to collaborate with each other."

Marc Lemoine, A.I.A, principal of Marc Lemoine Architecture, L.L.C., feels that in discussing their new home, clients are doing something that is very personal. So after the initial meeting, Marc relaxes them by chatting. They talk about restaurants, compare favorite sports teams and discuss entertainment venues. Inevitably, favorite movies come up, and when a client asks a house or a room that he or she saw in a film and would love to live in, Marc complies.

For a couple who fell in love with the movie, The Secret Garden, Lemoine designed a distressed wooden gate set in a stone arch. This magical gate opened onto a lush, secret garden in the flower-filled front courtyard of their Northern European home. For another client, Lemoine created a

tects

dramatic, two-story arched loggia from the movie, Parent Trap. And at yet another homeowner's request, he designed a large hidden closet, much like the one featured in the movie, Absolute Power, and secreted it behind an elegant paneled wall in the master bedroom. When asked about these re-creations Lemoine said, "What cinematographers do with lighting and sets, I do with color, texture and materials."

To a top architect, everything a client cares about is important, no matter how small. Jannotta asks his clients to tell him their likes and dislikes. Gearing welcomes contradictions, because he has found that they stimulate interesting design discussions and foster creative solutions. For example, when a husband envisioned a structured English Tudor home, but his wife wanted the home to be Art Deco, Gearing was able to please them both by taking elements of each style and creatively marrying them. By changing the pitch of the roof and replacing the traditional, exterior Tutor wood detail with 'Deco' insets of tile and glass, Gearing created an elegant residence that beautifully combines Tutor symmetry and Art Deco grace.

Clients' differing desires can be handled in many ways. For a couple who had divergent interests, Gearing created separate 'His' and 'Her' rooms. The husband's getaway featured a video-surround screen, for total immersion in sports events or videos. The wife's special room was designed as a play-room for the grandchildren, with plenty of space for a train set and toys.

A luxury custom home can, and should, celebrate a homeowner's lifestyle. For a client who has a menagerie of exotic animals, (Richard Luke designed an animal habitat off the master bath. There, behind a 20 ft. wall of glass, his client can watch the 'cats' play or rest on realistic-looking trees. Luke also created an aviary for this homeowner's exotic birds as part of the breakfast nook. So human swimmers could watch marine life while underwater, Luke constructed a special aquarium that could be viewed while in the swimming pool.)

For a top architect, no request is too complicated. When a client mentioned that he'd like to greet the morning by diving off his second story master bedroom deck into his first floor pool, Luke made it happen. For a homeowner who asked for a design that would create harmony in the environment, architect Jannotta utilized the 4,000-year-old principles of Feng Shui, specially orienting the rooms and courtyard water features.

A client's request can give rise to creative architectural solutions. For a couple who wished to separate their second floor master bedroom suite from their guest bedrooms, Jannota created a steel, serpentine bridge. This bridge not only connected the master bedroom on one side to the guest bedrooms on the other, it enhanced the dramatic, two-story volume of the first floor foyer and great room as well as adding a design element that is truly spectacular. Jannotta also created a bridge that made it possible for a client to access the separate structure that housed a client's art studio—a 40-ft. long structure that passes over a graceful waterfall.

The use of simple molding, half walls and a touch of ceiling color make this sleek, contemporary residence one-of-a-kind.

Photo courtesy of **Scott Gearing Architecture**
Photo by **Christopher Hukill**

tects

Sleek and high tech, this kitchen and dining area is neatly tucked away beneath a skylight enhanced loft.

Photo courtesy of **Jon J. Jannotta Architects-Planners, Inc.**

Archi

Today's top architects are ever aware of things that many clients often don't consider. A good architect will be sensitive to the unique qualities of the environment that might impact the design of a new home: where the sun comes up, the direction the wind blows, the look of the natural environment and the topography. Architects also consider changes in the family dynamic and design homes that can adapt as children grow or as couples face the "empty nest."

As your dreams begin to take shape, your architect will have countless ways to help you visualize your ideas, even in the earliest conceptual meetings. Many sketch ideas as they are verbalized. Some use 3-D computer imagery that allows clients to seemingly walk from room to room in a home that is still in the dream stage.

Never be shy about sharing visions with your architect. This sharing is the door to a collaboration that can be enjoyable and fruitful. You'll find that an architect is dedicated to shaping your dream and making it come true. And it will. ■

tects

Residential Designers

JEFF GROVER DESIGN ....**(702) 361-7576**
  7155 Polaris Avenue, Las Vegas   Fax: (702) 361-2200
  See Ad on Page: 103
  <u>Principal/Owner:</u> Jeff Grover
  <u>Website:</u> www.jeffgroverdesign.com <u>e-mail:</u> jgrover@jeffgroverdesign.com
  <u>Additional Information:</u> Residential Designer

JOHN C. MACKEY...**(702) 657-2277**
  7420 Stoney Shore Drive, Las Vegas   Fax: (702) 228-0198
  See Ad on Page: 102
  <u>Principal/Owner:</u> John C. Mackey
  <u>Website:</u> johncmackeyinc.com
  <u>Additional Information:</u> Licensed Nevada Residential Designer: Lake Las Vegas,
  Summerlin, Seven Hills, Spanish Hills, Acreage. Computer generated 3-D walk-throughs.

LARRY TINDALL RESIDENTIAL DESIGNER ....**(702) 597-5597**
  3531 East Russell Road Suite G, Las Vegas   Fax: (702) 597-5598
  See Ad on Page: 101
  <u>Principal/Owner:</u> Larry Tindall
  <u>e-mail:</u> ltrdcorp@aol.com

Specializing in Custom and
Production Homes

LARRY TINDALL
REGISTERED RESIDENTIAL
D E S I G N E R

3531 E. RUSSELL ROAD,SUITE G
LAS VEGAS, NV 89120

TEL:(702) 597-5597
FAX:(702) 597-5598
EMAIL LTRDCORP@AOL.COM

John C. Mackey
RESIDENTIAL DESIGNER

John C. Mackey, Inc.
7420 Stoney Shore Drive
Las Vegas, NV 89128
(702) 657-2277
ELN/johncmackeyinc@earthlink.ne
www.johncmackey.com

- Licensed Nevada
  Residential Designer
- Lake Las Vegas, Summerlin,
  Seven Hills, Spanish Hills &
  on acreage
- computer generated 3D
  walk-throughs
- references available upon
  request

we listen... then we design

JEFF GROVER DESIGN
Residential Architecture

7155 S. POLARIS AVENUE
LAS VEGAS, NV 89118

T 702.361.7576
F 702.361.2200
www.jeffgroverdesign.com
jgrover@jeffgroverdesign.com

Las Vegas Ho

Your Guide to Your Dream Home

Tired of being lost? Feel that you don't know where you're
going without a map? Can't find useful information regarding
home improvement? The Las Vegas Home Book website,
www.lvhomebook.com, provides you with a full color atlas
of information to map out the home of your dreams.

e Book.com

YOU WANT IT, WE'LL PROVIDE IT

The **Las Vegas Home Book** website covers a full range of resources for building, remodeling, decorating, furnishing and landscaping projects. The site also provides you with a number of unique, functional features designed to help you locate all the necessary information regarding the design or enhancement of your luxury home. Just log on at www.lvhomebook.com, and we'll do the rest.

YOUR RESEARCH SOURCE

The site enables users to search for professionals by specific category: architects, interior designers, kitchen and bath, and many more. Users can also search by keyword — company name and/or profession — right off the home page.

THE PERFECT PAIR

The **Las Vegas Home Book** website, www.lvhomebook.com is best used when complemented by a copy of the **Las Vegas Home Book**. The website picks up where the book leaves off, allowing consumers to further research their home improvement needs in depth. The two work in unison to provide consumers up-to-date and timely information regarding their most prized investment — their home.

WE'RE ONLY A FEW CLICKS AWAY

If you are planning to design or renovate your home, please don't hesitate to consult your local source to top design/build professionals, www.lvhomebook.com.
Allow us to be your road map, and we will gladly lead you to your final destination. Thank you from everyone at the **Las Vegas Home Book,** and we all hope to see you online!

There is only one premier resource provider for the luxury design and home enhancement market — the **Las Vegas Home Book!**

www.lvhomebook.com
www.homebook.com

Finally...
Las Vegas' Own
Home & Design
Sourcebook

The **Las Vegas Home Book** is your final destination when searching for home remodeling, building and decorating resources. This comprehensive, hands-on sourcebook to building, remodeling, decorating, furnishing, and landscaping a luxury home is required reading for the serious and discriminating homeowner. With more than 700 full-color, beautiful pages, the **Las Vegas Home Book** is the most complete and well-organized reference to the home industry. This hardcover volume covers all aspects of the process, includes listings of hundreds of industry professionals, and is accompanied by informative and valuable editorial discussing the most recent trends. Ordering your copy of the **Las Vegas Home Book** now can ensure that you have the blueprints to your dream home,
in your hand, today.

Order your copy now!

LAS VEGAS
HOME
BOOK

Published by
The Ashley Group
1740 Industrial Rd.,Las Vegas, NV 89118
702-614-4960 fax 702-263-6596
E-mail: ashleybooksales@cahners.com

CUSTOM HOME BUILDERS

& REMODELERS

D·I·S·T·I·N·C·T·I·V·E
GENERAL CONTRACTING

220 Commerce Park Ct.
North Las Vegas, NV 89032
Phone 702.395.2307

"The *beautiful* rests on the FOUNDATION of the *necessary.* "

Ralph Waldo Emerson

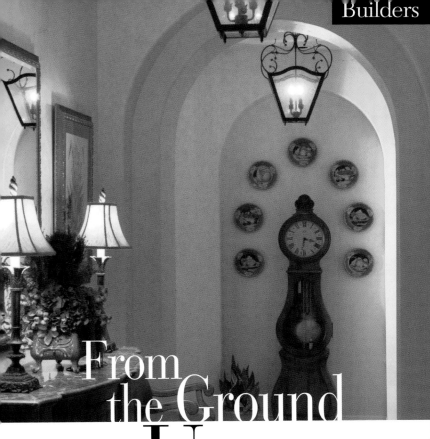

From the Ground Up

One of the key players in every homebuilding and remodeling success story is the builder. Architects envision possibilities, but builders create new realities. While design/build teams of architects and builders are becoming increasingly popular, the home in which you will be living will be the direct result of your contractor's efforts and expertise. So much of your satisfaction in the final outcome depends upon the selection of the right builder. It is essential to choose a company or individual with whom you have a good rapport, who has excellent references as well as experience with your type of project. While the planning phase of a new home or remodeling project may be exciting, creating the finished product is hard work. Seek out a builder whose attention to quality detail, willingness to listen to your concerns, and in-depth knowledge of the trades assures you a smoother road on the way to your new home.

Photo courtesy of **Loerwald Construction**
Photo by **Jeffrey Green**

THE TEARDOWN TREND

Land for new residential construction is getting harder to find, and "tear-down" renovations are becoming more common. There are often mixed emotions in an existing neighborhood as old structures come down. If you are considering a "tear-down" property, be sure you work with a builder and architect who are sensitive to the character of the neighborhood, and will help you build a home that fits in.

HOME BUILDER SOURCES

**Nevada Home Builders Association, and Southern Nevada Home Builders, Inc.
3685 Pecos McLeod
Las Vegas, NV 89121-3805
(702) 794-0117
www.nahb.org**

**National Association of the Remodeling Industry (NARI)
847.298.9200
www.nari.org**

SETTING THE STANDARD FOR QUALITY

A strong commitment to providing top quality materials and craftsmanship is the most important contribution a builder can make to your professional team. Working in concert with your architect, interior designer, kitchen and bath designer and landscape architect, a custom home builder will take the designs, and your dreams, and make them happen. Selecting a builder who shares your dedication to building only the best is how you build quality into your new home. This kind of quality is as tangible as it is intangible. You can see it in the materials used – not necessarily the most expensive, but always the best for the situation. More interestingly, you can feel it. There's an unmistakable sense of integrity in a well-built home, of a dream fulfilled.

IS IT A(ARCHITECT) BEFORE B(BUILDER) OR B BEFORE A?

Answering this question can seem like the "chicken or the egg" riddle: Do you hire the builder first, the architect first, or choose a design/build firm, where both functions are under the same roof?

If you work first with an architect, his or her firm will recommend builders they know who have a track record in building homes of the same caliber you desire. Most likely, your architect contract will include bidding and negotiation services with these builders, and you may expect help in analyzing bids and making your selection. Your architect contract also may include construction administration, in which the architect makes site visits to observe construction, reviews the builder's applications for payment, and helps make sure the home is built according to the plans.

Perhaps you've seen previous work or know satisfied clients of a custom home builder, and wish to work with him. In this scenario, the builder will recommend architects who are experienced in successfully designing homes and/or additions similar to what you want. The builder will support you, and the architect will cost-control information through realistic cost figures, before products are integrated into the house.

If you like the idea of working with one firm for both the architectural design and building, consider a design/build firm. Design/build firms offer an arrangement that can improve time management and efficient communication, simply by virtue of having both professional functions under the same roof. There is also added flexibility as the project develops. If you decide you want to add a feature, the design/build firm handles the design process and communicates the changes internally to the builder. When you interview a design/builder firm, it's important to ascertain that the firm has a strong architectural background, with experienced custom home architects on staff.

All scenarios work and no one way is always better than the other. Make your choice by finding professionals you trust and with whom you feel comfortable. Look for vision and integrity and let the creative process begin.

FINDING THE RIGHT BUILDER

The selection of a builder or remodeler is a major decision, and should be approached in a thoughtful, unhurried manner. Allow plenty of time to interview and research at least two candidates before making your choice. Hours invested at this point can save months of time later on.

At the initial interview, the most important information you'll get is not from brochures, portfolios, or a sales pitch, but from your own intuition. Ask yourself: Can we trust this person to execute plans for our dream home, likely the biggest expenditure of our lifetime? Is there a natural two-way communication, mutual respect, and creative energy? Does he have the vision to make our home unique and important? Is his sense of the project similar to ours? Will we have any fun together? Can we work together for at least a year?

If you answer "Yes!" you've found the most valuable asset – the right chemistry.

TAKE TIME TO CHECK REFERENCES

The most distinguished builders in the area expect, even want, you to check their references. More luxury home clients are taking the time to do this research as the move toward quality workmanship continues to grow.

Talk to clients. Get a list of clients spanning the last three to five years, some of whom are owners of projects similar to yours. Call them and go visit their homes or building sites. Satisfied customers are only too happy to show you around and praise the builder who did the work. If you can, speak with a past client not on the builder's referral list. Finding one unhappy customer is not cause for concern, but if you unearth a number of them, cross that builder off your list.

Visit a construction site. Clients who get the best results appreciate the importance of the subcontractors. Their commitment to quality is at the heart of the job. Do the subcontractors appear to be professional? Are they taking their time in doing their work? Is the site clean and neat?

TEN GOOD QUESTIONS TO ASK A BUILDER'S PAST CLIENTS

1. Are you happy with your home?
2. Was the house built on schedule?
3. Did the builder respect the budget and give an honest appraisal of costs early on?
4. Did the builder bring creativity to your project?
5. Were you well informed so you properly understood each phase of the project?
6. Was the builder accessible and on-site?
7. Does the builder provide good service now that the project is complete?
8. How much help did you get from the builder in choosing the products in your home?
9. Is the house well built?
10. Would you hire the builder again?

113

IT TAKES HOW LONG?

Some typical construction time frames:

Total Kitchen Remodel: From total demolition to installation of new cabinets, flooring, appliances, electrical, etc. **SIX – EIGHT WEEKS**

A 1,400 Sq. Ft. Addition: New first floor Great Room & powder room, extension of the existing kitchen; master suite upstairs. **FOUR – SIX MONTHS**

Total Home Remodel: An 1,800 sq. ft. Colonial expanded to 4,000 sq. ft. All spaces redefined, added third floor, three new baths, new high-end kitchen, deck. **SIX - NINE MONTHS**

These estimates depend on factors such as the size of the crew working on your project, the timeliness of decisions and the delivery of materials.

Contact subcontractors with whom the builder has worked. If they vouch for the builder's integrity and ability, you'll know the firm has earned a good professional reputation. Meeting subcontractors also provides a good measure for the quality of workmanship you'll receive.

Visit the builder's office. Is it well-staffed and organized? Does this person offer the technology for virtual walk-throughs? Do you feel welcome there?

Find out how long the builder has been in business. Experienced custom builders have strong relationships with top quality subcontractors and architects, a comprehensive knowledge of products and materials, and skills to provide the best service before, during and after construction.

Ask how many homes are currently being built and how your project will be serviced. Some builders work on several homes at once; some limit their total to 10 or 12 a year.

LAYING A FOUNDATION FOR SUCCESS

Two documents, the contract and the timeline, define your building experience. The contract lays down the requirements of the relationship and the timeline delineates the order in which the work is done. While the contract is negotiated once at the beginning of the relationship, the timeline continues to be updated and revised as the project develops.

THE CONTRACT

The American Institute of Architects (AIA) provides a standard neutral contract which is widely used in the area, but some firms write their own contracts. As with any contract, get legal advice, read carefully, and assume nothing. If landscaping is not mentioned, then landscaping will not be provided. Pay careful attention to:

• Payment schedules. When and how does the builder get paid? How much is the deposit (depends on the total cost of the project but $10,000 to $25,000 is not uncommon) and will it be applied against the first phase of the work? Do you have the right to withhold any payment until your punch list is completed? Will you write checks to the builder (if so, insist on sworn waivers) or only to the title company? Remodeling contracts typically use a payment schedule broken into thirds – one-third up front, one-third half-way through the project, and one-third at completion. You may withhold a negotiated percentage of the contract price until you're satisfied that the terms of the contract have been met and the work has been inspected.

This should be stipulated in the contract. Ten percent is the average amount to be held back, but is negotiable based on the overall size of the project.

Builders and remodeling specialists who attract a quality-minded, high-end custom home client are contacted by institutions offering attractive construction or bridge and end loan packages. Ask your contractor for referrals if you want to do some comparative shopping.

• The total cost-breakdown of labor and materials expenses.

• Change order procedures. Change orders on the average add seven to ten percent to the cost of a custom home. Be clear on how these orders are charged and the impact they eventually will have on the timetable.

• The basic work description. This should be extremely detailed, including everything from installing phone jacks to the final cleaning of your home. A comprehensive list of specified materials should be given, if it hasn't already been provided by your architect.

• Allowances. Are they realistic? This is one place where discrepancies will be evident. Is Contractor A estimating $75,000 for cabinets while Contractor B is stating $150,000?

• Warranty. A one-year warranty, effective the date you move in, is standard in this area.

THE TIMELINE

This changeable document will give you a good indication if and when things will go wrong.

Go to the site often enough to keep track of the progress according to the timeline. Do what you need to do to keep the project on schedule. One of the main causes of delays and problems is late decision-making by the homeowner. If you wait until three weeks prior to cabinet installation to order your cabinets, you can count on holding up the entire process by at least a month. (You'll also limit your options to cabinets that can be delivered quickly.)

THE SECOND TIME'S A CHARM

Renovating a home offers the unique excitement of reinventing an old space to serve a new, enhanced purpose. It's an evolutionary process, charged with creative thinking and bold ideas. If you enjoy a stimulating environment of problem solving and decision making, and you're prepared to dedicate the needed time and resources, remodeling

TRUTH ABOUT CHANGE ORDERS

The building process demands an environment that allows for changes as plans move from paper to reality. Although you can control changes through careful planning in the preliminary stages of design and bidding, budget an extra seven to 10 percent of the cost of the home to cover change orders. Changes are made by talking to the contractor, not someone working at the site. You will be issued a change order form, which you will sign and return to the contractor. Keep your copies of the forms together in one folder. Avoid last minute sticker shock by being diligent in keeping a current tab on your change order expenses.

CLEAN UP TIME: NOW OR LATER?

Your remodeling contract should be specific about clean-up. Will the site be cleaned up every day, or at the end of the project? Everyday clean-up may add to the price, but is well worth the extra expenditure.

One Person's Project Estimate:

Creating a Custom Home

It's fun to imagine, but what might it actually cost to undertake a project described in this chapter? The example below describes a typical project and gives a general estimate of the costs involved.

Project Description

Construction of a 10,000 sq. ft., country-style home with brick and stone veneer and a slate roof.

Rough Lumber and Exterior Trim	Exterior	$15,000
	Rough framing	$95,000
Carpentry	Caulking	$2,000
	Rough framing	$90,000
	Interior trim	$12,000
Steel and Ornamental Iron	Ornamental iron	$5,000
	Structural steel	$7,500
Windows	Skylight	$1,500
	Windows and doors	$75,000
Exterior Doors	Front door	$12,000
	Service door	$2,500
Roof	Slate	$140,000
Plumbing	Fixtures	$25,000
	Labor	$25,000
Heating	HVAC forced air	$45,000
	Radiant heat	$12,500
Electrical	Electrical	$50,000
	Security system	$5,000
Masonry Veneer		$215,000
Insulation		$10,000
Drywall		$38,000
Wood Floors		$30,000
Tile	Ceramic tile	$30,000
	Hearth and surround	$10,500
Cabinets and Vanities		$125,000
Interior Trim	Mantel	$10,900
	Wine rack	$3,000
	Closets	$8,000
Shower Doors and Tub Enclosure		$9,000
Gutters and Downspouts		$13,000
Garage Doors and Opener		$4,800

Total: ....

$1,147,200

Note: This estimate covers the basic construction costs of the project. Other costs include insurance and legal fees, survey and site plans, grading, light fixtures and appliance installation, and clean up of the site.

Rough cut siding

Stone veneer

slate roof

will result in a home which lives up to all of your expectations. You'll be living in the neighborhood you love, in a home that fits your needs.

A WORD ABOUT FINANCING OF REMODELING PROJECTS

Payment schedules in remodeling contracts typically require a deposit or a first payment at the start of the project, with subsequent payments due monthly or in conjunction with the progress of the work.

It is within your rights to withhold a negotiated percentage of the contract price until you're satisfied that the terms of the contract have been met and the work has been inspected. This should be stipulated in the written contract. Ten percent is the average amount to be held back, but is negotiated based on the overall size of the project.

Remodeling specialists who attract a quality-minded clientele are kept abreast of the most attractive remodeling loans on the market by lenders who specialize in these products. Ask your remodeler for referrals to these financial institutions.

UPDATING THE CLASSICS

Many homeowners at the beginning of the new century are attracted to the historic architecture in older neighborhoods. Maturity and classicism are factors that persuade homeowners to make an investment in an old home and restore, renovate or preserve it, depending on what level of involvement interests them and the significance of the house. Renovations include additions and updating or replacing systems in the house. Restorations involve restoring the building to the specifications original to the house. Preservation efforts preserve what's there.

Like any remodeling project, it's an emotional and personal experience, only more so. Staying within the confines of a certain period or style is difficult and time consuming. That's why it's crucial to find an experienced architect and builder who share a reverence for tradition and craftsmanship. At your interview, determine if his or her portfolio shows competence in this specialty. It's vital to find a professional who understands historic projects and knows experienced and qualified contractors and/or subcontractors who will do the work for you. Ask if he or she knows experienced contractors who work in historic districts and have relationships with knowledgeable, experienced craftsmen. If you want exterior features, like period gardens or terraces, ask if they will be included in the overall plan. Make sure he or she has sources for you to find period furnishings, sconce shades or chimney pots.

There are many construction and design issues particular to old homes. The historic renovation and preservation experts featured in the following pages bring experience, creativity and responsibility to each project.

RESPECT YOUR ELDERS

Before you fall in love with an old house, get a professional opinion. Find out how much is salvageable before you make the investment. Can the wood be restored? Have the casings been painted too many times? Is the plaster wavy and buckled? Can the house support ductwork for central air conditioning or additional light sources?

Notable remodelers are often contacted for their expert advice prior to a real estate purchase, and realtors maintain relationships with qualified remodelers for this purpose. They also keep remodelers informed of special properties suitable for custom renovations as they become available.

PRIVACY? WHAT'S THAT?

Remodelers overwhelmingly agree their clients are happier if they move to a temporary residence during all, or the most intensive part, of the renovation. The sight of the roof and walls being torn out, the constant banging and buzzing of tools, and the invasion of privacy quickly take their toll on children and adults who are trying to carry on family life in a house full of dust. Homeowners who are well-rested from living in clean, well-lighted temporary quarters enjoy better relationships with each other, their remodeler and subcontractors.

Common hideaways are rental homes, suite-type hotels, the unoccupied home of a relative, or a long vacation trip. ■

A LUXURY ADDITION OF AN HISTORIC HOME

Suburban Arts and Crafts-Prairie Home, circa 1915.
• **All windows, trim, casings and other details to match the original brick.**
• **Full, finished basement, with bar and workout area.**
• **First level family room, dining room and new kitchen.**
• **Upper level master suite and office. Stone terrace and garden.**

Total Project Cost: $500,000, including architectural fees.

119

CREATE A RECORD

You have a team of highly qualified professionals building your home, but the ultimate responsibility is on your shoulders. So keep track of the project. Organize a binder to keep all of your samples, change orders and documents together. Make copies for yourself of all communication with your suppliers and contractor. Take notes from conversations and send them to the contractor. This can help eliminate confusion before a problem occurs.

CHRISTOPHER HOMES ....**(702) 360-3200**
9500 Hillwood Drive Suite 200, Las Vegas   Fax: (702) 228-7976
See Ad on Page: 122,123
Principal/Owner: J. Christopher Stuhmer
Website: www.christopherhomes.com   e-mail: dstocker@christopherhomes.com

DISTINCTIVE GENERAL CONTRACTING ....**(702) 395-2307**
220 Commerce Park Court, Las Vegas   Fax: (702) 656-1388
See Ad on Page: 108,109, 121
Principal/Owner: Jeffrey W. Gremore
Website: www.distinctivegc.com   e-mail: distinctive@aol.com

EXECUTIVE HOME BUILDERS ....**(702) 656-5955**
8670 Meadow Spring Mountain Road #102, Las Vegas   Fax: (702) 595-5005
See Ad on Page: 163
Principal/Owner: Yohan Lowie and Paul & Vicki DeHart

HILLTOP DEVELOPMENT, INC. ....**(702) 365-0000**
4132 South Rainbow Boulevard, Las Vegas   Fax: (702) 365-0002
See Ad on Page: 124, 125
Principal/Owner: Paul Trudeau
Website: www.hilltopdevelopmentinc.com
e-mail: hilltopdevelopment.inc@worldnet.att.net
Additional Information: A premiere design/builder of completely automated Luxury
Homes in California, Hawaii, Washington & Nevada. If you can dream it, we can
design & build it.

LOERWALD CONSTRUCTION ....**(702) 255-6006**
405 Club Court, Las Vegas   Fax: (702) 255-6006
See Ad on Page: 126, 127, 154
Principal/Owner: LeRoy Loerwald

MERLIN CONTRACTING ....**(702) 257-8102**
2801 South Valley View, Suite 14B, Las Vegas   Fax: (702) 257-8105
See Ad on Page: 130, 131
Principal/Owner: Bart Jones/Steve Jones

MF KELLER DEVELOPMENT ....**(702) 451-1940**
3531 East Russell Road, Las Vegas   Fax: (702) 948-9090
See Ad on Page: 128
Principal/Owner: Michael F. Keller
Additional Information: Over 25 years experience in Las Vegas and Henderson build-
ing luxury custom homes.

PHILIP MORGAN COMPANY ....**(702) 876-1192**
See Ad on Page: 150, 151   Fax: (702) 876-1099
Principal/Owner: Brent M. Philip
Additional Information: Please accept our invitation to tour some of our completed
projects, including, Anthem Country Club, Mountain Trails, Queensridge North, and
Canyon Fairways.

RAFTERY CONSTRUCTION ....**(702) 242-4475**
400 Club Court, Las Vegas   Fax: (702) 240-4674
See Ad on Page: 152, 153
Principal/Owner: Jack Raftery

120

continued on page **149**

D·I·S·T·I·N·C·T·I·V·E
GENERAL CONTRACTING

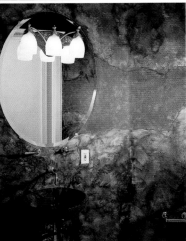

220 Commerce Park Ct.

North Las Vegas, NV 89032

702.395.2307

Thinking Custom?

Custom Homes

From $650's To Over $4 Million

We'll Build On YOUR Lot!

702-838-3000

www.christopherhomes.com

...Think Christopher!

H O M E S

CUSTOM HOME DIVISION

Photography by Chawla Associates

 **ILLTOP DEVELOPMENT, INC.**

LUXURY HOMES

Hilltop Developement, Inc. of Las Vegas, a premiere
design/ builder of completely automated Luxury Homes
in California, Hawaii, Washington and Nevada. If you can
dream it we can design and build it.

Paul Trudeau
702-365-0000
Fax 702-365-0002

4132 So. Rainbow Blvd. • Las Vegas, NV 89103 • Lic No. 42477
www.hilltopdevelopmentinc.com

Loe
CUSTO

DESIGN • BUILD • FURNISH
LOERWALD CONSTRUCTION
LAS VEGAS, NEVADA
702.255.6000 702.429.5151

wald
HOMES

BUILDING FUTURES

Merlin Contracting

2801 S. Valley View #14B
Las Vegas, NV 89102
702-257-8102
702-257-8105

Licence # 43785

Sparkling with lights and enhanced with glass brick detailing, this Las Vegas Home sparkles like a jewel.

Photo courtesy of **Philip Morgan Company**
Photo by **Studio West Photography**

HomeB

Detailing
THE DREAM

Wwhile architects interpret dreams, custom home builders make them reality. Their prodigious talents have created exquisite homes, true showcases for the lifestyles of their owners. Since these gifted builders have constructed homes in many different architectural styles, the Home Book asked four of Las Vegas' top custom builders to imagine their own dream home. If the sky was the limit and they could choose a site anywhere in the world, where would they build it, and what would it be like?

uilders

NATURAL ELEGANCE

Tim Stonestreet, owner of Six Star Construction, is in the process of building his dream home here in Las Vegas. When completed, it will be a grand Italian villa at the end of a graceful, cobblestone drive. Graced with hand-trowled, cut stone, the villa will boast a front courtyard with its own fireplace.

An imposing entrance will feature a solid Honduras mahogany door with the door knocker in the mouth of a brushed, antique brass lion's head. Once beyond the stone threshold, guests will be greeted by a graceful, cantilevered staircase topped with a faux-painted dome surrounded by tiny, inset windows. The 10,000 sq. ft. villa will have matte blonde travertine marble floors and hand-textured ceilings, faux-finished in a rich, caramel color. An abundance of hand-carved crown molding will enhance the elegant interior.

Designed for entertaining, the open floor plan will offer a view of the outdoor area through an expansive, 18 ft. wide window wall. An imposing fireplace will feature a mantle with sides carved to resemble a lion's legs and an adjoining bar will boast a striking curved glass window that overlooks the outdoor pool.

Because he has built media rooms for many of his clients, Stonestreet has come to love them. His personal media room will offer arena seating for a minimum of 10 guests. He also loves water features. As a result, the beach-entry, lagoon pool would feature a number of dramatic waterfall enhancements.

Stonestreet's home includes some thoughtful touches: an electronically lowered foyer chandelier for trouble-free cleaning, two cedar-lined, master bedroom closets of easily maintained Lucite,and even a laundry area in the master dressing room.

If architectural requirements allowed, this two-story Tuscan villa would command sweeping vistas on a large lot at the highest elevation in the Las Vegas Valley area—Promontory at the Ridges. But not all of the custom builders interviewed opted to locate their dream homes in the desert. One, initially, chose three locations for three separate homes.

TUSCAN TOUCHES

"I'd like to have a beach home, a mountain home and a city home," said Kathy Peterson, president of Specialized Development, L.L.C. If she had to choose one, however, she'd opt for a Tuscan home above the beach in Laguna Beach, California.

Blonde Utah sandstone would grace the drive and the path to the front door. Constructed of narrow, dry-stack stone, complemented with areas of hand-trowled, smooth finish stucco and an antiqued, barrel-tiled roof, her Tuscan home would present an Old World look. Faux-painted walls, distressed, knotty alder doors and natural maple floors with a scattering of designer area rugs would grace the interior.

HomeB

The barrel tiled roof, a multitude of architectural detailing and a dramatic entryway make this Valley villa truly spectacular

Photo courtesy of **Six Star Construction**

uilders

Peterson and her husband love to entertain, and her dream home would prove it. The floor plan would feature a combined great room and kitchen area large enough to hold up to 50 people. An expansive wall of sliding glass-paneled doors would open to a back patio for parties. Even the front courtyard with its English garden would feature an outdoor fireplace for company to enjoy.

LUSH ENVIRONMENT

Where Kathy Peterson would leave Las Vegas to build her dream home, Jeff Gremore, president of Distinctive General Contracting, would leave the continental United States. His home would also celebrate a greener, more watery and less desert-like environment in Hawaii.

Gremore's two-story contemporary home would sit high on a hill overlooking the ocean. His home would celebrate the lush tropical environment. There would be windows everywhere. So many, in fact, that when approaching the house, you could hardly see the walls for the abundance of tropical foliage.

Cool and welcoming, this pool area boasts delightful water features.

Photo courtesy of **Six Star Construction**

HomeB

Once through the etched glass front door, visitors would be greeted with a view of the blue Pacific Ocean through an 18 ft. by 8 ft. sliding glass-paneled door on the opposite wall of the great room. With a bow to the natural beauty outside, the interior would be simple and feature nature's colors and materials in the natural tawny beige walls and a highly polished, many-veined cream of Marfil marble floor. Gremore loves to create interesting ceilings. His would be a coffered ceiling with many architectural curves and angles. Painted to enhance its many dimensions, it would be the only bit of interior design that would not direct your gaze to the view outside.

"If you live in Hawaii, people are going to come and visit you," Gremore said. And with three guestrooms, a negative edge pool and landscape-lit, natural steps down to the beach, his home would be ready. Since Gremore is a gourmet cook, his functional, fitted kitchen would open into the great room so guests could chat with him as he cooked.

uilders

With its graceful staircase, natural stone fireplace and spectacular, coffered ceiling detail, this just completed grand home is a joy.

Photo courtesy of **Distinctive General Contracting**
Photo by **Jeffrey Green**

HomeB

Two-level curved windows and an abundance of architectural detailing give this great room an air of elegance while retaining a feeling of warmth.

LARGE, OPEN FLOOR PLANS

Brent Philip, owner of Philip Morgan Company, would also locate his dream home near water with lots of greenery in Northern California. "My dream home would contain a bit of the best of everything we've built," Philip said.

With its faux-finished exterior, Tuscan detailing and barrel-tiled roof, his home would exhibit the best of traditional Italian architecture. To support his personal lifestyle, Philip's fantasy home would boast a separate RV garage with extra space for his boat.

Warm and welcoming with plenty of room for Philip's wife, three children, and large extended family, his home would feature an open floor plan. The great room, with its earth-toned, matte finished stone floor and 6 ft. wide carved stone fireplace, would have an expansive sliding glass pocket door that would open onto an amazing back yard area.

Since the indoor kitchen would also play an important role in entertaining, Philip would surround the refrigerator and range with antiqued cabinetry. The dining room would be separate and formal, with a table that would seat up to 10 guests. Rich, mustard yellow or deep wine colors and wall sconces would grace the faux-finished walls. A few steps down would lead to a nearby wine room.

As these luxury home builders demonstrate every day, with thought and vision, dreams can become reality and fantasies can come true… even yours. ■

uilders

The Ashley Group Luxury Home Resource Collection

If you're searching for luxury home improvement resources, **The Ashle** **Group (www.theashleygroup.com)** is pleased to offer, as your final destination, the following **Home Books**: *Chicago, Washington DC, Sou* *Florida, Dallas/Fort Worth, Detroit, Atlanta, New York, Arizona,* *Philadelphia, Colorado* and the *Los Angeles* area. These comprehensive hands-on guides to building, remodeling, decorating, furnishing, and landscaping a luxury home are required reading for the serious and selective homeowner. With more than 700 full-color, beautiful pages per market, these hardcover volumes are the most complete and well-organized reference to the home industry. The **Home Books** cove all aspects of the building and remodeling process, include listings of hundreds of industry professionals, and are accompanied by informativ and valuable editorial discussing the most recent trends. Ordering you copy of any of the **Home Books** now can ensure that you have the blueprints to your dream home, in your hand, today.

Order your copies today and make your dream come true!

Building a **Custom** House

Interview and Select an Architect and Builder

This is the time to test the fit between what you want, what you need and what you can spend. It is advisable to interview two or three architects and builders and check their references before making a firm decision.

Site Selection

If you don't already own the land, meet with a realtor of your choice to describe the parameters of your future house. Also discuss future sites with your architect and builder.

Interview and Select an Interior Designer

A skilled designer will collaborate with the architect on matters such as windows and door location, appropriate room size and lighting plans.

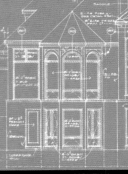

MONTH 1   MONTH 4

Design/Build Firms

A design/build firm is a company that employs architects, builders, estimators and sometimes interior designers and realtors. Read more about them in the Architects section.

• **Your architect and builder must work together.** The architect and contractor must be continually matching their budget and timelines. The architect converts the vision into buildable drawings. The contractor uses the drawings to make the plan work.

• **Final decisions:** Once you've received the initial drawings for the front, back and both sides of your house plus floor plans, you must make final decisions. You must decide on the exact footage of every level of your house and decide what unique elements you may want to include. For example, do you want your own home theater and entertainment center? Home automation and lighting?

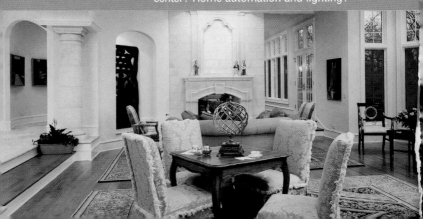

Project Description

Building an upscale, one-acre property, single-family home. This work includes planning the project (selecting an architect and builder), executing the project (the steps from breaking the ground to finishing the interior work) and finishing the project (closing on your new home).

Releasing the contractor

The client does a walk-through inspection and provides a "punch list"— a list of miscellaneous items the contractor needs to do to finish the work.

Final Close

Representatives for both the builder and the client will attend, along with a staff person from the closing company.

Final Inspection

Independent appraisals take place at this time.

MONTH 16

• **There are certain laws that protect the client.** Experts other than independent appraisers may be called upon to ensure that all agreements and building codes have been met. The client can, of course, make notes and have miscellaneous details taken care of.

• **Warranty:** Most states provide warranty protection for the client. The builder's warranty is typically one year for construction. Specific manufacturer warranties can last as long as five to 10 years.

Additional Information

For more information, contact the National Association of Home Builders (NAHB) 1201 15th St. NW Washington, DC 20005-2800 202-266-8111.

Mechanical Work Begins

This includes the rough plumbing, HVAC, electrical and low-voltage work. Allow two to three weeks each for the mechanical steps.

Interior Work Begins

Once the rough mechanical work is completed, the insulation and drywall can be installed. The hardwood floors and tile can be worked on concurrently. Next up are the stairs and the cabinets. Then the millwork (trim around the doors and windows) takes shape. The painting of trim, walls and ceilings follows. Then the mechanical work can be finalized.

Finishing the Work

Final sanding, sealing, carpeting and closet shelving complete the job. Allow three to four months for the interior work and final items to take place.

MONTH 10   MONTH 11   MONTH 15

• Environmental and energy concerns:

Of course, you will want to save on energy consumption, so make sure the builder doesn't forget these issues. Consider the selection of furnaces and water heaters. Ask your builder what their standard efficiency ratings are. Your initial investment might be more, but you could reap the benefit of lower energy costs in the long run. Where the sun rises and sets may seem inconsequential. But you'll want to make sure some key rooms allow natural light at particular times (for example, the greenhouse effect).

Also, as you build your house, you may want to ask your builder about different ways to protect the outside of the house using some sort of protective covering or wrap. That helps address your concerns about water intrusion.

Keeping on Schedule

Make sure the builder provides you with a schedule and completion date. The duration of the project should be clearly defined in the contract. However, you can almost depend on the schedule changing due to unforeseen delays such as weather-related items. But the homeowner can also affect the schedule by making late selections and desiring personal changes.

In
Conclusion

Your new house started as a dream with a piece of land. Now your custom-designed home has become a reality. It's time to start living in the special place you've created. Enjoy!

Special thanks to Orren Pickell Designers and Builders, Bannockburn, IL, and Centurian Development, Scottsdale, AZ, for their contributions to this article.

Breaking Ground

What a joy to see that construction of your new home is underway!

Foundation Work

This will include footings and dampproofing. The cement will need a few days to solidify.

Framing Begins

Rough framing of the house begins. At the end of this phase the structure will be in place, and you'll be able to see the rooms as they're going to look. This phase will take two to three months.

Roofing Begins

Since the time you broke ground until the time you get to this stage, probably four months have lapsed. With the exterior framing of the house completed, the contractor can start working on the interior (mechanical elements).

MONTH 5   MONTH 6   MONTH 9

Inspecting the Progress

At various times throughout the process, there will be building/municipal inspections to make sure the house meets all city codes and zoning issues. Often, a builder will insist on a six-month, follow-up courtesy inspection.

• **Choosing a contractor**: The builder is usually considered the general contractor for the job. The general contractor will line up the subcontractors and enter into an agreement with the vendors. The general contractor will be solely responsible for construction methods, techniques, schedules and procedures. The key is that teams need to be in place.

• **Seasonal costs**: The builder will keep in mind that different times of the year require different costs. The cost of lumber, for example, traditionally goes up in late spring to mid-summer. Good builders might also be able to figure when there will be occasional shortages in such items as drywall and brick. They might also know when to buy certain items in bulk to decrease your overall costs.

Building Your **Dream** Home

This timetable is included to support you in transforming your dream into reality. The sections of this book include specific categories to help you find the best quality craftsmanship available. This timeline will help you to understand the process from start to finish. How long might it take for you from designing the house to making it your own home? It could take from one year to a year and a half. Eighteen months is not unusual for a completely custom-built home. It can take four to six months to receive design approval and city permits alone. So be patient and plan ahead. Often delays occur because of a lack of communication. Take the initiative to keep in touch with all parties necessary. We hope this timeline will help give you an indication of how that dream home of yours will become a reality!

Custom Home Builders

continued from page **120**

SIX STAR CONSTRUCTION ....**(702) 243-6303**
10001 Moon Valley Place, Las Vegas   Fax: (702) 243-6289
See Ad on Page: 155, 156, 157, 158, 159, 160, 161, 162
<u>Principal/Owner:</u> Timothy Stonestreet

SOUTHERN HIGHLANDS ....**(702) 616-2500**
One Robert Trent Jones Lane, Las Vegas   Fax: (702) 616-2540
See Ad on Page: 164, 165

SPECIALIZED DEVELOPMENT ....**(702) 364-0656**
900 Granger Farm, Las Vegas   Fax: (702) 256-7510
See Ad on Page: 129
<u>Principal/Owner:</u> Kathy Petersen & Jay Weber
<u>e-mail:</u> weber01@lvcm.com
<u>Additional Information:</u> Custom, high-end home builder with attention to special
details and wine cellars.

SUMMER LAND CONSTRUCTION ....**(702) 616-2412**
5858 Juliano Street, Las Vegas
See Ad on Page: 166, 167
<u>Principal/Owner:</u> Chad Childress
<u>Additional Information:</u> Specializing in design/build construction from the purchase
of your lot through the final design.

Building Your Dream Home.

*Beyond this,
we believe
there should be
something more.*

Six Star Construction brings

Timothy Stonestreet,
President/Owner of Six Star Construction
"Over 21 years in Las Vegas"

Six Star Const

❊ Trust
  ❊ Quality
❊ Respect
  ❊ Dedication
❊ Value
  ❊ Pride

Six Star Constructi

★☆★☆★☆

No superintendents
Hands on management

The most important thing we build at Six Star Construction is trust. Our clients have become tr friends because of our word. No detail is too sma my personal attention. You'll never find me behi desk because I personally oversee every dream h build as if it were my own. I know what it takes the reward of a custom home and I am honored part of your dream. Every aspect is handled by u conception to completion.

We strive for 100% satisfaction. When you place trust in Six Star Construction you are guaranteed your project will be completed on time and on b More importantly, your dream home will be finis perfection.

And after you move into your new home, you ca easy knowing I'm just a phone call away. You ha word.

Timothy Stonestreet

0001 Moon Valley Place
s Vegas, NV 89134
nail: sixstarinc@aol.com

Cel: 702-218-
Ph: 702-243-
Fax: 702-243

action ★★★★★

your dreams to life...

EXECUTIVE HOME BUILDERS,

8670 Spring Mtn
Suite 102
Las Vegas, NV

02 • 656 • 5955
'02 • 562 • 0579 Fax

Many aspire.
Few have been chosen.

From the beginning, Southern Highlands Golf Club established a new benchmark for excellence in Las Vegas and beyond. Now, a select few custom homebuilders will continue this tradition as they create masterpieces of their own within The Estates at Southern Highlands. These extraordinary custom homes will feature:

- Half-acre to one-acre estate lots
- Breathtaking city, championship golf and mountain views
- Concierge-level amenities
- 24-hour guard-gated security

Homesites range from the $200,000s to more than $1 million.

PRIVATE GOLF   ESTATE LOTS

We invite you to tour our custom builder gallery.

Please call (702) 616-2500.

southernhighlands.com

SUMMER LAND CONSTRUCTION
Design • Build
702 • 616 • 2412

Only If You Want the Very Best...

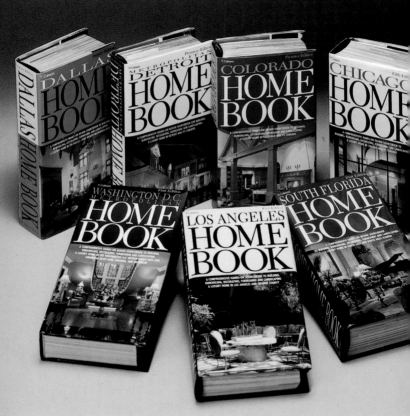

The
Ashley
Group

1350 E. Touhy Avenue, Des Plaines, Illinois 60018
888.458.1750   Fax 847.390.2902

www.theashleygroup.com • www.homebook.com

INTERIOR
DESIGNERS

Transform Your Imagination Into Reality

- INTERIOR DESIGN
  CONSULTATION

- SPACE PLANNING

- FINE FURNISHINGS
  AND ACCESSORIES

Interior Motives combines unique design elements with expertise to create the perfect ambiance for your home. We believe designing your home should be an exciting process. Creating an environment that reflects your taste, style, and personality is our top priority.

5260 Cameron Street
Suite A
Las Vegas, NV 89118
(702) 735-8151
Fax (702) 733-7079
www.interiormotivesly.com

"**Art** imitates **Nature** in this:

Not to dare is to dwindle. "

John Updike

173

Inner
Beauty

It may be as simple as a fresh look at the familiar. Or it may be an involved process requiring major renovation. In either case, interior designers can bring your ideas to life by demystifying the daunting task of designing a home. With their years of professional experience and the tools that they have at their fingertips, designers can orchestrate, layer by layer, design elements that compose an inviting and harmonious décor. For this collaboration to be a success, however, requires communication and trust. By listening to your dreams and by understanding your needs, designers can fashion workable rooms that are visual delights, reflecting your personality and your spirit. The end result of a productive partnership should be a happy homeowner who can exclaim, "I've always known that this was a great house, but now it's home!"

Photo courtesy of **Sydni Jay Associates**

WHERE STRUCTURE MEETS INSPIRATION

A great interior designer, like a great architect or builder, sees space creatively, applying years of education and experience to deliver a distinguished residence at the highest level of quality in an organized, professional manner. Intensely visual, these talented individuals imprint a home with the spirit and personality of the family living there.

Creativity, that special talent to see the possibilities in a living room, library, or little reading nook, is the most important asset an interior designer will bring to a project. Particularly in upper-end interiors, where the expense of sumptuous furnishings is often a secondary concern, the creative vision is what makes a room extraordinary.

A top quality interior designer who is licensed by the state is well educated in the field of interior design, usually holding a bachelor's or master's degree in the subject. This educational background coupled with practical experience is vital. You need not know where to get the best down-filled pillows or when French fabric mills close each summer. You need not learn the difference between French Country and English Country, how to match patterns, or how to correctly balance a floor plan. Rely on a knowledgeable designer for that information.

A great interior designer also handles the "nuts and bolts" business end of the project. With skill and experience in placing and tracking orders, scheduling shipping, delivery and installation, the designer can bring your project to its perfect conclusion.

AN INTERIOR DESIGNER IS A TEAM MEMBER

Choose an interior designer when you select your architect, builder, and landscape architect. A skilled designer can collaborate with the architect on matters such as window and door location, appropriate room size, and practical and accent lighting plans. In new construction and remodeling, try to make your floor plan and furniture choices simultaneously, to avoid common design problems, such as traffic corridors running through a formal space or awkward locations of electrical outlets.

CREATE THE BEST CLIENT-DESIGNER RELATIONSHIP

Talk to the best interior designers in the area and they'll tell you how exciting and gratifying it is for them when a client is involved in the process. This is happening as more homeowners turn their attention to hearth and home, dedicating their time and resources to achieve a style they love.

FIVE THINGS YOU SHOULD KNOW

1. Know what level of guidance you want: a person to handle every detail, someone to collaborate with you or simply an occasional consultation.
2. Know what you're trying to achieve. Start an Idea Notebook, filling it with pictures of rooms you like and don't like. This will help you define your style and stay true to your goal.
3. Know your budget. Prices of high-end furnishings know no upper limit. Adopt a "master plan" to phase in design elements if your tastes are outpacing your pocketbook.
4. Know what's going on. Always ask; don't assume. Design is not a mystical process.
5. Know yourself. Don't get blinded by beauty. Stay focused on what makes you feel "at home," and you'll be successful.

To establish the most successful and pleasant relationship with an interior designer, make a personal commitment to be involved.

Start by defining your needs, in terms of service and the end result. Have an interior designer involved during the architectural drawing phase of a new or renovation project, and get the process started early. Be clear about how much help you want from a designer. Some homeowners have a strong sense of what they want and simply need a consultant-type relationship. Others want significant guidance from a professional who will oversee the entire process.

Set up a relationship that encourages an open exchange of ideas. In pursuit of personal style, you need to trust a professional designer to interpret your thoughts and needs. You must be comfortable saying, "No, I don't like that," and receptive to hearing, "I don't think that's a good idea."

Be forthcoming about your budget. Not all interiors are guided by a budget, but the majority are. Your designer must know and respect your financial parameters and priorities. If a gorgeous dining room table is a top priority, objets d'art can be added later as you find them. Prices of exquisite furniture, custom-carved cabinets, and other high-end furnishings know no upper limit. Be realistic about what you will spend and what you expect to achieve. Do some research in furniture stores and specialty shops, starting with those showcased in this book. If your expectations temporarily exceed your budget, phase in the décor over a period of time.

Be inquisitive as the design unfolds. This is a creative effort on your behalf, so let yourself enjoy it, understand it and be stimulated by it.

START THINKING VISUALLY: STOP, LOOK AND CLIP

Before you start scheduling initial interviews with interior designers, start compiling an Idea Notebook – it's the best tool for developing an awareness of your personal style. Spend a weekend or two with a pair of scissors, a notebook, and a stack of magazines, (or add a section to the Idea Notebook you made to inspire your architecture and building plans). Make this a record of your personal style. Include pictures of your favorite rooms, noting colors, fabrics, tile, carpet, fixtures, the way light filters through a curtain, anything that strikes your fancy. On those pictures, circle the design elements that you'd like to incorporate into your own home décor and make comments regarding those elements you don't care for. Think hard about what you love and loathe in your current residence. Start to look at the entire environment as a rich source of design

UNDERSTANDING "ECLECTIC"

Eclectic means "not following any one system, but selecting and using what seems best from all systems."

Its popularity in interior design stems from the unique look it creates. Mixing the best from different styles creates a dynamic look that's totally different from an application of one chosen style. The overall effect is casual and comfortable, "dressed up" in a less formal way.

Eclectic can mean a mixing of styles within one room, like a rich Oriental rug paired with a denim sofa, or between rooms, like an 18th century dining room leading into an Early American kitchen. The possibilities for accents and appointments are unlimited because there are no restrictions.

One Person's Project Estimate:

Time To Redesign

It's fun to imagine, but what might it actually cost to undertake a project described in this chapter? The example below describes a typical project and gives a general estimate of the costs involved.

Project Description
Redesigning a 15 x 22 sq. ft. living room in a mid-scale price range.

Initial consultation $500
During the initial consultation, dimensions of the room are measured and photos taken of the room's distinctive qualities (unusual architecture, fireplaces, French doors, etc.). Next, a floor plan is done with recommendations of furniture placement.

Cost per hour (5 hour minimum) $100/hr
These charges apply to trips to local showrooms, the design center or antique shops to choose fabrics, furniture, and accessories. After the furniture is ordered, attention is turned to window treatments (photographing the windows and using the pictures as sketchboards to design various treatments, fabrics and colors). When designing kitchens and bathrooms, time may also be spent with clients and contractors discussing styles of cabinetry, countertops and flooring.

New rug (oriental or custom) $8,000

Furniture: Transitional (contemporary upholstery, traditional wood pieces)
     Sofa $3,000
     Chairs (2) .... $1,000 ea.
     Coffee table $2,000
     End tables (2) .... $1,000 ea.
     Sofa table $2,000
     French Be'rgre chair $3,000

Lamps (1 bronze, 2 porcelain) $1,200
Lighted wall sconces $1,000
Artwork $2,000
     1 large piece over sofa
     1 smaller piece over the fireplace
New paint
     Labor and paint (one color) $1,500
Accessories $3,000
     Silver tray with crystal decanter and 2 brandy snifters,
     large candlesticks.
     Crystal vase and several unusual picture frames in sterling and brass.

TOTAL $31,700

Note: The entire cost for a room design does not necessarily have to be paid at one time. Many designers are willing to work with a client over several years, adding a few items at a time, in order to create the look that is right for the client and his/her surroundings.

Lighted wall sconces to flank the fireplace

Contemporary chair

ideas. Movies, billboards, architecture, clothing – all are fascinating sources for visual stimulation.

Then, when you hold that initial meeting, you, too, will have a book of ideas to share. Although a smart designer will be able to coax this information from you, it's tremendously more reliable to have visual representations than to depend on a verbal description. It also saves a tremendous amount of time.

THE INTERIOR DESIGN PROCESS: GETTING TO KNOW YOU

Give yourself time to interview at least two interior designers. Invite them to your home for a tour of your current residence and a look at items you wish to use in the new environment. If you're building or remodeling, an interior designer can be helpful with your overall plans when he or she is given the opportunity to get involved early in the building process.

During the initial meeting, count on your intuition to guide you toward the best designer for you. Decorating a home is an intimate and very personal experience, so a comfortable relationship with a high degree of trust is absolutely necessary for a good result. You may adore what a designer did for a friend, but if you can't easily express your ideas, or if you feel he or she isn't interested in your point of view, don't pursue the relationship. Unless you can imagine yourself working with a designer two or three homes from now, keep interviewing.

You may wish to hire a designer for one room before making a commitment to do the whole house.

Some designers maintain a high degree of confidentiality regarding their clients, but if possible, get references and contact them, especially clients with whom they've worked on more than one home. Be sure to ask about the quality of follow-up service.

Be prepared to talk in specific terms about your project, and to honestly assess your lifestyle. For a home or a room to work well, function must be considered along with the evolving style. Designers ask many questions; some of them may be:

• What function should each room serve? Will a living room double as a study? Will a guest room also be an exercise area?

• Who uses the rooms? Growing children, adults, business associates? Which are shared and which are private?

• What safety and maintenance issues must be addressed? A growing family or a family pet may dictate the degree of elegance of a home.

IMMERSE YOURSELF

The more exposure you have to good design, the easier it becomes to develop your own style.

• Haunt the bookstores that have large selections of shelter magazines and stacks of books on decorating, design and architecture.
• Attend show houses, especially the Designer Showcase homes presented twice annually by ASID, and visit model homes, apartments or lofts.

EMBRACE THE MASTER PLAN

Gone are the days when Las Vegas Valley home-owners felt the need to move into a "finished" interior. They take their time now, letting the flow of their evolving lifestyle and needs guide them along the way.

- What kind of relationship do you want to establish between the interior and the landscape?

- Style: Formal, casual or a bit of both?

- Are you comfortable with color?

- Are you sentimental, practical?

- Are you naturally organized or disorganized?

- What kind of art do you like? Do you own art that needs to be highlighted or displayed in a certain way? Do you need space for a growing collection?

- Do you feel at home in a dog-eared, low maintenance family room or do you soothe your soul in an opulent leather chair, surrounded by rich cabinetry and Oriental rugs?

- What kind of furniture do you like? Queen Anne, contemporary, American Arts and Crafts, casual wicker, or eclectic mixing of styles?

- What words describe the feeling you want to achieve? Cheerful, cozy, tranquil, elegant, classic?

COMPUTING THE INTERIOR DESIGN FEE

Designers use individual contracts, standard contracts drawn up by the American Society of Interior Designers (ASID), or letters of agreements as legal documents. The ASID contract outlines seven project phases – programming, schematic, design development, contract documents, contract administration, project representation beyond basic services, and additional services. It outlines the designer's special responsibilities, the owner's responsibilities, the fees agreed upon, and the method of payments to the designer, including reimbursement of expenses.

Payment deadlines vary. Payments may be due at the completion of each project phase, on a monthly or quarterly basis, or as orders are made. You can usually expect to pay a retainer or a 50 percent deposit on goods as they are ordered, 40 percent upon the start of installation, and the balance when the job is completed.

Design fees, which may be based on "current market rate," are also computed in various ways. They may be charged on a flat fee or hourly basis, or may be tied to retail costs. Expect fees of approximately $100 an hour, varying by experience, reputation and workload. If an hourly rate is being used, ask if there is a cap per day, and if different rates are charged for an assistant's or drafter's time. Percentages may be figured as a certain amount above the retail or trade price, and can range from 15 to 100 percent.

MAKE LIGHTING A PRIORITY

The trend toward a comprehensive lighting programs as part of good interior design is catching on in Las Vegas Valley luxury homes. Appropriate light and well-designed accent lighting are very important to the overall comfort and functionality of a home. Neither the stunning volume ceiling nor the cozy breakfast nook can reach their potential if the lighting is wrong. Ask your interior designer for his or her lighting ideas. These choices need to be made in coordination with the building timeline, so plan and place orders early.

Make sure you understand your fee structure early on. Separate design fees may be charged by the hour, room, or entire project. It is imperative to trust your designer and rely on his or her reputation of delivering a top quality project in an honest, reliable fashion. You must feel you're being given a valuable service for a fair price.

If you work with a designer at a retail store, a design service fee ranging from $100 to $500 may be charged and applied against purchases.

FROM THE MIND'S EYE TO REALITY

Once you've found a designer who you like and trust, and have signed a clear, specific agreement, you're ready to embark on the adventure.

A good designer knows his or her way around the masses of products and possibilities. Such a person will guide you through upscale retail outlets and to craftspeople known only to a fortunate few in the trade. You can be a "kid in a candy store."

Just as you've allowed time to carefully consider and reconsider architectural blueprints, temper your enthusiasm to rush into decisions regarding your interiors. Leave fabric swatches where you see them day after day. Look at paint samples in daylight, evening light and artificial light. If possible, have everyone in the family "test sit" a kitchen chair for a week before ordering the whole set, and play with furniture placement. This small investment of time will pay handsomely in the end.

Be prepared to wait for your interiors to be installed. It's realistic to allow eight months to complete a room, and eight to 12 months to decorate an entire home.

Decide if you want your interiors to be installed piecemeal or all at once. Many designers recommend waiting for one installation, if you have the patience. Homeowners tend to rethink their original decisions when pieces are brought in as they arrive. By waiting for one installation, they treat themselves to a stunning visual and emotional thrill. ∎

A DESIGNING WOMAN ....**(702) 364-1549**
5530 South Valley View #104, Las Vegas .... Fax: (702) 889-3036
See Ad on Page: 184
Principal/Owner: Shirley Barton
e-mail: shirley@lasvegasdesigncenter.com
Additional Information: A Designing Woman approaches interior design with a
special flair and a contagious excitement to put the fun into creating a fresh image.

DE ATELIER DESIGN GROUP ....**(702) 366-0180**
2120 West Oakey Boulevard, Las Vegas .... Fax: (702) 366-1670
See Ad on Page: 183
Principal/Owner: Becky Najafi/Cyrus Najafi
e-mail: deatelier@att.net

DIANE CABRAL IMPRESSIONS ....**(702) 367-6570**
5410 Cameron Street #205, Las Vegas .... Fax: (702) 367-2593
See Ad on Page: 223
Principal/Owner: Diane L. Cabral
Additional Information: I specialize at turn-key custom homes as well as one-room
transformations by paying attention to detail and listening to the client's needs.

HARMONY DESIGNS..**(702) 240-3046**
Las Vegas
See Ad on Page: 186, 187
Principal/Owner: Julie Pilkington
Additional Information: Full service interior design, space planning, decoration and
consultation from inception to completion for the residential or commercial client.
Specializing in traditional, contemporary, historical & European styles.

HERBERT GORDON PRESS DESIGN ....**(702) 650-6511**
4033 Industrial Road, Las Vegas .... Fax: (702) 650-6557
See Ad on Page: 188, 189
Principal/Owner: Herbert Gordon Press

INTERIOR MOTIVES ....**(702) 735-8151**
5260 Cameron Street, Las Vegas .... Fax: (702) 733-7079
See Ad on Page: 170, 171, 185
Principal/Owner: Alice Roussos
Website: www.interiormotiveslv.com e-mail: alice@interiormotiveslv.com
Additional Information: Full service design studio specializing in clubhouses, model
homes and high end residential creating exciting and dynamic environments.

JAN STEVENS DESIGN..**(702) 433-7657**
2503 Albemarle Way, Henderson .... Fax: (702) 995-0098
See Ad on Page: 190
Principal/Owner: Jan Stevens
e-mail: snowite@lvcm.com
Additional Information: Understanding the client's soul translates into years
of timeless comfort & design!

JOY BELL DESIGN ASSOCIATES, INC ....**(702) 734-7404**
750 Rancho Circle, Las Vegas .... Fax: (702) 734-7414
See Ad on Page: 222
Principal/Owner: Joy Bell

181

continued on page **205**

Prism Interiors

Janice Reichardt
Interior Designer
(702) 252-5990

Interior and Architectural Design

de atelier
design group

A Designing Woman

5530 S. Vally View # 104
Las Vegas, NV 89118
702 • 364 • 1549

OFFERING EXCLUSIVE ARCHITECTURAL INTERIORS AND FURNISHINGS FOR THE DISCRIMINATING HOMEOWNER

I·N·T·E·R·I·O·R
IM
M·O·T·I·V·E·S
CREATIVE INTERIOR DESIGN

5260 Cameron St. #A
Las Vegas, NV 89118
Phone 702.735.8151
Fax 702.733.7079
www.interiormotiveslv.com

Historical renovation of the Governer's
Mansion in Carson City, Nevada.

From Manor to Mansion
Julie Pilkington
Harmony Designs
240-3046

HGp

Herbert Cordon Press Design Assoc., Inc.

CREATING EXCEPTIONAL RESIDENCES
FOR DISCERNING HOME BUYERS
INTERIOR ARCHITECTURAL DESIGN

702.650.6511
4033 INDUSTRIAL ROAD, LAS VEGAS, NEVADA 89103

NEW YORK • LAS VEGAS • LOS ANGELES

Jan Stevens design

office 702-433-7657
fax 702-995-0098
snowite@lvcm.com

PANACHE INTERIOR DESIGN

Photography by Lynn Gates

2795 Barrow Downs Street
Las Vegas, Nevada 89135
phone: (702) 869-5120
email: TKPanache@AOL.com

*" A well designed space should be an
expression of each clients personality.
Proffesionally executed in partnership
with an Interior Designer. Utilizing
thier buying power and creative
resources."*

Paula M. Corvin
Interior Designs

Registered Interior Designer AIA & NCIDQ Certified
Over 15 years experience in all phases of design
phone (702) 247-6958
fax (702) 614-4095

...ANLEY & ASSOCIATES
Robert Stanley, ASID
an interior design firm

.59 renate dr.
vegas, nevada 89103
one & fax (702) 248-4841
nail: rstanleyasid@wizard.com

reg. 033-ID

Project
Description

The project included redesigning every existing room along with planning and decorating a 3,500 sq. ft. addition. In all, the home has two family rooms, a great room, a theater, kitchen and dining rooms, screen porches with dining, and six bedrooms and baths. There is also a two-bedroom, two-bath guest house on the property. The project took approximately 18 months, which is a long time for a design-only project, but not long for new construction.

Creating a Beautiful Interior

Select an Interior Designer

Meet with several designers and ask questions. Consider personality, style and business methods when making your decision. Look at the designer's portfolio, ask for references and call them. Be sure you are comfortable with your choice–you'll be working together a long time.

Create a Furniture Floor Plan

This very preliminary plan is done with furniture shapes and prototypical sizes. The purpose is to test the rooms and the lighting plan to determine such things as: Do the rooms seat the number of people you had in mind? Can you fit your existing furniture? Is traffic flow working?

Review Electrical Plan

Once the preliminary floor plan is in place, review it against the electrical design of the space to be sure it will support the demand of the lighting and technology planned for the room.

Determine Flooring Type

Wood, tile, area rugs or wall-to-wall carpeting? The rest of the design of the room will evolve from the style of the flooring materials you choose.

| 1 | MONTH 2 | MONTH 3 |

Why use an Interior Designer

A designer will help you define your style and keep your project focused to minimize costly decorating mistakes. Designers have knowledge, training and, most importantly, resources. They can handle the myriad of details while you enjoy the results.

• **As you begin,** take some time to ask yourself some questions regarding your project. For whom is the space being designed? What activities will take place there? What is your time frame for the project? What is your budget? What image do you want to project? Keep in mind, the more information you provide, the more successful the designer will be in meeting your needs and expectations.

• **Keep focused.** Your designer is responsible for providing all the information you will need to make decisions, but you must ultimately make the decisions in a timely manner to keep your project on track and meet the dates in your timeline.

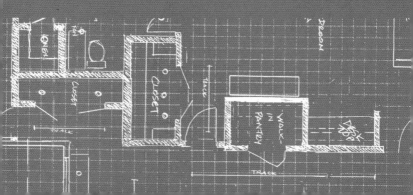

Begin Visiting Showrooms

Start looking at cabinetry, furniture, rugs, fixtures, and accessories to narrow down your choices. In some cases, clients visit the designer's studio to view selections. In others, the designer brings items, catalogs, swatches, etc. to the client's home.

Make Final Flooring, Cabinetry, Tile and Stone Selections

These items usually require professional installation, so they must be ordered first.

Workmen Begin Installation

First the flooring and tile will be installed, then cabinets and woodwork, countertops, plumbing fixtures and faucets.

MONTH 4   MONTH 5   MONTH 8

Communicate

It is important to establish parameters for updates on your project. The communication between you and your interior designer needs to be on-going.

• **Allow plenty of time.** Take as much time as you need to make your choices. You should be able to choose what you want and not be limited to choices because not enough time was allowed to view selections. Keep in mind that many decisions affect others, so once you have decided, try not to second guess or change your mind.

Creating a **Beautiful** Interior

You have found your paradise. You have fallen in love with the area around your new home. The views are spectacular. The entrance is grand and suitably impressive. The great room will be a place where family, friends and visitors will all feel at ease, and all will be welcomed within. You can envision it, but how do you get from dreaming the dream to living it? Beautiful rooms do not just happen. They are the result of careful planning by the homeowner and an interior designer. While you may have an idea of what you would like, or have a desire for a particular effect, it is the interior designer who can take your dream and turn it into something magnificent.

We have taken one family's dream, to create a spectacular, yet comforting home, and followed that project from the day the client bought the home to the day the rooms they once dreamed of became rooms they now live in.

The following timeline is designed to give you an idea of how long it may take to complete an interior design project of this magnitude, and what the steps will be along the way. While the steps will most likely remain the same, the timeline may shorten or lengthen depending on your individual project. We have also included a few helpful tips and ideas, to further ensure that your project can go as smoothly as possible.

In Conclusion

N ow that you have seen an interior design project guided from beginning to end, it's time to embark on your own project. Yes, it will take some time to complete. And it will require a certain amount of involvement from you and communication with the designer. But in the end, you will have a space that is uniquely yours. You will have rooms that welcome you in, views you enjoy, furnishings that fit and details that express who you are. It can be a long journey, but one with a remarkable payoff.

Thanks to Janet Mesic Mackie for her contribution of photography for this timeline.

Make Final Furniture Selections

Order furniture in plenty of time to account for inevitable delays. Custom furniture will take more time.

MONTH 11

Order Window Treatments

When window framing is complete, final measurements can be made for window treatments.

MONTH 14

Finishing the Work

Final sanding, sealing, carpeting and closet shelving complete the job. Allow three to four months for the interior work and final items to take place.

MONTH 15

• **Create a project file.** Keep carpet, fabric, wallpaper and paint samples, floor plans, a tape measure, calendar, phone list and your photo clippings together in an easy-to-carry file or project folder to reference at home and when out shopping for your rooms. With your project file in hand, decisions can be made on the spot without having to check if the upholstery matches or the piece fits into your overall plan.

Work Together

To ensure your project remains uniquely yours, continue to explore stores, websites, magazines and books for furnishings, styles, colors and accessories you like. Tell your designer your preferences. Be open to the new ideas your designer may offer, but pay attention to your gut feelings.

FINISHED PROJECT

Make Final Selections of Accessories and Artwork

Now is the time to select the accessories that will give the rooms your personal touch.

Schedule a Thorough House Cleaning

A professional cleaning is recommended to remove construction dust before moving final furnishings into place.

MONTH 16

Final Installations Begin

Workmen will be putting the final touches on the project, installing lighting fixtures, window treatments and rugs.

MONTH 18

Place Furniture and Accessories

Put the furniture in place, add accessories and artwork, relax and enjoy!

• **Show off your collection.** Many homeowners have a collection, be it antique cameras, sculpture, majolica, vintage perfume bottles, glass, art, or guns and swords. A well-designed display of your collection can put the finishing touch on your decorating project. Arrange a grouping in one area for a bold statement. Divide a very large collection into subsets and display them in several rooms to create a theme in your home. Vary heights and sizes for visual appeal, place small items at eye level, larger ones on the floor.

Stay Flexible
Be aware that product availability and contractor scheduling problems may cause unavoidable delays. Building extra time into your schedule can help avoid stress between you and your designer.

continued from page **181**

MAGDALENA'S ....**(702) 228-3924**
8125 West Sahara Ave, Las Vegas   Fax: (702) 228-6895
See Ad on Page: 412, 413, 429
Principal/Owner: Maggie Brandon
Website: www.magdalenaslasvegas.com e-mail: magdalenasvegas@aol.com
Additional Information: We invite you to tour our showroom, where you make your
dreams come true item by item, room by room.

MILTON HOMER FINE HOME FURNISHINGS ....**(702) 798-0707**
5455 South Valley View Boulevard, Las Vegas   Fax: (702) 739-1907
See Ad on Page: 191
Principal/Owner: Milton Homer

NEST FEATHERINGS ....**(702) 362-6707**
6425 West Sahara Avenue, Las Vegas   Fax: (702) 362-1231
See Ad on Page: 264, 434, 435
Principal/Owner: La Rayn Sorenson
Website: www.nest-featherings.com e-mail: nest_featherings@hotmail.com
Additional Information: Nest Featherings will enhance your home with an unequaled
combination of "investment" quality furniture and magnificent design expertise.

PANACHE INTERIOR DESIGN ....**(702) 869-5120**
2795 Barrow Downs Street, Las Vegas
See Ad on Page: 192
Principal/Owner: Tim Kain
e-mail: tkpanache@aol.com
Additional Information: No detail is too small; no ambition too great where
our clients needs are concerned.

PAULA CORVIN INTERIOR DESIGNS ....**(702) 247-6958**
2567 Corner Stone Circle, Henderson   Fax: (702) 614-4095
See Ad on Page: 194, 195
Principal/Owner: Paula Corvin
e-mail: paulacorvin@yahoo.com
Additional Information: Working directly with architects, builders, realtors & clients
to create pleasing designs ranging from custom residential to commercial properties.

PRISM INTERIORS ....**(702) 252-5990**
73 Prairie Dog Drive, Henderson   Fax: (702) 896-9769
See Ad on Page: 182
Principal/Owner: Janice Reichardt
Additional Information: Interior design, space planning and consultation.

RIO DÉCOR DESIGN & FINE ART ....**(702) 362-4500**
5530 South Valley View Suite 105, Las Vegas   Fax: (702) 362-4580
See Ad on Page: 193, 544, 545
Principal/Owner: Christine Rosa Lefkowitz
e-mail: riodecor@aol.com
Additional Information: Interior Design – Fine Art – Feng Shui.

RIO DESIGNS ....**(702) 304-1316**
605 Edgebrook Drive, Las Vegas   Fax: (702) 304-9616
See Ad on Page: 217
Principal/Owner: Rio Habbas
e-mail: riodesigns@hotmail.com
Additional Information: Personal service and attention given to every detail in order
to make your home truly unique.

205

continued on page **216**

RIO DÉCOR DESIGN & FINE ART

Christine Lefkowitz: "I use a significant amount of art in my designs because it represents many forms of emotions and feelings. When designing this room, I felt it was important to decorate parts of the area with art and other forms of expression which clearly demonstrated the connection between the room and its owner. I believe art brought life to this room, illustrated its history of generations and brought into perspective the constantly changing evolution of our world."

Photo by **Jerry Metellus**

Photo by **CHAWLA Associates**

Desi

Photo by **Catherine Tighe**

207

STANLEY & ASSOCIATES

Robert Stanley: "How do you design a hallway 40 ft. long by 6 ft. wide? Simplicity is the key. This unusual space is the main artery of the house and is the main access to the bedroom wing. The console table was specifically designed with clean, simple lines to provide a subtle background to a collection of art and unusual glass bottles. Vertical box shelving, positioned next to the three separate but continuous table pieces, augments the feeling of movement down the hall."

ners

Photo by **Dave Chawla**

208

A DESIGNING WOMAN

Shirley Barton: "I worked closely with the client in designing this home, and together, we decided on a soft, European style. The design of this room began with two custom hand-painted chests in a beautiful washed red. To help retain a sense of space in the room, we selected an iron bed with a canopy. The fabrics and colors were chosen for their soft and luminous elegance. To give the room weight, I used a broom-pleated fabric for the bed skirt. Accessories were kept to a minimum because this room is a special retreat for Grandma's visits."

Desi

DE ATELIER DESIGN GROUP

Becky Najafi: "Bring the outside in! The surrounding natural environment influenced the details, colors, textures, lighting and ambiance of this elegant living area. When looking out at the wondrous mountain range from this room, it is very comforting to see the beauty of the outside enhancing the beauty of this inside space."

ners

JAN STEVENS DESIGN

Jan Stevens: "This room was drenched in sunlight through multiple windows of different sizes, shapes and heights. How to address all the windows was a formidable task, and draperies everywhere was not the answer. The solution required inventiveness. I selected the tall, arched windows to crown with antique ox yokes, flanked with columns of soft, warm chenille. Another window became a simple pillar of light, topped with an accessory vignette. Finally, I took advantage of one more opening, using the natural light to accentuate the clients' glass collection, creating a colorful focal point."

210

Desi

SYDNI JAY ASSOCIATES

Samantha Sydni Michaels Badgley, IIDA Terry Jay Cohen, IIDA:
"Working closely with the builder and client, we designed the interior of this luxurious residence to embellish the client's collectibles and still retain warmth within massive spaces. After extensive consultation, it was decided that earthy yet elegant colors would be utilized throughout. To enhance and define the rotunda entry hall, we created the design for the floor and selected the various marbles, which were then lazer-cut to create the extraordinary entry floor. The intricate ironwork on the curving staircase, the decorative vertical wall panels and the traditional foyer table with a towering, exotic floral arrangement carry the interest upwards."

ners

JOY BELL DESIGN ASSOCIATES INC.

Joy Bell: "A warm atmosphere is created for this lovely detached office retreat by using corresponding colors, materials and finishes. The Silver Leaf curio cabinets and bronze leather sofa add character and balance to this pleasing environment."

Desi

PANACHE INTERIOR DESIGN

Tim Kain: "Our clients gave us two simple directives. First, accommodate three distinct functions within this singular space, and second, create an intimate, warm environment in which to showcase their diverse collection of art. We accomplished our task by careful utilization of space, color and texture. A petite baby grand piano hovers effortlessly between the living and dining rooms, crowned by the soft arch and framed by the opulent draperies. The sensuous slate floors and plush pumpkin carpet delineate areas without obstruction. The rooms flow from one to the other with a gracious capacity for comfort."

ners

RIO DESIGNS

Rio Habbas: "I believe that people crave the need to express their own individuality and tastes, whether they want to create a look that is simple yet elegant, or elaborate yet comfortable and impressive. In order to understand my client's desires, I ask questions, then listen and dig beneath the surface. In this room, the essence and core of my client's personal style was captured through the integration of colors, fabrics, furniture and accessories. The result is a room that achieves an elegant yet relaxing atmosphere."

Desi

INTERIOR MOTIVES

Alice Roussos: "My client was an empty nester coming from a large, very traditional home and desiring a new look. Because of my belief that interior design should reflect and enhance the architecture, I chose natural and textural materials to blend with the earthy but contemporary Prairie style of the home. The ledge stone used on the exterior was repeated on the interior, along with natural wood, granite, copper and glass, to create an environment that is both warm and sophisticated."

ners

continued from page **205**

STANLEY & ASSOCIATES..**(702) 248-484**
   3959 Renate, Las Vegas   Fax: (702) 248-484
   See Ad on Page: 196
   <u>Principal/Owner:</u> Robert Stanley
   <u>e-mail:</u> rstanleyasid@wizard.com
   <u>Additional Information:</u> NCIDQ-Certified. Nevada Registered Designer.

STATEMENT OF STYLE ....**(702) 871-417**
   3050 Sorrel Street, Las Vegas   Fax: (702) 871-968
   See Ad on Page: 220
   <u>Principal/Owner:</u> Susan Conboy
   <u>e-mail:</u> stmstyle@lvcm.com

SYDNI JAY ASSOCIATES – DESIGNERS ....**(702) 735-188**
   3355 South Highland Drive Suite 107, Las Vegas   Fax: (702) 735-673
   See Ad on Page: 218, 219
   <u>Principal/Owner:</u> Samantha Sydni Micheals Badgley,
   <u>Website:</u> www.sydnijay.com <u>e-mail:</u> sydnijsamantha@msn.com
   <u>Additional Information:</u> Cohen & Badgley have been working designers together
   in the Las Vegas area for 26 years. We are a complete design facility, offering
   consultation, supplying and installing all products required to complete projects, both
   residential and commercial.

R

ℛio Designs

RIO HABBAS
Interior Designer

PHONE: 702.304.1316
CELL: 702.306.3043
FAX: 702.304.9616

**SYDNI
JAY
associates**

3355 South Highland #107
Las Vegas, NV 89109
702.735.1885 • fax 702.735.6738

Statement Of Style

PHOTOGRAPHY: BY TRENT

" From Traditional to Contemporary, we are dedicated to providing timeless interiors with emphasis on comfort and warmth

Sue Conboy • Designer

3050 SORREL STREET • LAS VEGAS • 702.871.47

xperience

Furniture Showcase

JOY BELL design associates, inc.

750 Rancho Circle • Las Vegas, NV 89107
Office: (702) 734-7404 • Fax: (702) 734-7414

Finally... Las Vegas' Own
Home & Design Sourcebook

The **Las Vegas Home Book** is your final destination when search
for home remodeling, building and decorating resources. This
comprehensive, hands-on sourcebook to building, remodeling,
decorating, furnishing and landscaping a luxury home is required
reading for the serious and discriminating homeowner. With more
than 700 full-color, beautiful pages, the **Las Vegas Home Book** is
the most complete and well-organized reference to the home indus
This hardcover volume covers all aspects of the process, includes
listings of hundreds of industry professionals, and is accompanied
by informative and valuable editorial discussing the most recent
trends. Ordering your copy of the **Las Vegas Home Book** now ca
ensure that you have the blueprints to your dream home, in your
hand, today.

O R D E R   F O R

THE LAS VEGAS HOME BOOK

☐ YES, please send me _____ copies of the LAS VEGAS HOME BOOK at $39.95 per book, plus $3 Shipping & Handling per book.

Total amount enclosed: $_____   Please charge my: ☐ VISA   ☐ MasterCard   ☐ American Express

Card # _____   Exp. Date _____

Name _____   Phone: (   ) _____

Address _____   E-mail: _____

City _____   State _____   Zip Code _____

Send order to: Attn: Marketing Department—The Ashley Group, 1350 E. Touhy Ave., Suite 1E, Des Plaines, Illinois 60018
Or Call Toll Free: 888-458-1750   Fax: 847-390-2902   E-mail: ashleybooksales@cahners.com

All orders must be accompanied by check, money order or credit card # for full amount.

LANDSCAPING

Inspired by Nature, Created by

Oak Creek
LAWN & LANDSCAPE, LLC
NCL #0046205

phn 702-339-7747   fax 702-254-4067
Website - Portfolio at
www.OakCreekLandscape.com

Your Garden Environment
from Day...

to Night.

I trust in *nature* *for the* stable laws of *beauty.*

Robert Browning

Natural Selection

Landscaping is the only design area that is by nature intended to evolve over time. The philosophy behind landscape design has evolved as well. From traditional European formality to the naturalism of Prairie Style, to the simplicity and order of Far Eastern influences, your landscape should be as unique a design statement as your home itself. More and more people are blurring the divisions between inside and outside environments, with expanses of windows, patios designed to act as "outdoor rooms" and various types of glass and screened enclosures to enjoy the outdoors whatever the weather. Landscape becomes almost an architectural element at times, creating an interplay and synthesis of indoors and outdoors. Water gardens are growing in popularity as people learn that they are ecosystems in their own right, requiring little additional time or attention once they are established. Think of it: the soothing splash of a waterfall or babbling brook right in your own backyard!

VIEWS AND VISTAS

First you choose your views, then you build your home. To create a harmonious balance between your home and its surroundings, your architect should be invited to visit the site of your new home, and to meet with your landscape architect. The site can often serve as a catalyst, inspiring a design that responds to the uniqueness of the site. When all the team members are included, important details (like the location of your air conditioning units) can be discussed and settled, making for the best results for you and your family.

OUTDOOR DÉCOR

As Las Vegas Valley area homeowners get more involved in their yards and gardens, they learn to "see" outdoor rooms and take deep pleasure in decorating them. Arbors, sculpture, tables, benches, water features, or any piece of whimsy add delightful decorating. Hedges or fences create natural partitions. The results are appealing, comfortable and richly rewarding.

GETTING BACK TO THE GARDEN

Think of the land as a canvas for a work of environmental art. Think of the landscape professional as an artist who uses nature to translate your needs and desires into a living, breathing reality. A formal English garden or seemingly artless arrangements of native plantings, a winding cobblestone walkway leading from a hand-laid brick driveway — these are the kinds of possibilities you can explore. When you work with a professional who is personally committed to superior work and service, designing a landscape is full of creativity, new ideas and satisfying results.

GETTING A LANDSCAPE STARTED

Selecting a landscape professional to create and maintain a distinctive landscape is one of the most important decisions you'll make as a homeowner. In making your decision, consider these questions:

• Are you landscaping a new construction home? There are critical decisions to be made early in the home building planning process that concern the landscape. Interview and work with professionals who have considerable experience in doing excellent work with new construction projects. Make them part of your team and have them meet with your architect, interior designer and builder early in the project.

• Do you want to hire a landscape architect or a landscape designer? Landscape architects have met the criteria to be registered by the state. Many hold university degrees in landscape architecture. A landscape designer generally has had training and/or experience in horticulture and landscaping and may also have a background in art.

• Do you want full service? If you want to work with one source, from design through installation to maintenance, only consider those who offer comprehensive service.

Allow time to interview at least two professionals before making a decision. Start early, especially if you plan to install a swimming pool, which should be dug the same time as the foundation of a new home.

Invite the professional to your home to acquaint him or her with your tastes and personality through observing your choices in interior design as well as the current landscape. Have a plat of survey available. Be prepared to answer questions like:

• Do you prefer a formal or informal feel? The formality of symmetrical plantings or the informal look of a natural area?

• Is there a place or feeling you'd like to recreate? Somewhere where you've vacationed, or the place where you grew up?

• What colors do you like? This will impact the flowers chosen for your gardens.

• Are you a gardener? Would you like to be? If you're fond of flower, herb or vegetable gardening, your landscape professional will build the appropriate gardens.

• How will you use the space? Will children use the backyard for recreation? Will you entertain outdoors? If so, will it be during the day or at night? Do you envision a pool, spa, gazebo or tennis court?

• Are you fond of lawn statuary, fountains or other ornamental embellishments?

• What architectural features must be considered? A wrap-around porch, large picture windows? Brick or stone exteriors?

• To what extent will you be involved in the process? Most landscape architects and designers are happy to encourage your involvement in this labor of love. There is a great deal of pleasure to be derived from expressing your personality through the land. A lifelong hobby can take root from this experience. Landscapers say their clients often join garden clubs after the completion of their project, and that many of their rehabbing projects are done for clients who are already avid gardeners.

Landscape professionals expect that you will want to see a portfolio, inquire about their styles, and their experience. You may wish to request permission to visit sites of their installed landscapes. If you have special concerns, such as environmental issues, ask if the landscape professional has any experience in such areas.

COMPUTING LANDSCAPE FEES

It's important to create a workable budget. It's easy to be caught off guard when you get a landscape proposal – it is a significant investment.

To make sure you give the outside of your home the appropriate priority status, plan to invest 10 to 25 percent of the cost of a new home and property in the landscaping. Although landscape elements can be phased in year after year, expect that the majority of the cost will be incurred in the first year. Maintenance costs must also be considered.

Billing practices vary among professionals and depend on the extent of the services you desire. Some charge a flat design fee up front, some charge a one-time fee for a contract that includes everything, some charge a design fee which is

THE LANDSCAPE BUDGET

Basic:
10% of the cost of your home & property
In-depth:
The 10 to 25% rule of thumb applies to your landscapes too.
Starting at $90,000:
• Finish grading
• Sodded lawns
• Foundation plantings (all around the house) including some smaller trees
• Walkways of pavers or stone City Dwellers!
• Soft atmospheric lighting up to the front door and in the back yard
• Asphalt driveway
• Concrete unit pavers or stone patio, or deck
• Perimeter plantings of trees and shrubs for privacy and finished look

231

A PARTY OF GARDENS

As gardening attracts more devotees in Las Vegas Valley, people are rediscovering the satisfaction of creating imaginative gardens. Some ideas: one-color gardens, fragrance gardens, native plant gardens, Japanese gardens.

One Person's Project Estimate:

The Price of Being Green

It's fun to imagine, but what might it actually cost to undertake a project described in this chapter? The example below describes a typical project and gives a general estimate of the costs involved.

PROJECT DESCRIPTION

Landscape development of a typical property consisting of new paver patio and walk, retaining wall and approximately 600 sq. ft. of new planting beds along front foundation.

Initial consultation C

Design contract fees...$500

Hardscape construction
Cut Lanonstone retaining wall (85 face sq. ft.) $4,130
Concrete paver patio and walkway (480 sq. ft.) $7,785

Planting development
Bed preparation (600 sq. ft.) $9,000
Includes: Assorted foundation shrubs
    Four mid-size shade trees
    Assorted perennials
    Annual beds
    New sod for lawn areas

Landscape management...$3,648
One season (April – November) of maintenance of about one-half acre site.
Includes: Weekly mowing and trimming of maintained turf areas
    Monthly pavement edging of sidewalks, patios and driveway
    Weekly landscape debris clean-up of maintained areas
    Monthly cultivation of open bed areas
    Manual weeding
    Preventative weed control
    Granular fertilization of maintained bed areas
    Spade edging of beds
    Selective pruning of oriental trees (less than 12 feet high), shrubs and hedges
    Weekly perennial dead heading of faded flowers
    Groundcover maintenance and pruning
    Spring and Fall clean-up of maintained areas
    Weekly off-site disposal of landscape waste and grass clippings
    Turf fertilization program
    Broadleaf weed control in late Spring and late Summer

TOTAL: **$25,063**

Assorted annuals, perennials and shrubs

Cut Lanonstone retaining wall

Herringbone pattern for concrete patio pavers

LIGHTING YOUR LOT

"Less is more" is the best philosophy when designing an outdoor lighting system. Today's beautiful, functional fixtures are themselves worthy of admiration, but their purpose is to highlight the beauty of your home while providing safe access to your property. Well-established lighting companies and specialty companies offer extensive landscape lighting product lines.

DREAM POOLS

Yours for $60,000: Custom-designed mid-sized pool with a deep end, spa, custom lighting, cleaning system, remote control functions, cover, deck. Yours for $200,000: A custom-designed Roman-style pool with bar stools, a small wading pool, elevated spa and elaborate waterfall. Specialized lighting, built-in planters, automated hydraulic cover, top-of-the-line automated cleaning system, all with remote control functions.

waived if you select them to complete the project, and some build a design fee into the installation and/or maintenance cost.

A PROFESSIONAL DEVELOPS AN ENVIRONMENT

While you're busy imagining glorious gardens, your landscaper will be assessing practical issues like grading and drainage, the location of sewers, utility lines and existing trees, where and when the sun hits the land, and the quality of the soil.

This important first step, the site analysis, should take place before construction has even begun, in the case of a new house. Site work helps ensure that the blueprints for your house won't make your landscape dreams impossible to achieve, and vice versa. If you've told your builder you want a breakfast nook, you'll probably get one regardless of the fact that it requires taking out a tree you value.

If you're considering installing a custom driveway or sidewalk, this early stage is the time to inform your builder. Ask your builder not to do construction outside the building envelope. You and your landscape professionals will design and build your driveway and walkways.

Expect the design process to take at least six weeks. During this time, the designer is developing a plan for the hardscape, which includes all of the man-made elements of your outdoor environment, and the many layers of softscape, which are the actual plantings. You can expect to be presented with a plan view that is workable and in harmony with your home, as well as your budget.

Hardscape elements, like irrigation systems and pavements, will be installed first, before a new house is completely finished. Softscape will go in later.

During this landscape project, you most likely have begun to appreciate the special nature of landscape and will not be surprised if your completed project does not look "complete." A landscape should be given time in the hands of nature to come to maturity: three years for perennials, five years for shrubs, and 15 years for trees.

LUXURY LIVING WITH A CUSTOM-DESIGNED POOL

The beauty and value of a custom-designed swimming pool are unmatched. A welcome design element to the landscape, a pool adds to the overall property value of the residence, and creates greater use and enjoyment of the yard. As area families spend more and more of their leisure time at home, a pool answers their dreams of living well at home.

Deciding to build a swimming pool is best done as a new home is being designed so the pool can enhance the home and landscape architecture. By integrating the pool into the overall scheme, you'll be able to establish a realistic budget. One of the biggest mistakes homeowners make when purchasing a pool is not initially getting all the features they want. It's difficult and costly to add features later.

The design process is time-consuming. You may have four or more meetings with your pool professional before finalizing the design. Pool projects can be started at almost any time of year, so avoid getting caught in the busy season, spring to summer. Start getting approvals in January if you want to be enjoying your pool in the summer. The building process takes about two months, after obtaining permits. You should plan to have your pool dug at the same time as the home foundation. Pool construction is integrated with surrounding decking, so make sure your landscape architect, pool builder, or hardscape contractor is coordinating the effort.

OUTDOOR LIVING

Today's homeowners, having invested the time and resources to create a spectacular environment, are ready to "have it all" in their own backyards.

Decks, gazebos, and increasingly, screened rooms, are popular features of today's upscale homes. The extended living space perfectly suits our "cocooning" lifestyle, offering more alternatives for entertaining, relaxation, and family time at home. Many new homes tout outdoor living space as a most tantalizing feature.

Decks and outdoor rooms offer extra living space and are functional enough to host almost any occasion. With thoughtful and proper design, they fulfill our dreams of an outdoor getaway spot.

EVERY KID'S FANTASY

In a yard with plenty of flat area: a wood construction expandable play system with several slides, including a spiral slide, crawl tunnels and bridges to connect fort and structures, a tic-tac-toe play panel, three swings, climbing ropes, fire pole, gymnastics equipment (trapeze, turning bar), sandbox pit, and a built-in picnic table with benches. Price Tag: around $12,000

In a smaller yard: a wood construction expandable play system with a small fort, two swings and a single slide. Price Tag: around $1,400

235

THE FINAL EVALUATION

When the landscape is installed, conduct a final, on-site evaluation. You should evaluate the finished design, find out what elements will be installed later and learn more about how the plan will evolve over time. You, the landscape designer or architect, project manager, and maintenance manager should be involved.

A TYPICAL LANDSCAPE DESIGN TIMETABLE

- **One to two weeks to get the project on the boards**

  +
- **One to two weeks to do the actual site and design work and prepare plans**

  +
- **One week to coordinate calendars and schedule presentation meeting**

  +
- **One to two weeks to leave the plans with the client and get their feedback**

  +
- **One week to incorporate changes, create and get approval on a final design**

  =

FIVE TO EIGHT WEEKS

THE TIGHT SQUEEZE.

When homes get bigger, backyards get smaller. A landscape architect will be attentive to keeping all aspects of your plan in proper balance.

THINKING ABOUT OUTDOOR LIVING

An on-site meeting with a licensed contractor who is an expert in landscape building or a landscape architect is the first step in designing and building a deck, patio, or any outdoor structure. An experienced professional will guide you through the conceptualization by asking questions like these:

- Why are you building the structure? For business entertaining, family gatherings, child or teen parties, private time?

- Do you envision a secluded covered area, a wide open expanse, or both?

- Do you want a single level, or two or more levels (the best option for simultaneous activities)?

- Will it tie in with current or future plans?

- How do you want to landscape the perimeter?

- Do you want benches, railings, trellises, or other stylish options, like built-in counters with gas grills, or recessed lighting under benches or railings?

Don't let obstacles block your thinking. Your gas grill can be moved. Decks are often built around trees and can convert steep slopes into usable space.

Once a design has been settled upon, expect three to four weeks to pass before a deck or gazebo is completed. In the busy spring and summer months, it most likely will take longer. The time required to get a building permit (usually two to four weeks) must also be considered.

If you're landscaping during this time, be sure to coordinate the two projects well in advance. Building can wreak havoc on new plantings and your lawn will be stressed during construction.

DISTINCTIVE OUTDOOR SURFACES

Driveways, walkways, patios, decks and wood terraces, and hardscape features were once relegated to "last minute" status, with a budget to match. Today they are being given the full and careful attention they deserve. A brick paver driveway can be made to blend beautifully with the color of the brick used on the house. Natural brick stairways and stoops laid by master crafters add distinctive detail and value. Custom-cut curved bluestone steps, hand selected by an experienced paving contractor, provide years of pride and pleasure.

Hardscape installation doesn't begin until your new home is nearly complete, but for your own budgeting purposes, have decisions made no later than home mid-construction phase.

To interview a paving or hardscape contractor, set up an on-site meeting so you can discuss the nature of the project and express your ideas. Be ready to answer questions like:

• Will the driveway be used by two or three cars, or more? Do you need it to be wide enough so cars can pass? Will you require extra parking? Would you like a circular driveway? A basketball court?

• Will the patio be used for entertaining? Will it be a family or adult area, or both? How much furniture will you use? Should it be accessible from a particular part of the house?

• Do you have existing or future landscaping that needs to be considered?

• Would you like to incorporate special touches, like a retaining wall, a small koi pond, or a stone archway?

If you're working with a full-service landscape professional, and hardscape is part of the landscape design, be certain a hardscape expert will do the installation. A specialist's engineering expertise and product knowledge are vital to the top quality result you want. ■

WHY YOU NEED AN ARBORIST.

It's not just your kids, dogs and the neighborhood squirrels trampling through your yard during construction. Excavation equipment, heavy trucks and work crews can spell disaster for your trees. Call an arborist before any equipment is scheduled to arrive and let him develop a plan that will protect the trees, or remove them if necessary.

237

SOURCES

**American Society of Landscape Architects
636 Eye Street NW
Washington, DC 20001
(202) 898-2444**

Landscape Architects
& Contractors

GREEN PLANET LANDSCAPING ....**(702) 614-8866**
10890 S. Eastern Ave., Suite 102, Henderson, NV   Fax: (702) 614-6601
See Ad on Page: 250, 251
Principal/Owner: Damon Lang
Website: www.greenplanetlandscaping.com
Additional Information: Tropical/desert landscapes, maintenance, waterfalls, water features, fireplaces. firepits, barbecues. hardscapes, spascapes, putting greens, and lighting.

LANDACO LANDSCAPING & GRADING ....**(702) 895-7981**
4660 South Polaris, Las Vegas   Fax: (702) 895-7986
See Ad on Page: 276, 277
Principal/Owner: Clint Walcott
Website: www.landaco.com e-mail: landaco@cs.com
Additional Information: Design and build landscape contractors. Decorative hard-scape (Bomanite) and special site amenities.

MARJORIE SNOW LANDSCAPE CO., INC. ....**(702) 307-8080**
5301 West Charleston Boulevard, Las Vegas   Fax: (702) 307-8081
See Ad on Page: 252, 253
Principal/Owner: Marjorie L. Snow
Additional Information: Terra Cotta is my garden store featuring garden urns, fountains, furniture & statuary.

NEVADA SOURCES, INC. ....**(702) 255-3039**
9429 Low Tide Court, Las Vegas   Fax: (702) 255-0402
See Ad on Page: 249
Principal/Owner: Mark C. Kalbfleisch
Additional Information: Jay Pieggenkuhle is our in-house Landscape Architect.

OAK CREEK LAWN & LANDSCAPING, LLC ....**(702) 339-7747**
Las Vegas   Fax: (702) 254-4067
See Ad on Page: 226, 227, 247
Principal/Owner: Breck Bennion
Website: www.oakcreeklandscape.com
Additional Information: Original landscape design specializing in natural textures to bring your home alive. We also offer full service maintenance, outdoor lighting design, in-ground trampolines and pavers.

S & S LANDSCAPE DESIGN ....**(702) 870-4332**
270 Commerce Park Court, Las Vegas   Fax: (702) 251-9556
See Ad on Page: 248
Principal/Owner: Steven Hare
Website: www.landscapelasvegas.com e-mail: info@landscpaelasvegas.com
Additional Information: Collaborating to create stylish & timeless homes that express the client's taste and individual lifestyles. From concept to complete satisfaction since 1989.

SIERRA LANDSCAPE CONSTRUCTION, INC. ....**(702) 655-8786**
8855 West Craig Road, Las Vegas   Fax: (702) 646-4079
See Ad on Page: 254
Principal/Owner: Catherine Jaramillo
e-mail: sierralnd@aol.com

TERRA COTTA ....**(702) 307-8080**
5301 West Charleston Boulevard, Las Vegas   Fax: (702) 307-8081
4760 W. Sahara #6   **(702) 821-1400**
See Ad on Page: 252, 253   Fax: (702) 821-1788
Principal/Owner: Marjorie Snow

TRANQUILITY PONDS ....**(702) 270-3791**
8170 South Eastern #3, Las Vegas   Fax: (702) 270-3792
4760 W. Sahara Ave. #6, Las Vegas   **(702) 821-1400**
See Ad on Page: 273   Fax: (702) 821-1788
Principal/Owner: Jeffrey Reid/Holly Reid
Additional Information: We are the nation's largest pond supply company with stores in Washington, Oregon & Nevada.

Landscaping
Your
Dream Home

An important part of your dream home will be your outside surroundings, so, of course, you will want a beautiful landscape to complement your home. A great deal of thought will need to go into your landscaping project – this type of project does not solely consist of planting gorgeous flowers or deciding where to place trellises. The following guide will give you an idea of the steps and time that go into landscaping an upscale residential project.

Inspecting the Progress

Throughout the construction process keep an eye on the progress. Be checking for items listed on your contract. When you are completely involved with the process, you will be able to be vocal about it.

Inspection

Your landscaper will first have to inspect, evaluate and map out your site. He or she will take site measurements, which may include extensive grading details. The process should take about one to two weeks to complete.

WK16

Designing

If all goes smoothly, the landscape architect or designer will be able to complete the final designs of your project within a week. Keep in mind that modifications will likely have to be made, so you will need to leave time for negotiation.

WK18

Ordering Materials

Once you've had the pleasure of choosing the plants and hardscape you desire let your landscaper order them. This way, the responsibility for any problems is theirs alone.

WK19

Garden Styling

Imaginative theme gardens are becoming popular. Some ideas: a garden of native plants, a one-or two-color garden, a fragrance garden, a Zen garden, a moonlight garden. Don't forget to consider including arbors, sculpture, benches or water features.

• **Pretty Pathways:** Depending on where and how it's quarried, natural stone can vary in color, and brick can vary as well. To be certain that your bricks, cobbles or specialty stones perfectly match, have your contractor buy them from the same lot. There's nothing quite as disconcerting as a pathway where the bricks or stones are slightly different colors.

Landscaping a **Custom** House

Develop Your Vision

You will have to spend a large part of your planning stage deciding what will be most flattering to your home, what plants will work best in the climate you live in, what aspects will require the most upkeep and what is most cost effective. Plan on spending at least two to three months developing ideas for your landscape project.

WK 1

Research Landscapers

You may find the architect, designer or developer who can create your dreams, but plan on spending at least one month looking for that perfect fit. At this point, if you want to be fully involved with the overall process, it would be best to inform landscapers.

WK8

Choosing Subcontractors

The landscaper usually chooses the subcontractors who will assist on the project, but there are situations in which the client will choose. This process should take approximately one month.

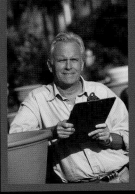

WK12

Design/Build Landscapers

A design/build landscaping firm offers its clients both the design of the project and the services to construct it. It differs from firms that may offer just design or construction services.

• **Who does what?** A landscape architect and a landscape designer perform similar tasks for projects, including surveying the land, discussing ideas with clients and drawing up plans. Due to an architect's more technical education, however, he or she is more eligible to handle the complicated projects. A landscape contractor installs the plants, trees, shrubs and hardscape of the project.

• **Who chooses the subcontractors?** This is a tedious process, because subcontractors are on other job sites and the new job has to be explained to each one. If you feel more comfortable meeting those who will potentially be working on your project, talk to your landscaper about being present at the interviews.

Project
Description

Landscaping an upscale, one-acre property, single family home. This project includes the installation of a swimming pool, masonry walls, fence, lighting, brick paving, a patio, and an assortment of shade trees and plants.

FINISHED PROJECT

Payment

When it comes to making the final payment of your landscaping bill, be sure to review the charges carefully. Additions, rare plants and specialty products all add on to the final cost of your project. An estimated price for the landscape project described here is around $200,000.

Final Inspection

Take an initial walk-through and get an overall sense of the finished project. Let your surroundings soak in and then take a second inspection. Bring your landscape architect along so you can let him or her know immediately if something just isn't right.

Grows on You: Keep in mind that some aspects of your completed landscape project may not be at their fullest potential when first implemented. Although good planning alleviates many surprises, it often takes one to three years for a landscape to mature. So if the flowers or shrubbery don't complement the walkway as you thought they would, give them some time. The flowers you want may not be available for another year, but you can always add a different variety. Larger, more permanent aspects of the landscape project, such as the swimming pool or a greenhouse, are, of course, much harder to change or alter, but can be done.

A Work in Progress

Landscapers expect their clients to freshen their landscaping every few years. So if you'd like to add more color or even move plants, don't be shy about giving your landscape professional a call.

The Pool

The installation of your swimming pool should take about five to six weeks. However, a pool with bar stools, an elevated spa or special water features may take longer.

Hardscape

The materials used for hardscape, such as brick paver paths, patios and retaining walls, will dictate the time needed to create them: brick or cobblestone paths take more time than flagstone stepping paths, and mortarless flagstone patios take more time than those joined with mortar.

Softscape

Softscape includes all your plantings and sodding. Once the hardscape is finished, the softscaping can begin. Depending on the amount of detail in your plan, a one-acre area may take from six days to two weeks. Water features and lighting are not considered part of the softscape; they are added last.

Lighting

After the major aspects of your landscaping project are complete, the installation of lighting will begin. The overall process of lighting installation is fairly straightforward and will take a few days at the most to complete. Keep in mind, though, that setbacks do arise.

Bumps in the Road: There are many reasons why your project may be delayed: materials are scarce or not in season, your new plants may not transplant well, or the specialty stones for your masonry walls are not available. Various problems can arise in the construction of a pool. And there will be numerous subcontractors working on your construction, who also work on other projects at the same time. For example, if the concrete layers are delayed two days and the electrician has other jobs scheduled, the added time could be significant. These setbacks are not pleasant, but they are realistic. Being emotionally prepared for such setbacks helps.

Types of Lighting

There are many ways to illuminate your garden. Do you entertain often? Try torches or tiki lights. Will you have a moonlight garden? Chinese hanging lanterns, floating candles in a glass bowl and lamp posts complement it well. Solar-powered lights are also popular now.

In Conclusion

The actual completion of a landscaping project varies greatly – a small project could take as little as one week and a large project can take as long as one year. There is no definite timeframe for a project like this. Talk to your landscaper in the initial interviewing and hiring process about timeframes. Ask if you can speak with past clients to find out how long their projects took to complete. This is not a small aspect of the overall completion of your dream home. Therefore, plan on dedicating a significant amount of time to the landscaping of your home. Eventually you will have a finished product that you can be proud of for years to come!

Special thanks to the American Society of Landscape Architects and Van Zelst Inc., Wadsworth, Illinios, for their contribution to this timeline and to Linda Oyama Bryan for her photography.

Original Landscape Design

Specializing in
Natural Textures
To Bring Your
Home Alive

Inspired by Nature,
Created by

Oak Creek
LAWN & LANDSCAPE, LLC
NCL #0046205

702-339-7747   fax 702-254-4067
Website - Portfolio at
www.OakCreekLandscape.com

CUSTOMIZE YOUR PIECE OF THE DESERT

Landscape, Design & Construction

- **Custom Concrete**
- **Decorative Stucco**
- **Covered Patio Structures**
- **Custom BBQs, Fire Pits....and more!**

If you can dream it ... We can build it

License # 0034747 • Nevada State Bonding: Unlimited

NEVADA SOURCES, INC.

A COMPLETE LANDSCAPE SERVICE COMPANY

9429 LOW TIDE COURT
LAS VEGAS, NV 89117
TEL: 702-255-3039
FAX: 702-255-0402

Creative Design...
Collaborative Planning...
Project Superintendent...
Pride...Personable...
Communications...Detail...
Fulfilled Visions...

"Landscape contracting
at it's finest

www.greenplanetlandscaping.com
hone 702-614-8866 • Fax 702-614-6601

terra cotta
a garden gallery

- French & Italian Urns
- Bronze Fountains
- Pedestals
- Garden Sculptures
- Birdbaths

5401 West Charleston • Las Vegas, NV 89146 • 702.214.4711
Located Next to Plant World Nursery

Building Paradise...
One Home at a Time

SIERRA LANDSCAPE CONSTRUCTION, INC.
EARNED ITS REPUTATION AS A PREMIUM LANDSCAPE COMPANY
BY CONSISTENTLY MAINTAINING A STANDARD OF EXCELLENCE,
QUALITY, AND EMPLOYING AN HONEST, THOUGHTFUL APPROACH
TO THE LANDSCAPE CONSTRUCTION OF YOUR HOME OR BUSINESS.
BY MAINTAINING THIS PHILOSOPHY, THE CUSTOMER
IS GUARANTEED A LIFETIME OF COMFORT AND SATISFACTION.

COMMERCIAL • RESIDENTIAL • INDUSTRIAL

- LANDSCAPE DESIGN
- IRRIGATION
- CUSTOM CONCRETE
- CUSTOM B.B.Q.'S
- LANDSCAPE LIGHTING
- RETAINING WALLS

SIERRA
LANDSCAPE CONSTRUCTION, INC.
(702) 655-8786   NCL #38432A

Swimming Pools,
Spas & Sport

OZZIE KRAFT ENTERPRISES, INC. ....**(702) 878-4206**
200 South Jones, Las Vegas   Fax: (702) 878-2058
See Ad on Page: 258, 259
Principal/Owner: Kevin Kraft
Website: www.ozziekraft.com e-mail: ozziekraft@iti.access.com
Additional Information: Award winning design and construction. Resort style pools,
spas & water features.
PRESTIGE POOLS, INC. ....**(702) 736-2345**
3530 West Hacienda Avenue, Las Vegas   Fax: (702) 736-2719
See Ad on Page: 256
Principal/Owner: William L. Palmer
Website: www.prestigepoolslv.com
SOUTHWEST PUTTING GREENS ....**(702) 263-0094**
1641 East Sunset Road, Suite B-108, Green Valley, NV   Fax: (702) 263-6930
See Ad on Page: 261
Principal/Owner: Randall J. Kleiner
Website: www.southwestgreens.com e-mail: swpgnv@aol.com
Additional Information: Nevada State Contractor Lic. # 50139
SPAS BY RENEE ....**(702) 458-8862**
2625 East Tropicana Avenue, Las Vegas   Fax: (702) 458-2315
See Ad on Page: 260
Principal/Owner: Renee Gibbs
SPAS UNLIMITED ....**(702) 258-4488**
5413 West Charleston Boulevard, Las Vegas
See Ad on Page: 257
Principal/Owner: Dianna Baldy
SUNDANCE POOLS & SPAS, INC. ....**(702) 363-2410**
8526 Del Webb Boulevard, Las Vegas   Fax: (702) 363-5313
See Ad on Page: 262, 263
Principal/Owner: Michael L. Specter
Website: www.sundancepoolsandspas.com

prestige Pools INC.

State License 18613A Unlimited
Las Vegas, Nevada 89118
3530 W. Hacienda Avenue
702·736·2345
prestigepoolslv.com

For The Discriminating

Featuring Marquis Spas

5413 W Charleston
Las Vegas, NV 89146
702.258.4488
Fax 702.258.0908
www.marquisspas.com

Celebrating 60 Years in Business

AWARD WINNING DESIGN & CONSTRUCTION
RESORT STYLE POOLS SPAS & WATERFEATURES
OZZIE KRAFT ENTERPRISES, INC.

OZZIE KRAFT

ENTERPRISES, INC.
200 SOUTH JONES BLVD.
LAS VEGAS, NV 89107
702.878.4206   FAX 702.878.2058
SINCE 1942   CONT. LIC #8646A
www.ozziekraft.com

SPAS BY RENEE

Spas • Saunas • Repairs • Accessorie

2625 E. Tropicana Ave.
Suite 1
Las Vegas, Nevada 89121
(702) 458-8862
Fax (702) 458-2315

2300 N. Rainbow Blvd.
Suite 101
Las Vegas, Nevada 8910
(702) 458-4135
Fax (702) 648-2151

SPAS BY RENEE

NV LIC. #017632

www.spasbyrenee.com

SUNDAN

Designers and Builders of Distinctive Pool
8526 Del Webb Blvd. Las Vegas, NV 8913

OLS & SPAS

as, and Water Features.
702-363-2410 fax 720-363-5313   www.sundancepoolsandspas.com

Nest Featherings

Patio Shop
6425 West Sahara Las Vegas, NV 89140
702/362-6707

Outdoor Lighting

OUTDOOR LIGHTING PERSPECTIVES OF LAS VEGAS ....**(702) 889-5004**
5554 Stomping Boots Avenue, Las Vegas   Fax: (702) 889-5033
See Ad on Page: 266, 267
<u>Principal/Owner:</u> Anthony Savignano Jr.
<u>Website:</u> www.outdoorlights.com <u>e-mail:</u> oldlasvegas@aol.com
<u>Additional Information:</u> The largest landscape and architectural lighting company
in Las Vegas and the nation.

SEE THE LIGHT...before you decide.

Our lighting consultants will show you how a complete lighting system will look with your home and landscaping. Our nighttime demonstrations are offered at no charge and are scheduled at your convenience. That way you can see how a proper lighting system ca enhance your home before you decide.

We will design, install and service our unique and distinctive low voltage halogen lights and also provide the following:

- Award winning solid copper fixtures
- Extend your living environment into the evening
- Accent your home and landscaping investment

- Home safety and security
- Unmatched 5 year warranty
- 37 locations nationwide

All fixtures and transformers Made In The USA

Outdoor Lighting Perspective is Las Vegas' and the Nation's largest home & landscape lighting company. We pioneered the FREE evening, home design and demonstration.

Call 702-889-5004 Today!

Outdoor
Lighting
Perspective's

Hardscape, Masonry &
Water Gardens

CHIEF CONCRETE, INC. ....**(702) 435-4038**
6275 Stevenson Way, Las Vegas   Fax: (702) 435-4075
See Ad on Page: 270, 271
Principal/Owner: Monte Walker
Website: www.chiefconcretelasvegas.com
Additional Information: In Las Vegas for 22 years, we can enhance the beauty
of your home, patio or pool area. Visit our showroom to see the wide selection of
applications to choose from.
DAYTON MASONRY ....**(702) 547-0225**
320 Sun Pac Court, Henderson   Fax: (702) 547-0226
See Ad on Page: 269
Principal/Owner: James T. Dayton
Website: www.daytonmasonry.com e-mail: jim@daytonmasonry.com
Additional Information: With unrivalled craftsmanship, we create harmony between
natural and built environments which have a profound effect on one's spiritual and
psychological health.
QUALITY MASONRY ....**(702) 270-2648**
Las Vegas   Fax: (702) 270-2647
See Ad on Page: 272
Principal/Owner: Robert G. Fullmer
Additional Information: Add durable richness, beautiful character and greater value
to your dream home with: brick, stone, glass block, pavers and block.
WATER FX ....**(702) 233-3200**
2200 East Patrick Lane #26, Las Vegas   Fax: (702) 597-9771
See Ad on Page: 274, 275
Principal/Owner: Tim Pangborn
e-mail: dancingfountains@earthlink.net
Additional Information: Custom design & construction of swimming pools, spas,
waterfalls, fountains, koi ponds and dancing fountains.

CUSTOM
MASONRY
APPLICATIONS

Patios

Fireplaces

Firepits

Barbeques

Pizza Ovens

Fountains

Waterfalls

Precast

Retaining
Walls

"Leading by example"

Dayton

M A S O N R Y

Corporate Headquarters
320 Sunpac Ct., Henderson, NV 89015
702.547.0225 Fax 702.547.0226
daytonmasonry.com
Nevada License No. 0037302
California License No. 404617

emical Staining and Overlayment

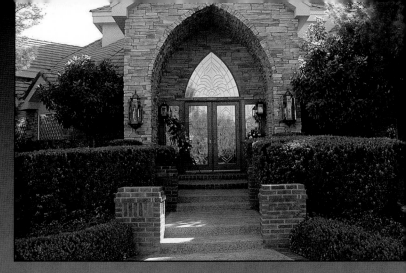

MASONRY AT IT'S BEST

QUALITY MASONRY

LIC. #32481

Phone: (702) 270-2648
Fax: (702) 270-2647

Designers & Builders of
Swimming Pools,
Spas, Fountains,
Natural Water Features &
Dancing Fountains
6200 East Patrick Lane #26
Las Vegas, NV 89119
(702) 233-3200
(702) 233-6925 Fax

...distinctive exterior environmen

Awnings

ACCENT AWNING CO. INC ....**(800) 397-663.**
1210 South Main Street, Las Vegas   Fax: (702) 388-297'
See Ad on Page: 279
<u>Principal/Owner:</u> Karl Desmakis
<u>Website:</u> www.accentawnings.com
<u>Additional Information:</u> Factory direct awnings, security shutters, solar screens.
Residential, commercial & new construction.

ACCENT AWNING COMPANY

Demand the Very Best

- Retractable Awnings
- Window Awnings
- Security Shutters
- Sun Screen Systems
- Vertical Drop Shades

"Cooling Las Vegas the Natural Way"

Call Today for a complimentary Consultation
Or Visit Our Factory Showroom
1210 S. Main Street • Las Vegas • Nevada

Residential • Commercial • New Contruction

Free Estimates ~ 800-397-6637

Nevada Contractor Lic. #51012

KITCHEN & BATH

Kiss Cabinet, Inc. & Design Center

5070 West Patrick Lane• Las Vegas, NV 89118

P: 702.739.6090 • F: 702.739.0391

**" A thing of
beauty
is a joy
*forever***

It's *loveliness*
increases;
it will never pass into
nothingness. **"**

John Keats

Form, Function... Fabulous!

Kitchens and baths were once designed for efficiency, with little attention to beauty. Today they are paramount to a home's comfort and style, places to nurture body and spirit. Without a doubt, today's larger kitchen is the real family room, the heart and soul of the home. Some kitchens serve as the control center in "Smart Houses" wired with the latest technology. With the kitchen as a focal point of the home, good design means the room must be both functional and a pleasure to be in, while reflecting the "feel" of the rest of the home. From the European "unfitted" look to super-high tech, there are styles and finishes to make everyone feel at home in the kitchen. The bath has evolved into a truly multipurpose "cocooning" area as well. Sufficient room for exercise equipment, spacious master closets, and spa features are all in high demand, resulting in master suites to allow one to escape from the world. The emphasis on quality fixtures and luxury finishes remains, whatever the size of the room.

Photo courtesy of **Loerwald Construction**

FIVE WAYS TO SPOT A TOP QUALITY KITCHEN OR BATH

1. A feeling of timelessness: Sophisticated solutions that blend appropriately with the home's overall architecture and smoothly incorporate new products and ideas.

2. A hierarchy of focal points: Visual elements designed to enhance – not compete with – each other.

3. Superior functionality: Rooms clearly serve the needs they were designed to meet, eliminate traffic problems and work well years after installation.

4. Quality craftsmanship: All elements, from cabinets, counters, and floors, to lighting, windows and furnishings, are built and installed at the highest level of quality.

5. Attention to detail: Thoughtful planning is evident – from the lighting scheme to the practical surfaces to the gorgeous cabinet detailing.

PLANNED TO PERFECTION
THE CUSTOM KITCHEN & BATH

In many ways, the kitchen and bath define how we live and dictate the comfort we enjoy in our everyday lives. Families continue to design their kitchens to be the heart of the home – in every way. It's the central gathering place. It's a work space. It's a command center for whole house electronic control systems. Bathrooms become more luxurious, more multi-functional. Having experienced the pleasures of pampering on vacations, in spas, beauty salons, and health clubs, sophisticated area homeowners are choosing to enjoy a high degree of luxury every day in their own homes.

Homeowners building a new home, or remodeling an existing one, demand flexible and efficient spaces, custom designed to fill their needs. Reaching that goal is more challenging than ever. As new products and technologies race to keep up with the creative design explosion, the need for talented, experienced kitchen and bath designers continues to grow.

The kitchen/bath designer will be a member of your home building team, which also includes the architect, contractor, interior designer and, in new home construction, the landscape architect.

Professional kitchen and bath designers, many of whom are also degreed interior designers, possess the education and experience in space planning particular to kitchens and baths. They can deliver a functional design perfectly suited to your family, while respecting your budget and your wishes. Their understanding of ergonomics, the relationship between people and their working environments, and a familiarity with current products and applications, will be invaluable to you as you plan.

SEARCH OUT AND VALUE
DESIGN EXCELLENCE

Designing a kitchen or bath is an intimate undertaking, filled with many decisions based on personal habits and family lifestyle. Before you select the kitchen/bath professional who will lead you through the project, make a personal commitment to be an involved and interested client. Since the success of these rooms is so important to the daily lives of your family, it's a worthwhile investment of your time and energy.

Choose a designer whose work shows creativity and a good sense of planning. As in any relationship, trust and communication are the foundations for success. Is the designer open to your ideas, and does he or she offer information on how you can achieve your vision? If you can't express your ideas reely, don't enter into a contractual relationship, no matter how much you admire this person's work. If these rooms aren't conceived to fulfill your wishes, your time and resources will be wasted.

What also is true, however, is that professional designers should be given a comfortable degree of latitude to execute your wishes as best as they know how. Accomplished designers earned their reputation by creating beautiful rooms that work, so give their ideas serious consideration for the best overall result.

Many homeowners contact a kitchen or bath designer a year before a project is scheduled to begin. Some come with a full set of complete drawings they simply want to have priced out. Some take full advantage of the designer's expertise and contract for plans drawn from scratch. And some want something in between. Be sure a designer offers the level of services you want – from 'soup to nuts' or strictly countertops and cabinetry.

Designers charge a design fee which often will be used as a deposit if you choose to hire them. If you expect very detailed sets of drawings, including floor plans, elevations, and pages of intricate detail, such as the support systems of kitchen islands, the toe kick and crown molding detail, be specific about your requirements. All contracts should be written, detailed and reviewed by your attorney.

TURNING DREAMS INTO DESIGNS— GET YOUR NOTEBOOK OUT

The first step toward getting your ideas organized is to put them on paper. Jot down notes, tape photos into your Idea Notebook, mark pages of your Home Book. The second step is defining your lifestyle. Pay close attention to how you use the kitchen and bath. For example, if you have a four-burner stove, how often do you cook with all four burners? Do you need a cook surface with more burners, or could you get by with less, freeing up space for a special wok cooking module or more counter space? How often do you use your bathtub? Many upper-end homeowners are forgoing the tub in favor of the multi-head shower surround and using bathtub space for a dressing or exercise area or mini-kitchen. As you evaluate your lifestyle, try to answer questions like these:

THINKING ABOUT KITCHEN DESIGN

• What feeling do you want to create in the kitchen? Traditional feel of hearth and home? The clean, uncluttered lines of contemporary design?

• Is meal preparation the main function of the kitchen? Gourmet cooks and gardeners want a different level of functionality than do homeowners

THE LATEST APPLIANCES

There's a revolution in kitchen appliances, guaranteed to make your life simpler and more enjoyable: High-performance stainless steel cook-top ranges with a commercial level of performance; Cook-tops with interchangeable cooking modules (like woks, griddles); Down draft ventilation on gas cook-tops; Convection ovens with oversize capacity, and electronic touchpad controls; Refrigeration products and systems you can put wherever you could put a cabinet or drawer; Flush-design appliances; Ultra-quiet dish-washers with stainless steel interiors; Refrigerators that accept decorative door panels and handles to match your cabinets; State-of-the-art warming drawers.

One Person's Project Estimate:

Ingredients of a New Kitchen

It's fun to imagine, but what might it actually cost to undertake a project described in this chapter? The example below describes a typical project and gives a general estimate of the costs involved.

PROJECT DESCRIPTION

Designing and installing a high-end, kitchen, 16' x 33' sq. ft.

Consultation: retainer, applied towards cabinet purchase $2,500

Cabinetry $44,000
> Kitchen, Island, Pantry, Desk
> 36"- 42" high wall cabinets to ceiling
> Maple w/med. stain, modified Shaker styling, custom solid wood construction
> Cabinet Accessories

> To allow for an ergonomic, efficient use of space, roll-out shelves, an appliance garage, a lazy susan, a trash pull-out, cutlery dividers, tray dividers, a tip-out at sink and cabinet hardware were incorporated.

Glass $3,500
> Stained glass doors, glass shelves

Countertop $12,000
> Granite, 1" thick, large beveled edge

Backsplash $2,500
> Tumbled marble with accent mosaic

Appliance Package, all stainless steel..$20,000
> 36" gas cooktop with hood
> Two electric ovens, 48" built-in refrigerator,
> Two dishwashers, under counter refrigerator,
> Warming drawer, microwave, disposal, hot water dispenser

Plumbing Fixtures $2,900
> Undermount double bowl main sink, prep sink,
> pull-out faucets, soap dispensers, water filter system

Flooring $4,000
> Stone-look porcelain tile

Lighting $2,500
> General, task, accent, combination of low voltage, halogen and xenon

Labor $7,000
> Installation of cabinets, appliances, counters,
> and backsplash. Room preparation, floor installation,
> electric and plumbing hook-ups, by general contractor.

TOTAL...**$98,400**

288

Note: A very similar look can be had at several price points. For a less expensive installation, custom cabinets can be replaced with stock or semi-custom. The granite tops could be made of butcher block or laminate. Clear or frosted glass can be substituted for custom glass. Depending on the choice of materials, prices could be cut back by half the quoted cost.

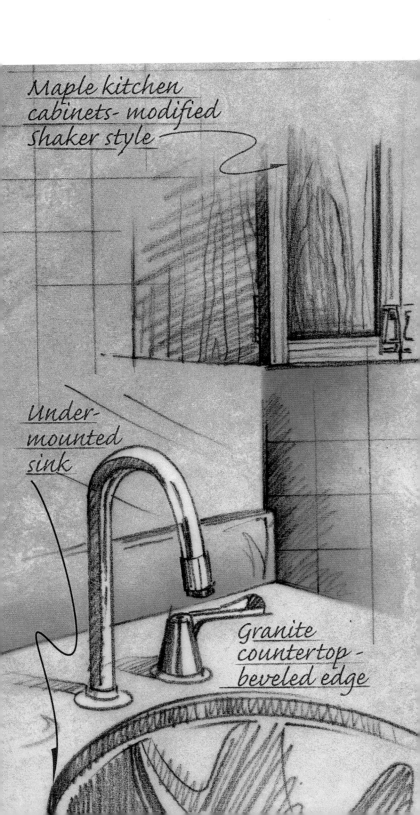

Maple kitchen
cabinets- modified
Shaker style

Under-
mounted
sink

Granite
countertop -
beveled edge

WHAT DESIGNERS OFFER YOU

1. Access to the newest products: With their considerable knowledge of products and solutions, your remodeling or budget limitations can be more easily addressed.
2. Ergonomic design for a custom fit: Designers consider all the measurements – not just floor plan space – but also how counter and cabinet height and depth measure up to the needs of the individual family members.
3. A safe environment: Safety is the highest priority. As kitchens and baths serve more functions, managing traffic for safety's sake becomes more crucial.
4. Orderly floor plans: When an open refrigerator door blocks the path from the kitchen to the breakfast room, or you're bumping elbows in the bathroom, poor space planning is the culprit.
5. Smart storage: Ample storage in close proximity to appropriate spaces is essential.

who eat out often or want to be in and out of the kitchen quickly.

• How does the family use the kitchen? How will their needs change your requirements over the next ten years? (If you can't imagine the answer to this question, ask friends who are a few years ahead of you in terms of family life.)

• Do you want easy access to the backyard, dining room, garage?

• Is there a special view you want preserved or established?

• Do you want family and friends to be involved and close to the action in the kitchen?

• What appliances and amenities must be included? Do some research on this question. Warming drawers, refrigeration zones, wine coolers, ultra-quiet dishwashers that sense how dirty the dishes are, cooktops with interchangeable cooking modules, convection ovens with electronic touchpad controls, are all available.

• What are your storage needs? If you own a lot of kitchen items, have a relatively small kitchen, or want personally tailored storage space, ask your kitchen designer to take a detailed inventory of your possessions. Top quality cabinets can be customized to fit your needs. Kitchen designers, custom cabinet makers, or space organization experts can guide you. Consider custom options such as:

  • Slotted storage for serving trays
  • Pull-out recycling bins
  • Plate racks and wine racks
  • Cutlery dividers
  • Angled storage drawer for spices
  • Pivoting shelving systems
  • Pull-out or elevator shelves for food processors, mixers, televisions or computers

• Is the kitchen also a work area or home office? Do you need a location for a computerized home management or intercom system?

THINKING ABOUT BATH DESIGN

• What look are you trying to create? Victorian, Colonial, contemporary, whimsical?

• What functions must it fill? Exercise area, sitting room, dressing or make-up area?

• Who will use the bath? Children, teens, guests, (and how many)?

- What is the traffic pattern? How do people move in and around a bathroom? (Set up your video camera in the corner one morning to get a realistic view.)

- What amenities are desired? Luxury shower systems, whirlpool tub, ceiling heat lamps, heated towel bars, spa, heated tile floors, audio and telephone systems

- What are your storage needs? Linen or clothes closets? Stereo and CD storage? Professionals will customize spaces for your needs.

- Do you want hooks for towels or bathrobes? Heated towel bars or rings?

THE SKY'S THE LIMIT

New high-end kitchen budgets can easily reach the $100,000 range, so it's important to identify your specific needs and wishes. The sky's the limit when designing and installing a luxury kitchen or bath in the 2000s, so don't get caught by surprise by the cost of high quality cabinetry, appliances and fixtures. Know what you're willing to spend and make sure your designer is aware of your budget. Projects have a way of growing along the way. If you've established a realistic budget, you have a solid way to keep the project moving forward and prioritizing your wishes. As you establish your budget, think in terms of this general breakdown of expenses:

Cabinets	40%
Appliances	15%
Faucets and Fixtures	8%
Flooring	7%
Windows	7%
Countertops	8%
Labor	15%

THE NEW KITCHEN – THE FLAVOR OF THE PAST – A TASTE OF THE FUTURE

Many of the fabulous new kitchens being built now don't look "new." The desire for an inviting, lived-in look that encourages friends and family to linger over coffee and conversation is leading homeowners to embrace European design ideas of furniture-quality cabinetry and dedicated work zones. Consumers are investing in restaurant-quality appliances, gorgeous imported natural stone countertops and floors, and luxury options like dedicated wine coolers, stem glass holders, and plate racks. Tastes are turning to more classical, traditional detailing in cabinetry, with Georgian, Greek and Roman influence in its architecture.

"WHAT ABOUT RESALE?"

This is a question designers hear when homeowners individualize their kitchens and baths. It's only prudent to consider the practical ramifications of any significant investment, including investing in a new custom kitchen and bath. Beautiful upscale kitchens and baths will only enhance the value of your home. Indeed, these two rooms are consistently credited with recouping much of their original cost. Research by professional builders' organizations and real estate companies bears this out year after year. The greatest return, however, is in the present, in the enjoyment of the space.

YOUR KITCHEN.COM

Technology has arrived in the kitchen. On-line grocery shopping, computers, multiple phone lines, intercom, security system and "smart house" controls. Right by the breakfast table.

A STEP UP

Custom counter height is an idea whose time has arrived in new and remodeled homes in the Las Vegas Valley. Multiple heights, appropriate to the task or the people using the particular area, are common. When one permanent height doesn't work as a solution to a problem, consider asking for a step to be built into the toe kick panel of the cabinetry.

GET TWO DISHWASHERS

**Homeowners today are installing extra dishwashers:
1. To make clean up after a party a one-night affair.
2. To serve as a storage cabinet for that extra set of dishes. They're also installing dishwashers at a more friendly height to eliminate unnecessary bending.**

That's not to say that homeowners no longer demand state-of-the-art features; quite the contrary. New, smart ideas play an ever more important role in a kitchen's daily life. Kitchens are often equipped as a central hub in a computer automated home, with everything from ovens and entertainment systems accessible by remote control. Home office or homework areas equipped with telephones, computers, printers, and fax machines are included in most every new project. With advances in refrigeration technology, homeowners now have separate integrated refrigerators and freezer drawers installed near the appropriate work zone – a refrigerated vegetable drawer near the sink, a freezer drawer by the microwave, dedicated refrigerators to keep grains or cooking oils at their perfect temperatures. Ultra-quiet dishwashers, instant hot water dispensers, roll-out warming drawers and versatile cooktops are just some of the products that meet the demands of today's luxury lifestyle.

THE NEW BATH – PRACTICALITY DRENCHED WITH PANACHE AND POLISH

Imagine it's a Thursday night at the end of a very busy week. You come home, have a great work out while listening to your favorite CDs over the loudspeakers in your private exercise room, then jump into an invigorating shower where multiple shower heads rejuvenate your tired muscles, and a steaming, cascading waterfall pulls all the stress from your body. You wrap yourself in a big fluffy bath sheet, toasty from the brass towel warmer, as you step onto the ceramic tile floor that's been warmed by an underfloor radiant heating unit. You grab something comfortable from your lighted, walk-in closet, and then head out of your luxurious bathroom to the kitchen to help with dinner.

A master bath such as this, built in custom luxury homes, fills a growing demand for private retreats replete with nurturing indulgences.

Master bathrooms are being rethought, with the emphasis shifting from form to function. These baths are still large, up to 400 square feet, but the space is organized differently. The newly defined master bath is actually an extension of the master suite, often including his and her walk-in closets, mirrored exercise space, (in remodeling projects, carved out of a spare bedroom) and separate areas for dressing, applying make-up, listening to music or making coffee.

Large whirlpool tubs are often replaced with custom shower systems with built-in seats and steam capabilities. Other stylish alternatives are Victorian style claw-foot tubs, or smaller whirlpool tubs.

REALITY OF REMODELING

Dollar-smart homeowners know that in cost versus value surveys, kitchen renovations and bath additions or renovations yield a very high return on the original investment. These homeowners rarely embark on such remodeling projects with resale in mind. However, knowing their investment is a wise one gives them the freedom to fully realize their dreams of the ultimate sybaritic bath or the friendliest family kitchen that accommodates them now and well into the future.

For more information on remodeling, see "The Second Time's The Charm" in the Custom Home Builders and Remodelers section.

CONTEXTUALISM IN THE KITCHEN AND BATH

Like any other rooms in the home, continuity and contextualism in the kitchen and bath are important to the overall appearance of the home. This is an important point to consider in a remodeling project, especially in an historic home. There often are restrictions on the materials and structural changes that may be made in historic buildings. Your kitchen or bath designer should be aware of these kinds of restrictions.

A REMODELING CONTINGENCY FUND

Kitchen and bath remodeling projects are well known for unexpected, unforeseen expenses, so put a contingency fund in your budget from the beginning. This fund can cover anything from structural changes to your sudden desire to install skylights in the kitchen.

THE BEAUTY OF TOP QUALITY SURFACES

Luxury surfaces continue to add astonishing beauty to kitchens and baths in new and remodeled homes throughout the area. Solid surfaces now are available in an ever-widening range of colors, including a granite look, with high degrees of translucence and depth. Granite and stone add a beautiful, natural look, with an abundance of choices and finishes. Tile, stainless steel, laminates, and wood – even concrete – are other possibilities. Each surface has its benefits, beyond the inherent beauty it can add to your design.

Your kitchen designer will advise you on the best choices for your project, based on overall design and budget. Use the professionals showcased in these pages to find the best quality materials and craftsmanship. ■

TAKING A TEST DRIVE

You wouldn't invest in a new car without taking it out for a test drive, so take the opportunity up front to test the individual fixtures and elements of a new kitchen or bath. Don't be hesitant to grab a magazine and climb into a bathtub, or to test sit a number of possible toilet choices or shower seats. Take your family to a showroom to evaluate counter heights and faucets. The more involved you can be in the planning, the more fun you'll have, and the better the end result will be.

293

Kitchen & Bath
Designers

CABINET WEST DISTRIBUTORS, INC. ....**(702) 362-4774**
3400 West Desert Inn #11, Las Vegas   Fax: (702) 362-1499
See Ad on Page: 322
Principal/Owner: Rick Wilder
e-mail: cabinetwest@aol.com

EBENISTE, INC. ....**(702) 368-2280**
2972 South Rainbow Boulevard Suite B, Las Vegas   Fax: (702) 368-1986
See Ad on Page: 300, 301
Principal/Owner: Gail Buy

FERGUSON BATH & KITCHEN GALLERY ....**(702) 876-8100**
3033 South Valley View Boulevard, Las Vegas   Fax: (702) 876-7846
See Ad on Page: 306
Principal/Owner: Ron Kern
Website: www.ferguson.com

GOLAN CABINETS ....**(702) 696-7106**
2324 South Highland, Las Vegas   Fax: (702) 696-7104
See Ad on Page: 296, 297
Principal/Owner: David Levy
Website: www.geocities.com/golancabinets   e-mail: golancabinets@cs.com,
Additional Information: At Golan Cabinets, we use all-wood construction methods.
Our multi-step process in applying our stains and enamels produces a strong,
enduring product. We install cabinetry to meet your individual needs.

IDEAL SUPPLY COMPANY ....**(702) 731-3445**
2935 South Highland Drive, Las Vegas   Fax: (702) 796-7467
See Ad on Page: 295
Principal/Owner: Brad Englert
Additional Information: Custom kitchens & baths.

KISS CABINET, INC. AND DESIGN CENTER ....**(702) 739-6090**
5070 Patrick Lane, Las Vegas   Fax: (702) 739-0391
See Ad on Page: 282, 283, 323
Principal/Owner: Stephen & Sophia Kiss
e-mail: kisscabinet@invegas.com

KITCHENLAND, INC. ....**(702) 896-0265**
6455 Industrial Road Suite K, Las Vegas   Fax: (702) 896-0335
See Ad on Page: 298, 299
Website: www.kitchenland-lv.com   e-mail: kitchenland00@earthlink.net
Additional Information: Modern showroom. In business since 1977.

ULTIMATE KITCHENS ....**(702) 248-7117**
9775 South Maryland Parkway #F11, Las Vegas   Fax: (702) 263-2303
See Ad on Page: 302, 303
Principal/Owner: Peggy Halliday
Website: www.ultimatekitchens.com   e-mail: ultimatekitchens@hotmail.com
Additional Information: Award winning cabinetry design firm, as featured on
"The Food Network", Street of Dreams, and Great American Kitchens.

Bath Design
by Ideal

Golan Cabinets

"The Difference is the Service"

If you're dreaming of fine cabinetry in your...

Bathroom...

Kitchen.

Or Home
Office...

Talk To A Specialist at Golan Cabinets

324 S. Highland Las Vegas, NV 89102
ffice (702) 696-7106 • Fax (702) 696-7104
olancabinets@cs.com

s one of the premier cabinet companies in Las Vegas, Golan Cabinets
-ives on quality of products as well as excellent customer service. With
.arge variety of cabinet styles and color to choose from, we can meet
your individual needs.

isit our beautiful showrooms featuring displays of our exquisite
abinetry, and let out friendly professional staff make your vision a
eality!

Wood·Mode®
FINE CUSTOM CABINETRY

Kitchenland, Inc
6455 Industrial Road Suite K
Las Vegas NV 89118
(702) 896-0265

Ébéniste
Finely Crafted Cabinetry

Kitchens

Baths

Home Offices

Entertainment
Centers

Libraries

Wet Bars

...and more!

ULTIMATE KITCHENS

LAS VEGAS

702.248.7117

WWW.ULTIMATEKITCHENS.COM

*Award Winning Kitchen Design &
Cabinetry for the Executive Home*

Fixtures
& Hardware

FERGUSON BATH & KITCHEN GALLERY ....**(702) 876-8100**
3033 South Valley View Boulevard, Las Vegas   Fax: (702) 876-7846
See Ad on Page: 306
Principal/Owner: Ron Kern
Website: www.ferguson.com

GLASSIC ART ....**(702) 658-7588**
5850 South Polaris Avenue Suite 500, Las Vegas   Fax: (702) 658-7342
See Ad on Page: 305, 354, 355
Principal/Owner: Leslie Rankin
Website: www.glassicart.com e-mail: glassicart@glassicart.com
Additional Information: This creative and diverse form of glass art will transform
your custom home into the most visually impressive living environment.

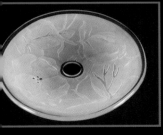

HOME SUITE HOME.

The Fables and Flowers™ bathroom suite
by Kohler® makes home sweeter than ever.
Available from Ferguson Bath & Kitchen Galleries.

FERGUSON
Bath 🔔🔔 Kitchen Gallery ✱FERGUSON
Products You Know. *People You Trust.*®

THE BOLD LOOK
OF **KOHLER**®

Las Vegas, 3033 S. Valley View Boulevard, (702) 876-8100

www.ferguson.com

Appliances

SUNWEST..**(480) 784-6611**
   8370 South Kyrene Road, Tempe, AZ   Fax: (480) 784-6633
   See Ad on Page: 310
   <u>Principal/Owner:</u> Robert Stamm
WESTAR APPLIANCES & HOME PRODUCTS................................**(702) 798-6060**
   7370 S. Industrial Rd. #401, Las Vegas   Fax: (702) 798-1610
   See Ad on Page: 308, 309
   <u>Website:</u> www.westar-sw.com

Viking Professional Series

Viking, the only manufacturer offering complete kitchen packages in two elegant, yet distinctly different designs. The Professional Series, offering consumers the styling for which Viking Range Corporation has become famous and now the more contemporary styling of the Designer Series

VIKING DESIGNER SERIES

8370 S. Kyrene Road Suite 107 • Tempe, AZ 85284 • 480 784 6611 office

Building Your **Dream** Kitchen and Bath

You may live in a house you love, in a neighborhood that suits you perfectly. However, your home may not fit your changing lifestyle or desires. The following timeline shows the steps involved in planning, executing, and finishing the major remodeling of a kitchen and full bath. It will help you to see the major tasks involved, and give you helpful information to make this process go more smoothly.

Mechanical Work & Whirlpool Bath

All electrical, plumbing, heating, ventilating and air conditioning work is finished. Low-voltage work is completed and whirlpool bath is installed.

Demolition

Walls, flooring, etc. are torn up and removed. Generally takes three days.

Framing

Rough framing and room modifications are completed.

Interior Work

Drywall is installed, walls are taped and primed.

Flooring

Floors are completed. Depending on the complexity of the materials used, this may take up to three more days than anticipated.

WK12	WK13	WK14	WK15	WK16

Windows

Attempt to keep existing window locations during any remodeling project. Moving windows is not a cost-saving endeavor.

• **Whenever you are adding on** new space to a home, have a heating contractor determine whether your existing heating system can accommodate and heat the extra space. You don't want to overwork and thereby damage your existing equipment and be forced to replace the entire unit.

• **Consider your cabinet options carefully.** Those choices will drive the overall price. You can add some options at a later date to defray some of the initial cost. Some that are easy to add include tilt front doors, spice racks and slide-out wire baskets. However, if you decide to wait, make certain that the option you want will be available and can be added after installation.

Building Your **Dream** Kitchen and Bath

Examine your Options

Contact three to five remodelers. Make appointments to discuss ideas and begin the basis for a cost estimate.

Narrow the Field

Hold initial meetings with the remodelers. These visits to the house include a walking inspection with measurements taken of specific rooms, etc.

Select Your Partner

Choose a designer/remodeler and blueprints will be created. Expect that it will take three weeks for a project of this size. A retainer will probably be required.

Review Designs

Meet with your remodeler to review the designs. Establish a budget per design.

Approve Drawings

Finalize and sign off on drawings and hold a "rough budget" meeting.

Approve budget and sign the contract.

WK 1   WK5   WK9

Your Vision

The first appointment is the time to discuss your vision and the remodeler's suggestions for potential layout of the rooms, such as how to squeeze more features into an existing space, etc.

• **In some cases, designers and remodelers** are employed by the same firm; in other cases, they could be separate firms. There are advantages to going to a company that has both services under one roof, but you are not obligated to hire a design/build firm for both services. Many firms are willing to do one or the other.

• **To prevent ending up with an addition that doesn't fit** the style of your home, look at pictures of a company's work and make certain to visit homes that it has remodeled.

Project Description

The remodeling of a kitchen and full bath. For the kitchen, the cabinets will be replaced, an island added, new flooring installed, and a breakfast nook with a bay window constructed. For the bath, a whirlpool will be installed, new flooring and new countertops will replace the old, and a closet will be carved out of the existing space.

FINISHED PROJECT

Project Completed!

After the final clean-up, be sure to make a final inspection to ensure that everything is done to your satisfaction.

WK21

• While most states provide warranty protection for the client, the remodeler will include a warranty as well. This may last as long as five years for general items and as long as 10 years for manufacturing products. Certain laws also protect the client. Experts may be called upon to ensure that all agreements and building codes have been made.

Additional Information

For more information, contact the National Association of the Remodeling Industry (NARI), 780 Lee Street, Suite 200 Des Plaines, IL 60016 847-298-9200.

Cabinetry and Kitchen Island

Kitchen island and all cabinetry are installed. Complicated cabinetry may take up to three more days than anticipated.

WK17

Countertops, Plumbing & Back Splash

It only takes a day to install countertops but you must wait two weeks after the cabinetry is installed before you can begin. If, during the wait, you change your mind and order different countertops, this will delay installation by three extra weeks. All plumbing is hooked up.

Depending on the materials used, it can take from one to four days to complete the back splash.

WK19

● All painting is completed.

WK20

• **If you are going to add a large jetted tub** to your project, consider adding a water heater dedicated to that tub. A large jetted tub can hold up to an average of 75 gallons or more, which can easily overextend your existing water heater and cause problems down the road.

Gaining Space

Examine how you are utilizing space. You may be able to steal some space from a neighboring room or closet. If your bathroom space is limited, purchase a jetted tub and shower combination or install a pedestal lavatory instead of a vanity cabinet with a sink.

In
Conclusion

The process of remodeling a kitchen and bath can be somewhat mysterious, sometimes perplexing, and often frustrating. At the end of the process, however, will be two of the most beautiful, comfortable, and enjoyable rooms of your home well into the future!

Special thanks to Neff Kitchens (Toronto, Ontario, Canada), the National Association of the Remodeling Industry, Inc. and the Design Guild of Chicago, Illinois for their contributions to this article.

Custom Cabinets

CABINET WEST DISTRIBUTORS, INC. ....**(702) 362-4774**
3400 West Desert Inn #11, Las Vegas   Fax: (702) 362-1499
See Ad on Page: 322
<u>Principal/Owner:</u> Rick Wilder
<u>e-mail:</u> cabinetwest@aol.com

KISS CABINET, INC. AND DESIGN CENTER ....**(702) 739-6090**
5070 Patrick Lane, Las Vegas   Fax: (702) 739-0391
See Ad on Page: 282, 283, 323
<u>Principal/Owner:</u> Stephen & Sophia Kiss
<u>e-mail:</u> kisscabinet@invegas.com

319

KISS CABINETS
Old World Styling:
We are pleased to offer hand-rubbed, two-toned custom cabinet styling. Designed to complement the popular Tuscan look, the detailing enhancement on each mitered cabinet door may go through as many as four stages, depending on the depth of the color desired.

KITCHENLAND, INC.
Wood-Mode Barcelona:
Old World elegance is evident in Wood-Mode's new Barcelona cabinetry, combining traditional beauty with frameless design. Drawn from the elaborately carved moldings of a by-gone era, the fine furniture elements of this period include the gracefully arched hood and fluted details. Here, it is shown in Fireside Cherry with a distressed, low-sheen finish.

GLASSIC ART
Shower Enclosures:
Traditionally, shower enclosures have been made of clear glass. Now, your bathroom can be enhanced by our distinctive designs, customized to your wishes.

Showroom

FERGUSON BATH & KITCHEN GALLERY
Kohler® Sink:
Simple, yet sophisticated, the unmistakably elegant Soliloquy™ bowl features a hand-painted orchid in purple-red tones.

CABINET WEST DISTRIBUTORS
Rustic Cabinetry:
Our new cabinetry finish on maple hardwood allows the natural knots and mineral streaks to show through. Available on any style cabinet, this finish is also glazed for an antique look.

GOLAN CABINETS
The Odyssey Collection:
Customized to your needs, these cabinets come in a choice of hickory, cherry, maple or oak and can be stained in any of over 130 decorator colors. We also offer a selection of eight different door styles.

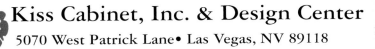

Kiss Cabinet, Inc. & Design Center

5070 West Patrick Lane• Las Vegas, NV 89118

P: 702.739.6090 • F: 702.739.0391

Finally...
Las Vegas' Own
Home & Design
Sourcebook

The **Las Vegas Home Book** is your final destination when searching for home remodeling, building and decorating resourc

This comprehensive, hands-on sourcebook to building, remodeling, decorating, furnishing, and landscaping a luxur home is required reading for the serious and discriminating homeowner. With more than 700 full-color, beautiful pages, tl **Las Vegas Home Book** is the most complete and well-organiz reference to the home industry. This hardcover volume covers aspects of the process, includes listings of hundreds of indust professionals, and is accompanied by informative and valuab editorial discussing the most recent trends. Ordering your cop of the **Las Vegas Home Book** now can ensure that you have t blueprints to your dream home, in your hand, today.

Order your copy now!

LAS VEGAS
HOME
BOOK

Published by
The Ashley Group
1740 Industrial Rd.,Las Vegas, NV 89118
702-614-4960 fax 702-263-6596
E-mail: ashleybooksales@cahners.com

CUSTOM WOODWORKING, METALWORKING, HARDWARE & GLASS

MAJESTIC CONSTRUCTION

**SPECIALIZING IN ALL PHASES OF
CUSTOM WOODWORKING
&FINE FURNITURE.**

4755 NEVSO DR. STE.# 7 LAS VEGAS, NV 89103
(702) 399-7411 (702) 210 2351 Fax (702) 399-7151

Our skilled craftsmen will work with you to create a true expression of
your personal style. Whether you prefer traditional, contemporary or
country, we can create the look you desire
Each order is handcrafted and one of a kind.

"God
is in the
details."

Ludwig Mies van der Rohe

329

Elegant
Touches

Fine, handcrafted interior architectural elements are the details that distinguish the highest quality custom-designed homes. They lend richness and elegance, infusing a home with character and originality. Even an empty room can speak volumes about the personal taste and style of its owners with cabinetry, moldings, ceiling medallions, chair rails, staircases, mirrors and mantels. Windows, doors, and hardware must endure the rigors of regular use, synthesizing beauty and function into high quality design statements made to stand the test of time. Bring your eye for detail as you explore the finest in architectural elements on the following pages.

Photo courtesy of **Kiss Cabinets**

WALL TO WALL ELEGANCE

Nowhere is the commitment to elegant living through quality materials more apparent than in the selection of cabinets and millwork. Representing a significant percentage of the overall cost of a new or renovated home, sophisticated homeowners use this opportunity to declare their dedication to top quality.

Architectural millwork, made to order according to a set of architectural drawings, is becoming an increasingly popular luxury upgrade. Such detailing creates a richly nostalgic atmosphere that reminds homeowners of the comfort and security of a grandparents' home or the elegance of a club they've been in.

Elegant libraries, dens or sitting rooms dressed with fashionable raised panel cabinetry and special moldings are often included in the plans for new homes and remodeling projects. As a homeowner considering how and where to install millwork, ask yourself questions like these:

• How is the room used? Will a study be used for work or for solitude? Entertaining or a second office? Will it have to function as both a working office and an elegant room?

• How are the cabinets and shelves used? Books, collectibles, audio-video equipment, computer, fax or copy machines?

• What look do you want? You may want to consider "dressing" your rooms in different woods. You may like the rich look and feel of cherry paneling in your library, mahogany in the foyer, oak in a guest room and plaster in a dining room.

• Will the interior millwork choices work with the exterior architecture? A colonial home reminiscent of Mount Vernon should be filled with authentic details, like "dog-ear" corners, that create classic luxury. Using millwork inside a modern home can add interest and warmth to one or many rooms.

TIME IS OF THE ESSENCE

Hand-crafted high quality woodwork cannot be rushed. Millwork specialists encourage clients to contact them as early as possible with a clear idea of what kind of architectural statement they wish to make. The earlier you plan these details, the more options you'll have. Wainscoting with raised panels has to be coordinated with electrical outlets, window and door openings; beamed ceilings with light fixtures, and crown moldings with heating vents.

Hold a preliminary meeting before construction begins while it's early enough to incorporate innovative or special requirements into your plans. The more time you can devote to design (two to

PRICING A POWER LIBRARY

• A 15- by 16-foot library, fully paneled in cherry, mahogany or oak, some cabinets, with moldings, desk with hidden computer, coffered ceilings: $20,000 to $30,000.

• In a 16- by 24-foot two-story study, less paneling and more cabinetry of cherry, mahogany or oak, heavy with moldings, and radius work, desk with more pull out and hidden compartments for fax machine, small copier, bar with leaded glass cabinet fronts and a marble top, built-in humidor, and heavily coffered ceilings with multiple steps: $40,000.

330

Custom Woodworking, Metal & Glass

three weeks is recommended), the better your result will be. You're creating a custom millwork package that's never been designed for anyone before. Investments made on the front end are the most valuable. Ask about design fees, timelines and costs per revision. Keep your builder up to date on all of your millwork plans.

Drawings can be as detailed as you require. If you want to see the intricacies of a radius molding before you contract for it, let the millwork specialist know your requirements. Ask to see wood samples, with and without stain or paint.

Try to visit installed projects to get a firsthand feel for the quality of a specialist's work and to develop clearer ideas for your own home.

Changes made after an order is placed are costly. Therefore, if you're unsure, don't make a commitment. Add accessory moldings and other details as you see the project taking shape.

Expect a heavily laden room to take at least five to eight weeks to be delivered, about the time from the hanging of drywall to the installation of flooring. Installation takes one to three weeks, depending on the size and scope of the project.

THE ELEGANT REFINEMENT OF CUSTOM CABINETRY

Handcrafted custom cabinets are a recognizable standard of excellence which lend refinement and beauty to a home. Built in a kitchen, library, bathroom, or closet, or as a free-standing entertainment system or armoire, custom cabinets are a sophisticated signature statement.

There are no limits to the possibilities of custom cabinets. The requirements of any space, no matter how unusual, can be creatively met. The endless combinations of style and detail promise unique cabinetry to homeowners who are searching for an individual look, while the first class craftsmanship of experienced, dedicated woodworkers promises unparalleled quality.

DESIGNING HANDSOME CABINETRY

Cabinetry is a major element in your dream home, so let your imagination soar. Collect pictures of cabinets, noting the particular features you like. Cabinet makers appreciate visual examples because it's easier to interpret your desires from pictures than from words. Pictures crystallize your desires.

When you first meet with a cabinet maker, take your blueprints, and if possible, your builder, architect or designer. Be prepared to answer questions like:

HOW TO RECOGNIZE CUSTOM CABINET QUALITY

1. Proper sanding which results in a smooth, beautiful finish.
2. Superior detail work, adding unexpected elegance.
3. Classic application of design features and architectural details.
4. Beautiful, functional hardware selections.
5. High-quality hinges and drawer glides.
6. Superior overall functionality.

WHY YOU WANT A PROFESSIONAL DESIGNER

• They rely on experience to deliver you a custom product. Computer tools are great, but nothing replaces the experienced eye.
• They have established relationships with other trades, and can get top-quality glass fronts for your cabinets, or granite for a bar top.
• Their design ability can save you significant dollars in installation.
• They know how to listen to their clients and help them get the results they dream of.

One Person's Project Estimate:

Adding a Winding Elegance

It's fun to imagine, but what might it actually cost to undertake a project described in this chapter? The example below describes a typical project and gives a general estimate of the costs involved.

Project Description
Construction of a high-end, cherry wood circular staircase, 16-rise (stairs)

Scenario I
Staircase is constructed as part of a new home construction, based on previous blueprint renderings.

Raw Materials (lumber)	$ 9,630
Labor (Shop time)	$34,295
Labor (Installation)	$ 4,680
Total:	**$48,605**

Scenario II
Staircase is constructed as an addition to an existing home.
In addition to the above prices, the following quotes would be added.

Consultation (Quote)	$265
Field measurement	$210
Job site measurements are taken	
Preliminary drawings	$0
Estimating	$360
Processing the information from a blueprint and determining the cost of the raw materials, labor and any other type of subtiers (paint, special material).	
Proposal	$100
Engineering	$360
Total:	**$50,030**

Cherry wood
circular
staircase

Optional
baluster
detail

• What is the exterior style of your home and do you want to continue that style inside?

• How will you the use the cabinets? Cutlery trays, pull-out bins? Shelves for books, CDs, computer software, collections?

• What styles and embellishments do you like? Shaker, Prairie, Country English, contemporary? Fancy moldings, wainscoting, inlaid banding? Use your Idea Notebook to communicate your preferences.

• Do you prefer particular woods? Cherry, oak, sycamore, or the more exotic ebony, Bubinga or Swiss pearwood? (Species must be selected on the basis of the finish you want.)

• Will cabinetry be visible from other rooms in the house? Must it match previously installed or selected flooring or countertops? (Take samples.)

PRICING OF CUSTOM KITCHEN CABINETS

• **Deluxe Kitchen - Face frame-style cabinets of oak, maple or pine, with raised panel doors; crown molding on upper cabinetry, decorative hardware, wood nosing (cap) around counter tops: $10,000 - $20,000**
• **Upgrade to Shaker inset-style cabinets in cherrywood, painted finish: $20,000 additional.**

334

MANAGING THE LENGTHY PROCESS OF A CUSTOM CABINET PROJECT

With plenty of unhurried time, you can be more creative, while allowing the woodworkers the time they need to deliver a top quality product. Take your blueprints to a cabinet maker early. Although installation occurs in the latter part of the construction, measuring usually takes place very early on.

If your project is carefully thought out, you won't be as likely to change your mind, but a contingency budget of 10 to 15 percent for changes (like adding radiuses or a lacquered finish) is recommended.

Custom cabinets for a whole house, (kitchen, butler's pantry, library, master bath, and three to four additional baths) may take 10 to 15 weeks, depending on the details involved (heavy carving adds significant time). Cabinets for a kitchen remodeling may take two months.

THE DRAMATIC EFFECT OF EXCEPTIONAL STAIRCASES

Take full advantage of the opportunity to upgrade your new or remodeled home with a spectacular staircase by contacting the stairmakers early in the design phase. Their familiarity with products, standards and building codes will be invaluable to you and your architect, contractor or interior designer.

Visit a stair showroom or workroom on your own or with your architect, interior designer or builder during the architectural drawing phase of your project. Discuss how you can achieve what you want at a cost-conscious price. Choosing a standard size radius of 24 inches, in place of a custom 25 1/2 inch radius, for example, will help control costs.

Although your imagination may know no bounds in designing a staircase, hard and fast local building codes may keep your feet on the ground. Codes are not static, and stairmakers constantly update their files on local restrictions regarding details like the rise and run of a stair, and the size and height of rails.

THE STAIR-BUILDING PROCESS

The design of your stairs should be settled in the rough framing phase of the overall building project. If you work within this time frame, the stairs will be ready for installation after the drywall is hung and primer has been applied to the walls in the stair area.

Stairs can be built out of many woods. The most popular choice is red oak, but cherry, maple, walnut and mahogany are also used. If metal railings are preferred, you'll need to contact a specialist.

A top quality stair builder will design your stairs to your specifications. Consider the views you want of the house while on the stairs, and what kind of front entrance presentation you prefer. You may want to see the stairs from a particular room. An expert also can make suggestions regarding comfort and safety, and what styles will enhance the overall architecture.

Plans which are drawn on a computer can be changed with relative ease and can be printed at full size. This is very helpful to homeowners who want to see exactly what the stairs will look like in their home. The full-size plans can be taken to the job site and tacked to the floor to be experienced firsthand.

THE POLISHED ARTISTRY OF CUSTOM GLASS AND MIRROR

A room can be transformed through the use of custom decorative glass and mirrors. Artists design intricately patterned, delicately painted glass to add light and architectural interest in all kinds of room dividers and partitions. Glass artistry can be based on any design, playing on the texture of carpet, the pattern of the brick, or repeating a fabric design. A glass block wall or floor panel can add the touch of distinction that sets a home above the others. Stained glass, usually associated with beautiful classic styling, can be designed in any style – from contemporary to art deco to traditional.

Top specialists, like those presented in the following pages, take great care in designing and delivering unique, top quality products. They work with top quality fabricated products, with the highest quality of beveling and edge work.

USING PLASTER DETAILING

Plaster architectural detailing and trim add a distinctive look to any home. Most often used in out of the way places, like in ceiling medallions or crown moldings, the high relief detailing is especially impressive.

PRICES OF CUSTOM STAIRS

Stairs can cost anywhere from $200 to $95,000, depending on size, materials and the complexity of design:
• Red Oak spiral staircase, upgraded railing: $10,000
• Red Oak circle stairs, standard railings on both sides and around upstairs landing: $13,000
• Six flights of Red Oak circle stairs stacked one atop the next, with landings at the top of each stair: $95,000
• Walnut or mahogany adds 50 percent to the overall cost.

DOOR #1, #2, OR #3?

• **Door #1 - Six panel oak door with sidelights of leaded glass: $1,700 - $2,000**

• **Door #2 - Six panel oak door with lead and beveled glass: $3,000**

• **Door #3 - Oversized, all matched oak, with custom designed leaded glass and brass, sidelights, elliptical top over door: $15,000**

• **Allow $500 to $1,500 for doorknobs, hinges and other hardware.**

THREE TIPS FOR DOOR HARDWARE

1. Use three hinges to a door - it keeps the door straight.
2. Match all hardware - hinges, knobs, handles, all in the same finish. Use levers or knobs - don't mix.
3. Use a finish that will last.

THE ARTISTIC PROCESS

Glass specialists will visit your home or building site to make recommendations and estimate costs and delivery time. Study their samples and if they have a showroom, go take a look. Perhaps you could visit an installed project. Seeing the possibilities can stimulate your imagination and open your eyes to new ideas in ways pictures simply cannot.

Allow a month to make a decision and four weeks for custom mirror work delivery, and ten to 14 weeks for decorated glass.

In order to have the glass or mirror ready for installation before the carpet is laid, decisions must be made during the framing or rough construction phase in a new home or remodeling job. Mirrored walls are installed as painting is being completed, so touch-ups can be done while painters are still on site.

Expect to pay a 50 percent deposit on any order after seeing a series of renderings and approving a final choice. Delivery generally is included in the price.

THE DRAMATIC EFFECT OF CUSTOM WINDOWS AND DOORS

Just as we're naturally drawn to establish eye contact with each other, our attention is naturally drawn to the "eyes" of a home, the windows, skylights and glass doors.

These very important structural features, when expertly planned and designed, add personality and distinction to your interior while complementing the exterior architectural style of your home.

After lumber, windows are the most expensive part of a home. Take the time to investigate the various features and qualities of windows, skylights and glass doors. Visit a specialty store offering top of the line products and service and take advantage of their awareness of current products as well as their accumulated knowledge.

Visit a showroom with your designer, builder or architect. Because of the rapidly changing requirements of local building codes, it's difficult for them to keep current on what can be installed in your municipality. In addition, the dizzying pace of energy efficiency improvements over the past five years can easily outrun the knowledge of everyone but the window specialist. Interior designers can help you understand proper placement and scale in relation to furnishings and room use.

As you define your needs ask questions about alternatives or options, such as energy efficiency, ase of maintenance, appropriate styles to suit the exterior architecture, and interior.

Top quality windows offer high energy efficiency, the best woodwork and hardware, and comprehensive service and guarantees (which should not be pro-rated). Good service agreements cover everything, including the locks.

Every home of distinction deserves an entry that exudes a warm welcome and a strong sense of homecoming. When we think of "coming home," we envision an entry door first, the strong, welcoming look of it, a first impression of the home behind it. To get the best quality door, contact a door or millwork specialist with a reputation for delivering top quality products. They can educate you on functionality, and wood and size choices and availability, as well as appropriate style. Doors are also made of steel or fiberglass, but wood offers the most flexibility for custom design.

Since doors are a permanent part of your architecture, carefully shop for the design that best reflects the special character of your home. Allow two to three weeks for delivery of a simple door and eight to 12 weeks if you're choosing a fancy front door. Doors are installed during the same phase as windows, before insulation and drywall.

FABULOUS HARDWARE ADDS DESIGN FLAIR

Door and cabinet hardware, towel bars and accessories add style and substance to interiors. Little things truly do make the difference - by paying attention to the selection of top quality hardware in long-lasting, great-looking finishes, you help define your signature style and commitment to quality in a custom home. There are hundreds of possibilities, so when you visit a specialty showroom, ask the sales staff for their guidance. They can direct you towards the products that will complement your established design style and help you stay within the limits of your budget. When a rim lock for the front door can easily cost $500, and knobs can be $10 each, the advice of a knowledgeable expert is priceless.

Most products are readily available in a short time frame, with the exception of door and cabinetry hardware. Allow eight weeks for your door hardware, and three to four weeks for cabinetry selections. Since accessory hardware is usually in stock, changing cabinet knobs, hooks and towel bars is a quick and fun way to get a new look. ∎

LUXURY GLASS & MIRROR

- **Mirrored Exercise Room: Floor to ceiling, wall to wall mirrors, on two or three walls. Allow at least a month, from initial measuring, to squaring off and balancing walls, to installation. Price for polished mirror starts around $9 per square foot. Cut-outs for vent outlets cost extra.**
- **Custom Shower Doors: Frameless, bent or curved shower doors are popular luxury upgrades. Made of clear or sandblasted heavy glass - 1/2" to 3/8" thick. $2,000 and up.**
- **Stained Glass Room Divider: Contemporary, clear on clear design, with a hint of color. Approximately 4' x 6', inset into a wall. $4,500.**
- **Glass Dining Table: Custom designed with bevel edge, 48" x 96" with two glass bases. $1,200.**

Stairs &
Metalworking

A.K.A. DESIGNS, INC. ....**(702) 233-8277**
3624 Deer Flats Street, Las Vegas   Fax: (702) 254-7012
See Ad on Page: 344
Principal/Owner: Amy Kline-Alley
Website: www.akadesignsinc.com   e-mail: aka@lvcm.com
Additional Information: Custom metalwork created and signed by Amy Kline-Alley
who is a master of metal sculpture, metal window scapes and more.

NEVADA STAIRS, INC...**(702) 739-3481**
6098 Topaz Street Suite 8, Las Vegas   Fax: (702) 739-3480
See Ad on Page: 340, 341
Principal/Owner: Russ Emerich & Pete Kueffner
Website: www.nevadastairs.com
Additional Information: We offer complete design services for creative stair-rail
systems in new residential homes and commercial offices.

SLATER DESIGN STUDIO ....**(702) 221-9112**
4355 West Reno Avenue #6, Las Vegas
See Ad on Page: 339
Principal/Owner: Doug Slater

TITAN STAIRS ....**(702) 221-9980**
4444 West Russell Road Suite A, Las Vegas   Fax: (702) 221-1489
See Ad on Page: 342, 343
Principal/Owner: Bob Gabour

Website: www.titanstairs.com   e-mail: titanstairs@aol.com
Additional Information: When only the best will do...Titan Stairs specializes in exquisite
stairways that will make your home a showplace. We also supply and install interior
and exterior columns and balustrades, wood and precast fireplace mantels.

phone: (702)739-3481
fax: (702)739-3480

6038 Topaz St. Suite 8
Las Vegas, NV 89120

NV LICENSE # 42454-A

Location,
Location,
Location!

Location,
Location,
Location!

What better LOCATION for your
advertisement than the
LAS VEGAS HOME BOOK!

Just as our readers realize how important
location is when choosing a home, we realize
that it's just as important to you when
allocating your advertising dollars.
That's why we have successfully positioned the
LAS VEGAS HOME BOOK to reach
the high-end consumers you want as clients.

**Call 702-614-4960 to find out about our
unique marketing programs and
advertising opportunities.**

Published by
The Ashley Group
7140 Industrial Rd., Las Vegas, NV 89118
702-614-4960 fax 702-263-6598
E-mail: ashleybooksales@cahners.com

Custom Cabinets

ANGIONE'S IN THE WOODS ....**(702) 367-1460**
    4560 Arville Road #C27, Las Vegas   Fax: (702) 367-2665
    See Ad on Page: 348
    <u>Principal/Owner:</u> Russ Angione
    <u>e-mail:</u> rangione@sprintmail.com
    <u>Additional Information:</u> From the concept to the finished product, let us help you
    express your thoughts & stretch your imagination.

CUSTOM CABINET FACTORY OF N.Y., INC. ....**(702) 739-9900**
    4350 West Sunset Road, Las Vegas   Fax: (702) 739-9911
    See Ad on Page: 349
    <u>Principal/Owner:</u> Israel Dorinbaum
    <u>e-mail:</u> idorinbaum@aol.com
    <u>Additional Information:</u> A family owned business spanning 300 years. Attention
    to detail is offered to the most discriminating customers.

HUNT'S WOODWORK & DESIGN, INC. ....**(702) 251-4748**
    4851 West Hacienda Ave Suite #4, Las Vegas   Fax: (702) 251-3940
    See Ad on Page: 350, 351
    <u>Principal/Owner:</u> Matt Hunt
    <u>Website:</u> www.huntswoods.com <u>e-mail:</u> mh88@ix.netcom.com
    <u>Additional Information:</u> Makers of fine furniture, cabinets, and interior accents.

MAJESTIC CONSTRUCTION, INC. ....**(702) 399-7411**
    4755 Nevso Drive Suite #7, Las Vegas   Fax: (702) 399-7151
    See Ad on Page: 326, 327, 347
    <u>Principal/Owner:</u> George Avendano

WOOD EXPRESSION STUDIO ....**(702) 894-9090**
    3160 South Highland Unit G, Las Vegas   Fax: (702) 894-5038
    See Ad on Page: 352
    <u>Principal/Owner:</u> Vlad Sretenovic

Kitchen & Bath an
Custom Cabinetry

"If you invest in beauty it will remain with you all the days of your life..."
Frank Lloyd Wright

ANGIONE'S
N THE WOODS
FINE WOODWORKING

4560 ARVILLE SUITE C27
LAS VEGAS, NV 89103
702.367.1460

CUSTOM KITCHEN AND BATH CABINETRY FEATURING **CORSI**™ AND **STARMARI**
ENTERTAINMENT CENTERS • OFFICES • LIBRARIES • CLOSETS
EXQUISITELY DESIGNED AND CRAFTED FOR YOU

legant Cabinetry...
...Functional Design

**Your
Imagination
Is
Our
Limit...**

Entertainment Centers

Libraries

Mantles

Wine Cellars / Coolers

e Custom Cabinet Factory of New York Inc. has been a family business for e generations. Spanning over 295 years from Europe to Las Vegas, the mpany uses old-world techniques to design, manufacture, and install wood binetry, kitchens, entertainment centers, libraries and other niture, crafted with painstaking expert design and attention to detail.

Free In-Home Estimates

**HOWROOM-FACTORY LOCATED AT:
57 West Sunset Road
s Vegas, NV 89118
702.739.9900
702.739.9911**

Five Generations In Wood Working
CUSTOM
CABINET FACTORY
OF
NEW YORK INC.

Exclusive Dealer
of HERTCO Kitchen

WOOD EXPRESSIONS STUDIO

WOOD EXPRESSIONS STUDIO
3160 South Highland Suite G
Las Vegas, NV 89109

www.894-9090.com

(702) 894-9090

Decorative
Glass & Mirrors

GLASSIC ART..**(702) 658-7588**
5850 South Polaris Avenue Suite 500, Las Vegas   Fax: (702) 658-7342
See Ad on Page: 305, 354, 355
<u>Principal/Owner:</u> Leslie Rankin
<u>Website:</u> www.glassicart.com   <u>e-mail:</u> glassicart@glassicart.com
<u>Additional Information:</u> This creative and diverse form of glass art will transform
your custom home into the most visually impressive living environment.

PERSPECTIVES ENGRAVING, INC. ....**(702) 871-3134**
5320 Cameron Suite #5, Las Vegas   Fax: (702) 871-3184
See Ad on Page: 358, 359
<u>Principal/Owner:</u> Ed Hughes, President/Pat Hughes, Vice President
<u>Website:</u> www.perspectivesengraving.com   <u>e-mail:</u> perspeceng@aol.com
<u>Additional Information:</u> Toll Free # 888-775-9937

YAMILE'S ART CENTER..**(702) 363-8044**
1000 South Rampart, Suite 4, Las Vegas   Fax: (702) 363-8773
See Ad on Page: 360
<u>Principal/Owner:</u> Yamile Gaez
<u>e-mail:</u> ygaez@aol.com
<u>Additional Information:</u> Enhance entry doors, side lights, windows and transoms
with stained and etched glass design. Traditional & contemporary designs by a
professional from concept to final project.

Consider the possibilities...

Welded Glass:
Taking glass into a new dimension and opulence...

arved, Painted Glass
assic Art's own innovative
ay to add color in glass,
ing beyond any traditional
ethod.

Strong, Durable, Easy to Clean, and Exquisite!

Founder and artist **Leslie Rankin** as featured on HGTV's "Modern Masters".

Commercial, Residential, Interior, and Exterior

GLASSIC ART

We Bring Glass To Life!

702-658-7588

www.GlassicArt.com

PASSING THRU

ESCAPE

THE PASSAGE

SIERRA AND THE SENT

STARGATE HANDLE

TONY MILICI
SCULPTOR

MILICI STUDIOS
95 E. SHELBOURNE AVE.
LAS VEGAS, NV 89123
TEL. (702) 270-4414
FAX. (702) 270-6315
www.milicistudios.com
email: tm@milicistudios.com

STARGATE

ALSO SEE PAGE -
ART &ANTIQUES

PERSPECTIVES ENGRAVIN INC.

he finest in custom engraved glass and
irror for home or office

Yamiles Art Center

Traditional and Contemporary
Stained and Etched Glass

Professional designer
From concept to final Project

363-8044

Boca Park Marketplace
1000 South Rampart, Suite 4

Windows
& Doors

GLASSY BUSINESS WINDOW TINTING, INC. ....**(702) 341-9677**
7441 West Lake Mead # 104, Las Vegas   Fax: (702) 341-6902
See Ad on Page: 374, 375
<u>Principal/Owner:</u> Jim Flihan
<u>Website:</u> www.glassybusiness.com <u>e-mail:</u> jflihan@aol.com
<u>Additional Information:</u> Specializing in commercial and residential applications since 1986. We are fully licensed and insured.

LAS VEGAS WINDOW TINTING ....**(702) 222-1710**
3380 West Hacienda, Las Vegas   Fax: (702) 251-3016
See Ad on Page: 373
<u>Principal/Owner:</u> Frank Friedlander
<u>Additional Information:</u> Serving the custom home market for 30 years.

MILICI STUDIOS ....**(702) 270-4144**
95 East Shelbourne, Las Vegas   Fax: (702) 270-6315
See Ad on Page: 356, 357, 496, 497
<u>Principal/Owner:</u> Tony Milici/Sculptor
<u>Website:</u> www.milicistudios.com <u>e-mail:</u> tm@milicistudios.com
<u>Additional Information:</u> Fine art glass sculpture with elements of rock, marble, steel & glass. Custom architectural furniture, public art, private commissions. "Glass is the perfect canvas for light. It increases the emotional and visual impact of my work".

SIERRA PACIFIC WINDOWS ....**(800) 824-7744**
3725 West Teco Avenue Suite #7, Las Vegas   Fax: (702) 837-8574
See Ad on Page: 363
<u>Website:</u> www.sierrapacificwindows.com <u>e-mail:</u> mghali@spi-ind.com
<u>Additional Information:</u> Factory Direct. Come see our showroom and meet our friendly sales team!

SUNBELT WINDOWS & DOORS ....**(702) 362-0144**
4390 West Tompkins #G, Las Vegas   Fax: (702) 362-6168
See Ad on Page: 362
<u>Principal/Owner:</u> Duane Crook & Phil Truman
<u>Additional Information:</u> We represent a variety of product lines to meet the styles, shapes and sizes of every home.

361

SUNBELT
WINDOWS & DOORS, IN

Sunbelt Windows

4390 W. Tompkins #G
Las Vegas, NV 89103
(702) 362-0144
Fax   362-6168

Featuring

WINDSOR
WINDOWS & DOORS

"We start with integrity and end
with customer satisfaction."

Fireplaces, Mantels
& Moldings

REALM OF DESIGN ....**(702) 566-118**
1188 Center Point Drive, Henderson   Fax: (702) 566-9318
See Ad on Page: 366, 367
Principal/Owner: Scott & Cindy McCombs
Website: www.realmofdesign.com   e-mail: sales@realmofdesign.com
Additional Information: Manufacturing & designing exquisite architectural details
since 1991. Such as, but not limited to, fireplace surrounds, columns, balustrades
& entry ways.

SILVER STATE FIREPLACES ....**(702) 474-409**
Las Vegas   Fax: (702) 474-4428
See Ad on Page: 365
Principal/Owner: Danny Check & Linda Kirkpatrick
e-mail: silverstatefp@aol.com
Additional Information: Complete service, installation and maintenance for fireplaces
(new & retrofit), surrounds, mantels, fire pits, custom mirrors and bath enclosures.

SUPERIOR MOULDING OF NEVADA ....**(702) 739-9663**
5585 South Valley View Boulevard, Las Vegas   Fax: (702) 739-9669
See Ad on Page: 370, 371
Principal/Owner: Bill Carr/Brian Oohs
Website: www.smnv.net   e-mail: bill@smnv.net
Additional Information: Superior Molding offers the quality material, from molding
to flooring to completion & customization of your home.

HEAT-N-GLO®
No one builds a better fire

ilver
tate
ireplaces

"The Fireplace Experts"

- Mantels
- Surrounds
- Skylights

- Custom Mirror
- Bath Enclosures
- Custom Wardrobes Doors

• Fireplaces (new and retrofit)

Phone 474-4099
Fax 474-4428

Specialize and Custom
Architectural Reproductio.

· Columns
· Fireplace Surrounds
· Crown Moldings
· Balustrades
· Entry Ways

Realm of Design

THE DIFFERENCE BETWEE

LIES IN TH

The

A

Grou

THE ASHLEY GROU

The Ashley Group is the largest provider of hor
quality designing, building, and decorating information a
For more on the many products of **The Ashl**
Cahners Business Information (www.cahners.cor
U.S. provider of business information to
manufacturing and retail. Cahners` rich content portfo
Publishers Weekly, Design News and 152 oth

shley

...ESOURCE COLLECTION

...al resource images and strives to provide the highest
...ources available to upscale consumers and professionals.
...oup, visit our website at www.theashleygroup.com.
...ember of the Reed Elsevier plc group, is a leading
...tical markets, including entertainment,
...compasses more than 140 Websites as well as *Variety*,
...rket-leading business-to-business magazines

SUPERIOR
MOULDING OF NEVADA

5585 South Valley View Blvd., Suite 4
Las Vegas, NV 89118
702.739.9663
Hours: Mon.- Fri. 7a.m. - 5p.m. • Sat. 8a.m.- 1p.m.
www.smnv.net

Custom
Window Tinting

LAS VEGAS WINDOW TINTING..**(702) 222-1710**
3380 West Hacienda, Suite 103, Las Vegas   Fax: (702) 251-3016
See Ad on Page: 373
<u>Principal/Owner:</u> Frank Friedlander
<u>Additional Information:</u> Serving the custom home market for 30 years.

EXPECTED

Every choice should be this clear. VISTA Window Film is the obvious choice for designers who demand the extraordinary. Your exceptional design, priceless works of art, delicate fabrics and furniture all need VISTA's protection to block out virtually all the cumulative damage from ultraviolet rays as well as heat and glare. The choice is yours.

Fully licensed and fully insured, **Glassy Business Window Tinting, Inc.** has been specializing in residential and commercial film applications since 1986. Please call for more information.

EXTRAORDINARY

Clear Quality & Protection
ASSURED

Glassy Business Window Tinting, Inc

7441 West Lake Mead Road, Unit 104
Las Vegas, Nevada 89128
Telephone: **702-341-9677** Fax: **702-341-6902**
www.glassybusiness.com

THE SKIN CANCER FOUNDATION
RECOMMENDED

VISTA®

W I N D O W   F I L M

Wine Cellars

VALENTINI'S FINE WINE LINE, INC. ....**(480) 991-1980**
See Ad on Page: 377   (888) 330-6371
<u>Principal/Owner:</u> Kathleen Valentini Bonner
<u>Website:</u> www.worldclasscellars.com <u>e-mail:</u> kathleen@worldclasscellars.com

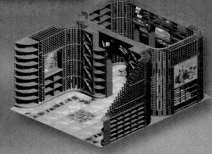

Only If You Want the Very Best...

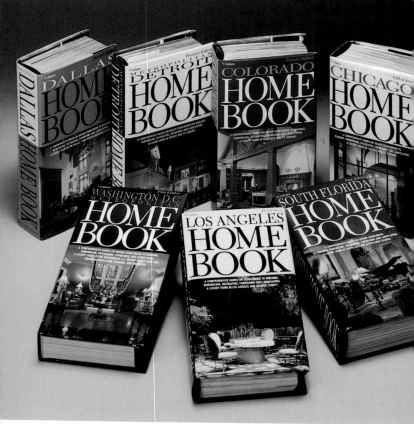

The Ashley Group

1350 E. Touhy Avenue, Des Plaines, Illinois 60018
888.458.1750   Fax 847.390.2902

www.theashleygroup.com • www.homebook.com

FLOORING

&

OUNTERTOPS

The welcoming warmth of your kitchen,...

versatile solid surfaces from DuPor

CORIAN®

SOLID SURFACES

DUPONT

www.corian.com

888 462 0865

...or the private sanctuary of the bath,

let you live your mood as it unfolds.

ZODIAQ®

QUARTZ SURFACES

"Things are *pretty*, *graceful*, rich, *elegant*, handsome, but, until they speak *to the imagination*, not yet *beautiful.*"

Ralph Waldo Emerson

383

Tops 'N Bottoms

The solid surfaces of a home, the floors and countertops are show-stopping design elements that add beauty and distinction to each room. From exquisite marble slabs, richly polished woods and luxurious carpets, to fabulous granites and ceramic tiles, the possibilities color, style and combination are unlimited. Custom homeowners are well traveled and sophisticated in their tastes and preferences, as shop owners and craftsmen who cater to this clientele will attest. Their strong desire for quality and beauty make for educated choices that add value and personality to the home. The following pages will introduce you to some of the most distinguished suppliers and artisans working with these products.

Photo courtesy of **Elite Tile**

FLOOR COVERINGS OF DISTINCTION...CARPETS & RUGS

From a room-sized French Aubusson rug to a dense wool carpet with inset borders, "soft" floor treatments are used in area homes to make a signatur statement, or blend quietly into the background to let other art and furnishings grab the attention.

Selecting carpeting and rugs requires research, a dedicated search, and the guidance of a well establish design plan. Because the floor covers the width and depth of any room, it's very important that your choices are made in concert with other design decisions—from furniture to art, from window treatments to lighting.

Your interior designer or a representative at any of the fine retail stores featured in the following pages is qualified to educate you as you make your selections.

Rug and carpet dealers who cater to a clientele th demands a high level of personal service (from advic to installation and maintenance) and top quality products, are themselves dedicated to only the best i terms of service and selection. Their accumulated knowledge will be a most important benefit as you select the right carpet for your home.

THE WORLD AT YOUR FEET

Today's profusion of various fibers, colors, patterns, textures, and weights make carpet selection exciting and challenging. Your search won't be overwhelming if you realize the requirements of your own home and work within those boundaries.

Begin where the carpet will eventually end up— that is, in your home. Consider how a carpet will function by answering questions like these:

• What is the traffic pattern? High traffic areas, like stairs and halls, require a stain resistant dense or low level loop carpet for top durability in a color or patter that won't show wear. Your choices for a bedroom, where traffic is minimal, will include lighter colors in deeper plush or velvets.

• How will it fit with existing or developing decors? D you need a neutral for an unobtrusive background, or an eye-catching tone-on-tone texture that's a work of art in itself?

• Will it flow nicely into adjoining rooms? Carpet or other flooring treatments in the surrounding rooms need to be considered.

• What needs, other than decorative, must the carpet fill? Do you need to keep a room warm, muffle sound protect a natural wood floor?

• How is the room used? Do teenagers and toddlers carry snacks into the family room? Is a finished basement used for ping-pong as well as a home office

ORIENTAL RUGS

The decision to invest in an Oriental rug should be made carefully. Buying a rug purely for its decorative beauty and buying for investment purposes require two different approaches. If you're buying for aesthetics, put beauty first and condition second. Certain colors and patterns are more significant than others; a reputable dealer can guide you. Check for quality by looking at these features:

• Regularity of knotting.
• Color clarity.
• Rug lies evenly on the floor.
• Back is free of damage or repair marks.

THE NUMBER ONE WAY TO DECIDE ON A RUG

Do you like the rug enough to decorate around it? There's your answer.

THE ARTISTRY OF RUGS

Nothing compares to the artful elegance of a carefully selected area rug placed on a hard surface. Through pattern, design, texture and color, rug designers create a work of art that is truly enduring. If you have hardwood, marble or natural stone floors, an area rug will only enhance their natural beauty. From Chinese silk, to colorful Pakistanis, to rare Caucasian antiques, the possibilities are as varied as the world is wide.

If you're creating a new interior, it's best to start with rug selection. First, it's harder to find the 'right' rug than it is to find the 'right' fabric or paint: there are simply fewer fine rugs than there are fabrics, patterns or colors. However, don't make a final commitment on a rug until you know it will work with the overall design. Second, rugs usually outlive other furnishings. Homeowners like to hang on to their rugs when they move, and keep them as family heirlooms.

In recent years, many rug clients have been enjoying a bounty of beautiful, well-made rugs from every major rug-producing country in the world. As competition for the global market intensifies, rugs of exceptionally high caliber are more readily available. Getting qualified advice is more important than ever.

Fine rug dealers, like those showcased in the following pages, have knowledgeable staff members who are dedicated to educating their clientele and helping them find a rug they'll love. Through careful consideration of your tastes, and the requirements of your home, these professionals will virtually walk you through the process. They'll encourage you to take your time, and to judge each rug on its own merits. They'll insist on you taking rugs home so you can experience them in your own light (and may also provide delivery). And their companies will offer cleaning and repair service, which may well be important to you some day.

ELEGANCE UNDERFOOT: HARDWOOD

A hardwood floor is part of the dream for many custom homeowners searching for a warm, welcoming environment. Highly polished planks or fine parquet, the beauty of wood has always been a definitive part of luxurious homes and as the design "warming trend" continues, a wood floor figures prominently in achieving this feeling.

With new product options that make maintenance even easier, wood floors continue to add value and distinction in upscale homes throughout the area and the suburbs. Plank, parquet, and strip wood come in a wide variety of materials, and scores of styles and tones. Consider what effect you're trying to achieve.

FOR SUCCESSFUL CARPET SHOPPING

1. Take along blueprints (or accurate measurements), fabric swatches, paint chips & photos.
2. Focus on installed, not retail price.
3. Take samples home to experience it in the light of the room.
4. Be aware of delivery times; most carpet is available within weeks; special orders or custom designs take much longer.
5. Shop together. It saves time in the decision-making process.

BUDGETING FOR WOOD FLOOR*

2 1/4" strip oak – $10/sq. ft.
Wider plank or parquet, glued & nailed – $15/sq. ft.
Fancy parquet, hand-finished plank or French patterns (Versailles, Brittany) – $30/sq. ft. and up.
* Estimates include finishing and installation; not sub-floor trim.

Plank wood complements a traditional interior, while parquet wood flooring offers a highly stylized look. Designs stenciled directly on to floorboards create an original Arts and Crafts feel.

The more exotic woods used for flooring, like Brazilian cherry wood, are often harvested from managed forests.

DON'T GET COLD FEET

Stone and tile floors are known for their chilly feel. Electrical products are available now to help warm the surfaces of natural products. Installed in the adhesive layer under the flooring, these warming units are available at the better suppliers and showrooms in the Las Vegas Valley and the suburbs.

CERAMIC TILE AS STONE

With textured surfaces and color variations, ceramic tile can look strikingly like stone. You can get the tone on tone veining of marble, or the look of split stone, in assorted shapes, sizes and color.

VINYL AND LAMINATES

Vinyl or laminated floor coverings are no longer considered candidates for immediate rehab.— as a matter of fact, they're among the most updated looks in flooring. Stylish laminates are made to convincingly simulate wood, ceramic tile and other natural flooring products, and are excellent choices for heavy traffic areas. They come in hundreds of colors and patterns, and offer great compatibility with countertop materials.

THE RENAISSANCE OF CERAMIC TILE

Ceramic tile has literally come out of the back rooms and into the spotlight with its color, beauty and unique stylistic potential. As sophisticated shoppers gain a better understanding of the nature and possibilities of tile, its use has increased dramatically. Homeowners who want added quality and value in their homes are searching out hand painted glazed tiles for the risers of a staircase, quirky rectangular tiles to frame a powder room mirror, and ceramic tiles that look exactly like stone for their sun porch or kitchen. From traditional to modern, imported to domestic, ceramic tile offers a world of possibilities.

It is the perfect solution for homeowners who want floor, walls, countertops or backsplashes made of top quality, durable and attractive materials. A glazed clay natural product, ceramic tile is flexible, easy to care for, and allows for a variety of design ideas. It is easily cleaned with water and doesn't require waxing or polishing. And, like other natural flooring and counter products, ceramic tile adds visible value to a luxury home.

SELECTING CERAMIC TILE

Not all tile works in all situations, so it's imperative that you get good advice and counsel when selecting ceramic tile for your home. Ceramic tile is wear-rated, and this standardized system will steer you in the right direction. Patronize specialists who can provide creative, quality-driven advice. Visit showrooms to get an idea of the many colors, shapes and sizes available for use on floors, walls and counters. You'll be in for a very pleasant surprise.

If you're building or remodeling, your builder, architect, and/or interior designer can help you in your search and suggest creative ways to enliven your interior schemes. Individual hand-painted tiles can be interspersed in a solid color backsplash to add interest and individuality. Tiles can be included in a glass block partition, on a wallpapered wall, or in harmony with an area rug.

Grout, which can be difficult to keep clean, is now being addressed as a potential design element. By using a colored grout, the grout lines become a contrast design element—or can be colored to match the tile itself.

THE SOPHISTICATED LOOK OF NATURAL STONE

For a luxurious look that radiates strength and character, the world of natural stone offers dazzling possibilities. As custom buyers look for that "special something" to add to the beauty and value of their homes, they turn to the growing natural stone marketplace. A whole world of possibilities is now open to involved homeowners who contact the master craftsmen and suppliers who dedicate their careers to excellence in stone design, installation and refurbishing.

Marble and granite, which have always been options for homeowners are more popular than ever. With luxurious texture and color, marble is often the choice to add dramatic beauty to a grand entryway or a master bath upgrade. Granite continues to grow in popularity especially in luxury kitchens – there is no better material for countertops. It's also popular for a section of countertop dedicated to rolling pastry or dough. Rustic, weathered and unpolished, or highly polished and brilliant, granite brings elegance and rich visual texture that adds easily recognizable value to a home. Beyond marble and granite, the better suppliers of stone products also can introduce homeowners to slates, soapstone, limestone, English Kirkstone, sandstone, and travertine, which can be finished in a variety of individual ways.

ADJUSTING TO STONE PRODUCTS IN THE HOME

Like Mother Nature herself, natural stone is both rugged and vulnerable. Each stone requires specific care and maintenance and homeowners often experience a period of adjustment as they become accustomed to the requirements of caring for their floors or countertops.

Ask an expert about the different requirements and characteristics. Soapstone, for example, is a beautiful, soft stone with an antique patina many

PRICING FOR NATURAL STONE

As with all flooring and countertop materials, get an installed, not a retail quote. Installation can drive the cost up significantly. Preparing a realistic quote may take days of research, due to the tremendous variety of factors that can influence price. As a general guideline, the installed starting price per square foot:
• Granite: $30
• Tumbled marble, limestone, slate: $20
• Engineered stone/quartzite: $25
•Antique stone, with intricate installation: $75
•Granite slab countertop: $70

One Person's Project Estimate:

Reflooring with Red Oak

It's fun to imagine, but what might it actually cost to undertake a project described in this chapter? The example below describes a typical project and gives a general estimate of the costs involved.

Project Description

Replacement of the tile floor of a kitchen and breakfast area with red oak flooring, 200 - 250 sq. ft.

Removal and disposal of old flooring...$875

Installation of red oak boards, 2 inches wide... $2,000*
(finishing fee included)

Toekick at base of cabinets $270

Inlaid vents that match the floor wood ($40 apiece).......................................$80

Threshold to different levels..$20

Furniture removed and replaced..$100

Cabinets wrapped during sanding $100

Total.. $3,445

*Price is based on room with cabinets ($9/sq. ft.). If no cabinets exist, then the price is $8/sq. ft.

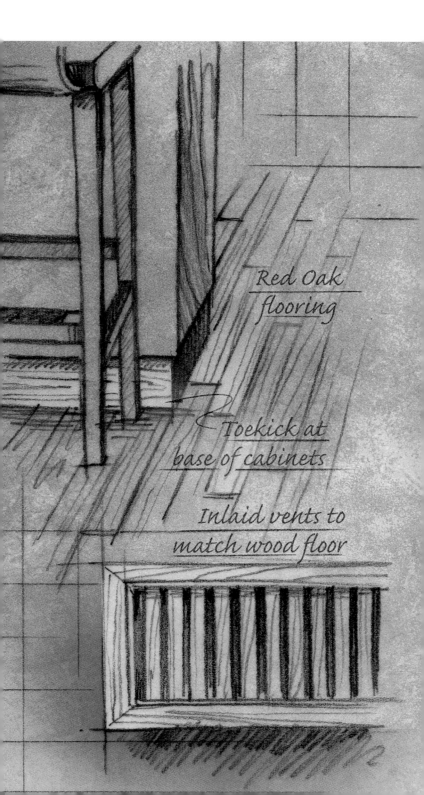

Red Oak
flooring

Toekick at
base of cabinets

Inlaid vents to
match wood floor

people love. Accumulated stains and scratches just add to the look. Granite, on the other hand, will not stain.

A professional can educate you about the specific characteristics of each stone product so you make an informed decision on what products will best serve the lifestyle of your family.

MAKE IT CONCRETE

This material is a versatile and indestructible choice, available in a variety of colors and textures. Sealed concrete can be made with creative borders, scored, sandblasted or stained. A strong, natural material, it can be made to look like other materials and natural stone.

SOLID SURFACING SHOWS UP ON TILES

Durable, non-porous solid surface materials are now being used to make decorative wall tiles. Check with your countertop supplier for information and ideas.

CHOOSING STONE – A UNIQUE EXPERIENCE

Once a decision to use a natural stone is made, begin your search right away. By allowing plenty of time to discover the full realm of choices, you'll be able to choose a stone and finish that brings luster and value to your home, without the pressure of a deadline. If you order imported stone, it can take months for delivery. Be prepared to visit your supplier's warehouse to inspect the stone that will be used in your home. Natural stone varies—piece to piece, box to box—a slab can vary in color from one end to the other. If you understand this degree of unpredictable irregularity is unavoidable, it will help you approach the selection in a realistic way.

STRONG AND ELEGANT COUNTERTOPS

The quest for quality and style does not stop until the countertops are selected. Today's countertop marketplace is brimming with manmade products that add high style without sacrificing strength and resiliency.

As the functions of kitchens become broader, the demand for aesthetics continues to increase dramatically. For lasting beauty with incredible design sensibilities, manmade solid surfaces are a very popular choice. The overwhelming number of possibilities and combinations in selecting countertops makes it vital to work with specialists who are quality-oriented. Countertops represent a significant investment in a custom home, and quality, performance and style must be the primary considerations in any decision. Established professionals, like those introduced in your Home Book, have a reputation for expert installation and service of the top quality products that define luxury.

MAKE COUNTERTOP CHOICES EARLY

Since decisions on cabinetry are often made far in advance, it's best to make a countertop choice concurrently.

Expect to spend at least two weeks visiting showrooms and acquainting yourself with design and materials. Take along paint chips, samples of cabinet and flooring materials, and any pictures of the look you're trying to achieve. Expect a solid surface custom counter order to take at least five weeks to arrive.

WEALTH OF COUNTERTOP OPTIONS

You'll face a field of hundreds of colors and textures of solid surfacing, laminates, ceramic tile, natural stone, wood and stainless or enameled steel. Poured concrete counters also are finding their way into luxury kitchens in the area.

Laminate or color-through laminate offer hundreds of colors, patterns and textures, many of which convincingly mimic the look of solid surfacing or granite. Enjoying growing popularity in countertop application, are the natural stones, those staggeringly gorgeous slabs of granite, marble or slate, which offer the timeless look of quality and luxury. Naturally quarried stone is extremely durable and brings a dramatic beauty and texture to the kitchen or bath. For endless color and pattern possibilities, ceramic tile is a highly durable option. Man made resin-based solid surfacing materials offer many of the same benefits as stone. These surfaces are fabricated for durability and beauty, and new choices offer a visual depth that is astounding to the eye. It can be bent, carved, or sculpted. Elaborate edges can be cut into a solid surface counter and sections can be carved out to accommodate other surface materials, such as stainless steel or marble. Best known for superior durability, solid surfaces stand up to scratches, heat and water.

FINDING THE BEST SOURCE FOR MATERIALS

If you're building or remodeling your home, your designer, builder or architect will help you develop some ideas and find a supplier for the material you choose. Reputable suppliers like those featured in the Home Book, are experienced in selecting the best products and providing expert installation. Go visit a showroom or office—their knowledge will be invaluable to you. The intricacies and idiosyncrasies of natural products, and the sheer volume of possibilities in fabricated surfaces, can be confounding on your own. ■

BEYOND TRADITIONAL

Solid surfacing is now being used to make custom faucets, decorative wall tiles, and lots of other creative touches for the home. Their rich colors (including granite), famed durability and versatility are perfect for bringing ideas to life. Check with your countertop supplier for information and ideas.

391

BE CREATIVE!

Mix and match counter top materials for optimum functionality and up-to-date style. Install a butcher block for chopping vegetables and slicing breads, a slab of marble for rolling pastry and bakery dough, granite on an island for overall elegance, and solid surfaces for beauty and durability around the sinks and cooktop areas.

Ceramic Tile

ARIZONA TILE ....**(702) 364-2199**
  4701 South Cameron Suites C & I, Las Vegas   Fax: (702) 364-5955
  See Ad on Page: 393
  <u>Website:</u> www.arizonatile.com
WALKER ZANGER...**(702) 248-1550**
  4701 Cameron Street Suite P, Las Vegas   Fax: (702) 248-1556
  See Ad on Page: 404
  <u>Website:</u> www.walkerzanger.com

iscover a World of Possibilities...

❖ Arizona Tile

eramic Tile • Natural Stone • Granite Slabs

4701 S. Cameron Street
Showroom - Suite C, 702.364.2199
Slabs - Suite I, 702.248.0954
Las Vegas, NV 89103

Other Locations: Phoenix · Tempe · Scottsdale · Glendale · Tucson · Prescott
Salt Lake City · Albuquerque · Miramar · San Diego · San Marcos · Temecula

visit us at www.arizonatile.com

&Flooring

CARPET ▲ WOOD

If you imagine your home as a
canvas for self-expression, then Corian®
is your palette of exciting possibilities.

888.462.0865
www.corian.com

CORIAN®
SOLID SURFACES

Flooring

ELITE TILE & FLOORING ....**(702) 221-5600**
5530 South Valley View #105, Las Vegas   Fax: (702) 221-5604
See Ad on Page: 394, 395
<u>Principal/Owner:</u> Bob Ahrens
<u>Additional Information:</u> Tile, flooring, carpet and counter-tops

FLOORS WITH STYLE...**(702) 364-5207**
9916 Charlemont Drive, Las Vegas   Fax: (702) 364-5209
See Ad on Page: 398, 399
<u>Principal/Owner:</u> Phillip Fileccia
<u>e-mail:</u> floorswithstyle@earthlink.net

PIANETA LEGNO FLOORS USA, INC....................................**(212) 755-1414**
1100 Second Avenue, New York   Fax: (212) 755-0112
See Ad on Page: 402
<u>Principal/Owner:</u> Mr. Ercan Elemek
<u>Website:</u> www.plfloors.com   <u>e-mail:</u> pianetalegno.cs.com
<u>Additional Information:</u> Importer & retailer of the highest quality Italian engineered
pre-finished hardwood flooring.

REVOLUTION ....**(702) 453-7500**
3061 French Creek Court, Las Vegas   Fax: (702) 453-8975
See Ad on Page: 400, 401
<u>Principal/Owner:</u> Abraham King
<u>e-mail:</u> rEvolution_vegas@msn.com
<u>Additional Information:</u> Hand painted, signed & numbered, beautiful concrete
flooring. Custom design in Las Vegas. Limitless as the imagination.

MALIBU CHAN'S

Floors With Style creates beautiful, practical, long lasting and low maintenance concrete floors that are perfect for today's lifestyle. Whether your Application is commercial, retail, office or residential, we can achieve a long lasting creative expression that enhances the appeal of any environment.

Our design team is very innovative and we offer many options that can accommodate most any budget and scheduling demands.

PROTEX

ESS FURNITURE

AUTO BUTLER

UTO BUTLER

Photography by Bob Wortham

rEvolution   *Abraham Kir*

3061 French Creek Court
las Vegas, NV 89156
p 702.453.7500
f 702.453.8975
rEvolution_vegas@msn.com

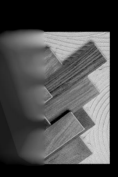

Marble & **Granite**

GLOBAL LINK SERVICES ....**(702) 639-9881**
6620 Escondido, Suite #E, Las Vegas   Fax: (702) 639-6331
See Ad on Page: 405
Website: www.globallinkservices.com e-mail: ironconsulting@aol.com
Additional Information: Worldwide supplier of marble, granite and hardwood flooring.
Custom marble fireplaces that are one of a kind!

GRANITE WORLD ....**(702) 614-4520**
6280 South Valley View #308, Las Vegas   Fax: (702) 614-4522
See Ad on Page: 406, 407
Principal/Owner: Burt Paul
Website: www.granite-world.com

STONE SOURCE ....**(702) 364-0394**
3575 South Decatur Blvd. #102, Las Vegas   Fax: (702) 597-2152
See Ad on Page: 408
Additional Information: Everything to do with the fabrication & maintenance
of stone. Artistic displays to assist with design layout.

STONEWERKS, INC....**(702) 682-4410**
535 Chelsea Drive, Las Vegas   Fax: (702) 456-7957
See Ad on Page: 409
Principal/Owner: Eric Hill

Lasting
Impressions.

Ceramic Tile • Stone Tile & Slabs • Mosaics • Terra Cotta • Glass Tile

GLOBAL LINK SERVICES, INC.

24FT. CUSTOM LIMESTONE MARBLE MANTEL AND RISERS

WORLDWIDE DISTRIBUTOR
SPECIALIZING IN:

HARDWOOD FLOORING, FEATURING EXOTIC
ASIAN ROSEWOOD AND HEART PINE
MARBLE AND GRANITE SLABS AND TILES
TRIM PACKAGES - BASE, CASE, CROWN, FLEX
MOSAICS
CUSTOM WOOD AND MARBLE FIREPLACES

6620 ESCONDIDO, SUITE E-3
LAS VEGAS, NV 89119
TEL 702.639.9881
FAX 702.639.6331
WWW.GLOBALLINKSERVICES.COM
EMAIL: UNIVTRADE@AOL.COM

*Like fine art, our Marble and
Granite will enhance your
residence with a grace
unparalleled*

*You're always welcome at
The Granite World Showroom*

Allow our marble & granite
to grace the presence of your home....

- Kitchen Counters
- Master Suites
- Wet Bars
- Flooring
- Wall Tile

STONE SOURCE

"People in the industry know that my name means first quality."

3575 South Decatur Boulevard
Suite 102
Las Vegas, NV 89103
P702.364.0394

STONEWERKS INC.

TEL. 702-682-4410
FAX 702-456-7957
HENDERSON, NV 89014
Specializing in custom
marble & granite
furniture and artwork

Solid Surfaces

PINNACLE DISTRIBUTION CONCEPTS ....**(480) 551-2234**
15300 North 90th Street, Suite 200, Arizona   Fax: (480) 657-6869
See Ad on Page: 380, 381, 396
<u>Principal/Owner:</u> Paul D. Clegg
<u>Website:</u> www.pdc4surfaces.com <u>e-mail:</u> lrodriguez@pdc4surfaces.com
<u>Additional Information:</u> Authorized distributor & marketer of DuPont Corian® solid
surfaces & DuPont Zodiaq® quartz surfaces.

HOME
FURNISHINGS
&
DECORATING

MAGDALENA'S
Home Furnishings & Accessories

Shop of Interior Inspirations

P: (702) 228-3924

F: (702) 228-6895

8125 W. Sahara Ave.

Suite 160

Las Vegas, NV 89117

"One may do
whate'er one likes

In Art:

the only thing is,

to make sure

That one does

like it. "

Robert Browning

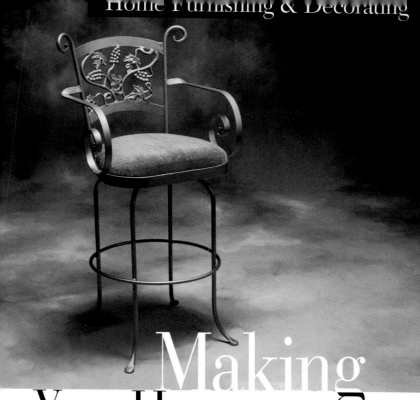

Making Your House A Home

A beautiful designed, meticulously planned house becomes a home when the furnishings are set in place. Comfortably upholstered sofas and chairs in the family room, a unique faux-finished foyer, richly appointed windows in the dining room, all give a home its individual flair and welcoming livability. Today's homeowners, whether they're in their first or final home, have the elevated taste that comes from exposure to good design. They know what quality furniture looks and feels like and they want it in their homes. In the home furnishing industry, one item is more outrageously gorgeous than the next, and anything you can imagine can be yours. This freedom can be overwhelming, even intimidating, if you don't keep a sharp focus. By visiting the finest stores, specialty shops, and artisans, like those presented in the following pages, you can be certain your desire for top quality is already understood and that knowledgeable people are ready to guide you. Enjoy.

Photo courtesy of **Zo'Calos**

MODERN IDEAS

With an evolutionary array of styles, contemporary furnishings add excitement, elegance and personality to a home. From Bauhaus, Retro, and Deco, to pure modern, these artful furnishings satisfy the desire for unique, individual expression.

KEEP IT ALIVE!

Regardless of your budget, you needn't sacrifice quality or style. Set your priorities and let your home take on a dynamic, ever-changing feel as you add or replace furnishings over a period of time.

TAKE TIME TO CHOOSE FURNITURE

You'll be living with your choices for many years to come, so take your time. Try to define why you like what you like. Look through shelter magazines, visit decorator homes and furniture showrooms. When you see a piece or arrangement you like, try to analyze what you like about it. Is it the color, the style of the piece, the texture of the fabric? Recognizing common elements you are drawn to will help you hone and refine your personal style.

As you start out, be sure to ruthlessly assess your current interior. Clear out pieces that need to be replaced or no longer work with your lifestyle, even if you have no clear idea of what you'll be replacing them with. Sometimes empty space makes visualizing something new much easier.

When furnishing a new room, consider creating a focus by concentrating on an architectural element, or selecting one important piece, like a Chinese Chippendale-style daybed or an original Arts & Crafts spindle table. Or, make your focus a special piece you already own.

To make the most of your time when visiting showrooms, take along your blueprint or a detailed drawing with measurements, door and window placements, and special architectural features. If your spouse or anyone else will be involved in the final decision, try to shop together to eliminate return trips. The majority of stores can deliver most furniture within eight weeks, but special custom pieces may take up to 16 weeks.

Be open-minded and accept direction. Rely on your interior designer, or a qualified store designer, to help direct your search and keep you within the scale of your floor plan. Salespeople at top stores can help you find exactly what you're seeking, and, if you ask them, guide you away from inappropriate decisions toward more suitable alternatives. His or her firsthand knowledge of pricing, products and features is invaluable when it comes to finding the best quality for your money.

As you seek these tangible expressions of your personal style, keep these thoughts in mind:

• What are your priorities? Develop a list of "must have," "want to have," and "dreaming about."

• What major pieces will be with you for a long time? Allow a lion's share of your budget for these.

• What colors or styles are already established through the flooring, walls, windows, or cabinetry? Keep swatches with you, if possible.

• Does the piece reflect your tastes? Don't be influenced too strongly by what looks great in a showroom or designer house.

• Does the piece fit the overall decorating scheme? Although the days of strict adherence to one style per room are over, it's still necessary to use coordinated styles.

• Is the piece comfortable? Before you buy, sit on the chair, recline on the sofa, pull a chair up to the table.

• Can you get the furnishings through the doorway, up the elevator, or down the stairs?

• Will a piece work for your family's lifestyle? Choose upholstery fabrics, colors and fixtures that will enhance, not hinder, your everyday life.

• Do you have accessories (a lamp, antique candlesticks, a framed picture) you can put on the table you're considering? If not, choose accessories when you choose the table.

CONSIDERING CUSTOM FURNITURE

The ultimate in expression of personal style, a piece of custom designed furniture is akin to functional art for your home. A custom furniture designer can create virtually any piece you need to fill a special space in your home and satisfy your desire for owning a unique, one-of-a-kind.

Some of the most-talented, best known designers working in this area today are listed in the following pages of the Home Book. You can contact them directly, or through your interior designer. At an initial meeting you'll see examples of the designer's work and answer questions like:

• What kind of piece do you want? Freestanding entertainment system, dining table, armoire?

• What functions must it serve? It is a piece of art, but the furniture still must function in ways that make it practical and usable. Explain your needs clearly.

• Do you have favorite woods, materials or colors? As with ordering custom woodwork, the possibilities are almost unlimited. Different woods can be painted or finished differently for all kinds of looks. It's best to have some ideas in mind.

• Are you open to new ideas and approaches? If you'd like the designer to suggest new ways of reaching your goal, let him or her know.

Seek out a furniture designer whose portfolio excites you, who you can communicate with, and you trust to deliver your project in a top quality, professional manner. Ask for a couple of design options for your piece. Make sure you and the designer are in agreement regarding finishes, materials, stain or paint samples you want to see, and a completion date. Most charge a 50 percent deposit at the beginning with the balance due upon

THREE IS THE MAGIC NUMBER

In accessorizing a home, thinking in "threes" is a good rule of thumb: Three candlesticks with candles of three different heights. Three colors of pottery grouped together, one less vibrant to highlight the others. Three patterns in a room.

417

One Person's Project Estimate:

Custom Designing a Cherry Wood Table

It's fun to imagine, but what might it actually cost to undertake a project described in this chapter? The example below describes a typical project and gives a general estimate of the costs involved.

Project Description

Custom design and construction of a 48" x 96" dining room table.

A couple moving to a new home in another region had trees from their old home site harvested, sawed into lumber, dried, and built it into a Cherry table for their dining room.

Trees harvested (felled) ($30/hr x 2 hours)... $60

Trees sawn and dried.. $175

Design (included in the project cost)
    Clients were first asked about their desires for the table, then books and catalog research was done for examples. Once a basic concept is formulated, a full-scale drawing is done. Generally, clients may or may not see it these drawings. In this case, the clients only saw rough sketches before it was delivered to them.

Labor Cost $5,000
    Fine sanding, construction, varnishing

Special materials (included in cost)... $0
    Varnish, etc.

*Delivery (local) $0

Total:... $5,235

*If more than 100 miles away, delivery is $250

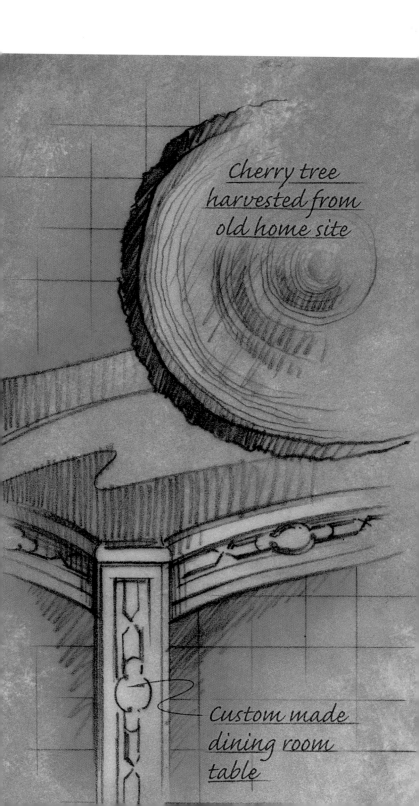

Cherry tree
harvested from
old home site

Custom made
dining room
table

LOFT LIGHTING

Lofts do have large windows, but they're usually on one wall. That presents a lighting challenge that is often met with new low-voltage systems. The transformer is hidden in a closet or soffit; decorative transformers are mounted on a wall. The halogen bulbs last thousands of hours — very important given the height of loft ceilings.

A BRIGHT IDEA

Buy a few clip-on lights with 50-watt bulbs and take them home with you to pinpoint your needs and favorite lighting looks. Experiment with them to create different effects. See if you like up—or downlights to highlight an architectural feature. Get an idea of how much light it takes to illuminate a room.

completion. If you decide not to go ahead with construction of a piece, expect to be billed a designer's fee. A commissioned piece of furniture requires a reasonable amount of time to get from start to finish. If you want an entertainment system for Super Bowl Sunday, make your final design decisions when you take down the Halloween decorations. Keep in mind that the process cannot be rushed.

SPOTLIGHT ON LIGHTING

Lighting can be the focal point of a room, or it can be so subtle that it's almost invisible. The trick is knowing what you want to accomplish. Indeed, when we remember a place as cozy, elegant, or dramatic, or cold and uncomfortable, we're feeling the emotional power of illumination.

The industry is filled with options and combinations, from fixtures and bulbs to dimmers and integrated systems. Top lighting retailers in the area employ in-house design consultants to guide you, or you can employ a residential lighting designer.

To deliver a superior lighting scheme, a designer must know:

• What is your budget? One of the biggest mistakes custom home owners make is under budgeting for their lighting program.

• What are your needs? Lighting falls into three categories—general, task, and atmospheric. A study/work area, a cozy nook, and a kitchen each require different lighting.

• What feeling are you trying to create?

• What "givens" are you working with? Where are your windows or skylights? The use of artificial, indoor light depends to a great degree on the natural light coming in.

• What materials are on the floor and what colors are on the walls and ceiling? This affects how well your lighting will reflect, or "bounce."

• Where is your furniture placed, and how big are individual pieces? This is especially important when you're choosing a dining room chandelier.

• If you're replacing lighting, why are you replacing it? Know the wattage, for instance, if a current light source is no longer bright enough.

• Are there energy/environmental concerns? Lighting consumes 12 to 15 percent of the electricity used in the home. An expert can develop a plan that maximizes energy efficiency.

• Who lives in the house? Will footballs and frisbees be flying through the kitchen? Take a pass on the hanging fixture and choose recessed lighting instead.

WINDOW DRESSING

The well-appointed room includes window treatments in keeping with the style of the home and furnishings. Yet it's also important to consider how your window treatments will need to function in your setting. Will they be required to control light, or provide privacy as well? Some windows in your home may need just a top treatment as a finishing touch, while a soaring window wall might require sun-blocking draperies or blinds to minimize heat build-up or ultraviolet damage.

How window treatments will be installed is another design question to consider–inside or outside the window frame, from the top of the window to the sill or from ceiling to floor? Take these points into consideration when designing your window treatments:

• How much privacy do you require? If you love the look of light and airy sheers, remember they become transparent at night and you may need blinds or shades as well.

• Is light control necessary? This is usually a must for bedroom window treatments, as well as for windows with southern or western exposures.

• Are your windows a focal point of the room or the background that puts the finishing touch on your room design?

• What role will the choice of fabric play? The fabric can unify the whole, standout as the focus, or add another note to the rhythm of the room.

PAINTING OUTSIDE THE FRAMES

Through their travels, reading and exposure to art and design, sophisticated homeowners are aware of the beauty that can be added to their homes with specialty decorative painting. They see perfect canvases for unique works of art in walls, furniture and fabrics. The demand for beautiful art applied directly to walls, stairs or furniture has created a renaissance in decorative painting. Faux finishes, trompe l'oeil and murals have joined the traditional finishes of paint, wallpaper and stain for consideration in outstanding residential interiors.

Specialty painters of the highest caliber, such as those on these pages, can help you fine-tune your idea, or develop a concept from scratch. At your initial meeting, discuss your ideas, whether they're crystal clear or barely there. Don't be apprehensive if you don't have a clear idea. Artists are by profession visually creative, and by asking questions and sharing ideas, you can develop a concept together. If all decision-makers can attend these meetings, the process will move along more quickly.

THE GLOBAL MARKET-PLACE

There are so many exciting lighting designs available from all over the world, a lighting retailer can't possibly show you even half of them in the showroom. Allow yourself enough time to pour over the catalogs of beautiful chandeliers, luminaries (lamps) and other lighting fixtures available to you. A special order may take up to eight weeks, but it may net you the most beautiful piece of art in your room!

421

LIGHTING YOUR ENTERTAINMENT ROOM

One suggestion for properly lighting a 20-foot by 20-foot room to be used for watching television, listening to music and entertaining friends:
• General lighting provided by recessed fixtures
• A wall-mounted dimming package, with remote control
• A decorative ceiling fixture for more lighting when entertaining.

THE PRICE OF GETTING ORGANIZED

- **An eight-foot closet, round steel chrome-planted rods, double and single hang, with a five-drawer unit: $800 to $1,000**

- **His and Hers walk-in closet, full length and double hang rods, two five-drawer units, foldable storage space, mirrored back wall, shoe rack: $1,000 to $4,000**

- **Conversion of a full-size bedroom into closet area with islands, custom designed cabinets with full extension drawers and decorative hardware, mirrors, jewelry drawers, and many other luxury appointments: $15,000**

- **Customized desk area, with file drawers, computer stand and slide shelves for printer, keyboard and mouse pad, high pressure surface on melamine with shelves above desk: $1,000**

- **Average garage remodel, with open and closed storage, sports racks for bikes and fishing poles, a small workbench, and a 4-by-8-foot pegboard, installed horizontally: $2,500**

Ask to see samples of his or her other work, and if possible, visit homes or buildings where the work has been done. Ask for, and call, references. Find out if the work was completed on time and on budget. Based on your initial conversations, a painter can give you a rough estimate based on the size of the room and the finish you've discussed. You can expect the artist to get back to you with sample drawings, showing color and technique, usually within a week.

A deposit is generally required, with balance due at completion. Discuss payment plans in the initial meeting. Surface preparation, such as stripping and patching, is not usually done by the specialty painter. Ask for recommendations of professionals to do this work if you don't have a painter you already use.

Before painting is begun in your home, the artist should provide you with a custom sample large enough to provide a good visual sense of what the technique will look like in your home, with your fabric, woodwork and cabinetry.

"DECKED OUT" FOR OUTDOOR LIVING

As homeowners strive to expand comfortable living space into their yards, top quality outdoor furniture manufacturers respond with new and innovative styles. Before you shop for outdoor furniture, think about:

- What look do you like? The intricate patterns of wrought iron? The smooth and timeless beauty of silvery teak wood? The sleek design of sturdy aluminum?

- What pieces do you need? Furnishing larger decks and terraces requires careful planning.

- Will you store the furniture in the winter or will it stay outdoors under cover?

- Can you see the furniture from inside the house? Make sure the outdoor furnishings won't distract from the established inside or outside design.

THE SPECIAL QUALITY OF PIANOS

A new or professionally reconditioned piano makes an excellent contribution to the elegance and lifestyle of a growing number of area homes. Pianos add a dimension of personality that no ordinary piece of furniture can match. They are recognized for their beauty, visually and acoustically.

First time piano buyers may be astonished at the range of choices they have and the variables that will influence their eventual decision. Go to the showrooms that carry the best brand name pianos. Not only will you be offered superior quality instruments, but you'll also get the benefit of the sales staff's professional knowledge and experience. Questions that you need to answer will include:

• Who are the primary players of the instrument?

• What level of players are they (serious, beginners)?

• Who are their teachers?

• What is the size of the room the piano will be placed in?

•• What are your preferences in wood color or leg shape?

• Are you interested in software packages that convert your instrument into a player piano?

Pianos represent a significant financial investment, one that will not depreciate, and may actually appreciate over time. If a new piano is out of your financial range, ask about the store's selection of reconditioned instruments that they've acquired through trades. The best stores recondition these pieces to a uniformly high standard of excellence and are good options for you to consider. These stores also hold occasional promotions, when special pricing will be in effect for a period of time.

THE HOME OFFICE COMES INTO ITS OWN

The home office is rapidly becoming a "must have" room for many homeowners. More businesses are being operated from home, and increasing numbers of companies are allowing, even encouraging, telecommuting. Spreading out on the dining room table or kitchen table is no longer an efficient option.

Because the home office often requires specific wiring and lighting, be sure your architect, designer and builder are involved in the planning process. If you're simply outfitting an existing room to be your home office, designers on staff at fine furniture stores can guide you. However, it's still most practical to get some architectural input for optimum comfort and functionality of the space.

Unless you're designing a home office that will be architecturally separated from the rest of your home (such as a 'loft' office over the garage) it's a challenge to effectively separate work and home. As you plan a home office, ask yourself these questions:

• How do I work best? Close to the action or tucked away where it's quiet?

• How much space do I need? More than one desk, space for computer equipment and other technology, or reference books and files? Space for seeing clients?

• How many phone lines will I need? Do I like a window view? Consider natural light as well as artificial light.

• How will I furnish the office? Will the space also serve as a library or guest room? ■

'FAUX' FINISH TROMPE L'OEIL?

Any painting technique replicating another look is called a 'faux' (fake) finish. There are many methods to achieve wonderful individual effects. Trompe l'oeil (fool the eye) is a mural painting that creates illusion through perspective. A wall becomes an arched entry to a garden.

AMEN WARDY HOMES ....**(702) 734-1433**
4230 South Decatur Suite A, Las Vegas   Fax: (702) 734-1470
See Ad on Page: 425
<u>Principal/Owner:</u> Amen Wardy
<u>Website:</u> www.amenwardy.com   <u>e-mail:</u> amen@amenwardy.com

CITY CENTER GALLERY..**(702) 294-1510**
410 Nevada Highway, Boulder City   Fax: (702) 294-1409
See Ad on Page: 436
<u>Principal/Owner:</u> Donna Taylor Draney
<u>Website:</u> www.citycentergallery.net
<u>Additional Information:</u> Offering the most sought after collection of unique
and traditional furniture and accessories in the Las Vegas area.

CORONADO CONSULTING...**(702) 497-4188**
P.O. Box 36664, Las Vegas   Fax: (702) 804-9255
See Ad on Page: 443
<u>Principal/Owner:</u> Marcy DeLatorre Grubbs
<u>e-mail:</u> coronadoconsulting@hotmail.com
<u>Additional Information:</u> A company of professionals with experience stemming from
the most prestigious home builders, Coronado Consulting provides our elite clientele
with the mastery necessary to dress an elegant home.

COTTURA ....**(702) 892-9353**
3570 South Las Vegas Boulevard, Las Vegas
See Ad on Page: 448
<u>Principal/Owner:</u> Jim Zimmerman
<u>Website:</u> www.cottura@msn.com   <u>e-mail:</u> customerservice@cottura.com
<u>Additional Information:</u> Located in The Caesar's Palace Forum Shops

CUSTOM BED SOURCE..**(702) 362-1167**
8789 Spanish Mountain Drive, Las Vegas   Fax: (702) 579-9702
See Ad on Page: 426, 427
<u>Principal/Owner:</u> Deborah Parness
<u>Website:</u> www.ultraking.com   <u>e-mail:</u> info@ultraking.com

424

DANIEL'S WEST ....**(702) 990-8300**
8878 South Eastern Avenue Suite 102, Las Vegas   Fax: (702) 990-8303
See Ad on Page: 430, 431
<u>Principal/Owner:</u> Harry & Marianne Freeman
<u>Website:</u> www.danielswest.com   <u>e-mail:</u> design@danielswest.com
<u>Additional Information:</u> For over 15 years in Las Vegas, Daniel's West specializes
in creating your perfect interior environment – from home furnishings and draperies
to fine art and custom framing.

DANIEL'S WEST ....**(702) 243-6410**
2291 South Ft. Apache Road Suite 100, Las Vegas
See Ad on Page: 430, 431
<u>Principal/Owner:</u> Harry & Marianne Freeman
<u>Website:</u> www.danielswest.com   <u>e-mail:</u> design@danielswest.com
<u>Additional Information:</u> For over 15 years in Las Vegas, Daniel's West specializes
in creating your perfect interior environment – from home furnishings and draperies
to fine art and custom framing.

EUROPEAN HOME LIVING INC. ....**(702) 214-3905**
6959 Speedway Boulevard Suite W-103, Las Vegas   Fax: (702) 214-3970
See Ad on Page: 432, 433
<u>Principal/Owner:</u> Giro Katsimbrakis
<u>e-mail:</u> europeanhome@aol.com
<u>Additional Information:</u> We import all of our furniture from Europe. We also
specialize in contract for hotels & restaurants. We carry a full line of bedrooms,
living & dinning rooms.

FURNITURE SHOWCASE ....**(702) 891-9246**
6231 South McCleod Suite B, Las Vegas   Fax: (702) 891-9247
See Ad on Page: 221, 437
<u>Principal/Owner:</u> Ben Spano
<u>Additional Information:</u> Furniture Showcase is the largest exclusive Mitsubishi
Big Screen dealer in Southern Nevada.

continued on page **428**

"Your Source for Complete Luxury and Oversized Bedding "

Patented, Hand Crafted Mattresses
Fine Grain Case Goods with many finishes
Upholstered Headboards - Luxury Linen Selections
Premium Down Products - All at competitive prices

Custom Bed Source, Inc.
8789 Spanish Mountain Drive
Las Vegas, NV 89148
(702) 362-1167
Fax (702) 579-9702

www.UltraKing.com

continued from page **424**

LLADRO CENTER...**(702) 414-3747**
   3377 Las Vegas Boulevard South Suite 2245, Las Vegas   Fax: (702) 733-0400
   See Ad on Page: 455
   <u>Principal/Owner:</u> Lladro Brothers
   <u>Website:</u> lladro.com <u>e-mail:</u> lasvegas-center@us.lladro.com
MILTON HOMER FINE HOME FURNISHINGS ....**(702) 798-0707**
   5455 South Valley View Boulevard, Las Vegas   Fax: (702) 739-1907
   See Ad on Page: 191
   <u>Principal/Owner:</u> Milton Homer
MORTISE & TENON ....**(702) 880-4400**
   4590 West Sahara Avenue, Las Vegas   Fax: (702) 880-4459
   See Ad on Page: 439
   <u>Principal/Owner:</u> Felix Rodriguez
NEST FEATHERINGS ....**(702) 362-6707**
   6425 West Sahara Avenue, Las Vegas   Fax: (702) 362-1231
   See Ad on Page: 264, 434, 435
   <u>Principal/Owner:</u> La Rayn Sorenson
   <u>Website:</u> www.nest-featherings.com <u>e-mail:</u> nest_featherings@hotmail.com
   <u>Additional Information:</u> Nest Featherings will enhance your home with an unequaled combination of "investment" quality furniture and magnificent design expertise.

428

home furnishings

interior design

custom draperies &

bedding

fine art

custom framing

gifts

ery single element in your home expresses

ur individuality. At Daniels West, our

verse showrooms feature collections from

e world over. From home furnishings and

aperies to fine art and custom framing, let

aniels West create an environment that is

nique just to you.

DanielsWest

European Home Living, Inc., along with Francesco Molon GieMme, provide distinct, elegant furniture to hotels and restaurants. Our mission is to supply our clients with a quality product that will enhance their place of business. We deliver the best.

Il Gattopardo Restaurant

Mini Suite

European Hom Living, Inc.
Contract Division

LeGrand Bar

Deluxe Guest Room

Featuring the finest furniture, accessories, and unique gifts. Discover the world's most beautiful, superbly hand crafted and custom made fine furniture from Italy, Dall'Agnese and Francesco Molon GieMme.

Sleigh Bed - Rialto

Armoire - Murano

th Century Walnut Carved Sideboard

New Empire Dining Table & Chairs

Fine Furniture & Interior Design
6425 W. Sahara
Las Vegas, NV 89146
702/ 362-6707

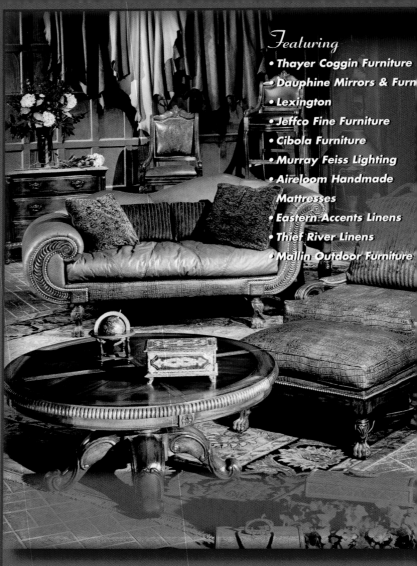

Featuring
- **Thayer Coggin Furniture**
- **Dauphine Mirrors & Furn**
- **Lexington**
- **Jeffco Fine Furniture**
- **Cibola Furniture**
- **Murray Feiss Lighting**
- **Aireloom Handmade Mattresses**
- **Eastern Accents Linens**
- **Thief River Linens**
- **Mallin Outdoor Furniture**

Offering the most sought after collection o distinctive furniture, accessories, linens and g items in the Las Vegas Area.

CITY CENTER
Gallery
BOULDER CITY, NEVADA

Fine Home Furnishings
410 NEVADA HIGHWAY • BOULDER CITY, NEVADA 89005
(702) 294-1510 • (702) 294-1409 FAX
WWW.CITYCENTERGALLERY.NET

Experience
Furniture Showcase

Luxurious Living

An Inspiring Collection of Traditional, Classic, Contemporary Home Furnishings and Accessories from the World's Finest Resources.

Complimentary Design Service

9340 W Sahara
Las Vegas, NV
702 320 8421

4500 E Sunset
Henderson, NV
702-451-8421

Custom
Furniture

MORTISE & TENON ....**(702) 880-4400**
4590 West Sahara Avenue, Las Vegas   Fax: (702) 880-4459
See Ad on Page: 439
<u>Principal/Owner:</u> Felix Rodriguez

ZO'CALOS, LLC...**(702) 269-6550**
7470 South Industrial Road, Las Vegas   Fax: (702) 269-6659
See Ad on Page: 440, 441
<u>Principal/Owner:</u> Chris & Lori Taplett
<u>Website:</u> zocaloslasvegas.com   <u>e-mail:</u> zocaloslv@aol.com

Accessories

ACRYLIC TANK MANUFACTURING ....**(702) 387-2016**
6125 Annie Oakley Dr., Las Vegas   Fax: (702) 387-2075
See Ad on Page: 444, 445
Principal/Owner: Brett Raymer
Website: acrylicaquariums.com e-mail: atmoflv@aol.com
Additional Information: We specialize in custom aquariums from 50 to 50,000 plus
gallons!

BILLARD WORLD ....**(702) 259-6010**
5411 W. Charleston Blvd., Las Vegas   Fax: (702) 259-6046
See Ad on Page: 488
Principal/Owner: Jim Roach

LIFE LIKE BOTANICALS ....**(702) 795-0010**
731 Pilot Road #B, Las Vegas   Fax: (702) 260-8888
See Ad on Page: 459
Principal/Owner: Robin

MAGDALENA'S ....**(702) 228-3924**
8125 West Sahara Avenue Suite 160, Las Vegas   Fax: (702) 228-6895
See Ad on Page: 412, 413, 429
Principal/Owner: Maggie Brandon
Website: www.magdelenaslasvegas.com e-mail: magdelenasvegas@aol.com
Additional Information: We invite you to come to our showroom where you make
your dreams come true item by item, room by room.

NORITAKE FACTORY STORE ....**(702) 897-7199**
7400 South Las Vegas Boulevard Box 108, Las Vegas Fax: (702) 897-7281
See Ad on Page: 458
Principal/Owner: Hope Marshall-Pasinski (Manager)
e-mail: lasvegas.fstore@noritake.com
Additional Information: We stock active, first quality china and crystal patterns.

PACIFIC FITNESS ....**(702) 227-9850**
3850 West Desert Inn Road Suite 105, Las Vegas   Fax: (702) 227-9858
See Ad on Page: 486, 487
Principal/Owner: Peter Oh
e-mail: zateeny-angela@hotmail.com
Additional Information: We specialize in fitness room design and equipment, sauna
installation, rubber flooring, mirrors, and ballet bars. Delivery and install available by
qualified factory-trained service technicians.

SAGE ....**(702) 562-4438**
9410 West Sahara Avenue #130, Las Vegas
See Ad on Page: 451
Principal/Owner: Carol & Rick Sage

SHOWCASE SLOTS & ANTIQUITIES ....**(702) 740-5722**
4305 South Industrial Road Suite B-110, Las Vegas Fax: (702) 740-5733
See Ad on Page: 489
Principal/Owner: Pete Castiglia
Website: www.showcaseslots.com e-mail: info@showcaseslots.com

SILKEN GARDENS ....**(702) 878-0944**
5243 West Charleston Boulevard #4, Las Vegas   Fax: (702) 878-7508
See Ad on Page: 456, 457
Principal/Owner: Beth Olsen

THE IVY ....**(702) 360-0800**
9350 West Sahara Ave., Las Vegas
See Ad on Page: 449
Principal/Owner: John Nicolai

continued on page **454**

CORONADO CONSULTING
interiors

rnishings ∿ Accessories ∿ Window Treatments
ooring ∿ Art Selection ∿ Design Services

unique and unusual
selections

to create the home
of your dreams

from flooring to finish

Coronado Consulting provides it's elite clientele
with the mastery necessary to dress an elegant home
down to the finest detail

Phone: 702.497.4188 ∿ Facsimile: 702.804.9255
e-mail: coronadoconsulting@hotmail.com

ACRYLIC TANK MANUFACTURING

A R T

6125 Annie Oakley Dr.
Las Vegas, NV 89120
702.387.2016 / 702.387.2075 fax

the Ivy
house & garden

photos by Jan Baldwin

artistic floral creations for the
discerning taste.

9340 west sahara avenue #100
las vegas, nevada 89117
702.360.0800   702.360.0900 f

Las Vegas RUGS
DESIGNER & DISTRIBUTION SHOWROOM

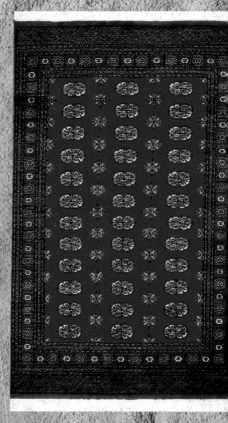

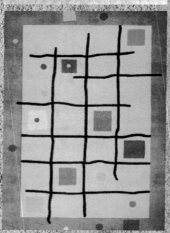

Large selection of area rugs from around the world.
Variety of sizes and shapes. Runners, tapestries, cowhide,
chain stitch, needle point, pillows. Handmade and
machine made.

6330 South Pecos Rd.
Suite 115
Las Vegas, NV 89120

Tel (702) 458-4466
Fax (702) 458-2770

www.lasvegasrugs.com

the Plantworks

www.plantworks**now**.com

The Plantwork

3930 GRAPHICS CENTER DR.
LAS VEGAS, NEVADA 89118
702-795-3600
www.plantworks**now**.com

Home Furnishings & Decorating

continued from page **442**

THE NATURAL TOUCH..**(702) 365-0197**
    5480 South Valley View Boulevard, Las Vegas   Fax: (702) 876-8271
    See Ad on Page: 446, 447
    <u>Principal/Owner:</u> Jan & Steve Shaw
    <u>Website:</u> www.thenaturaltouch.com
    <u>Additional Information:</u> Since 1979, The Natural Touch has provided quality silk
trees, plants, floral design, holiday décor and accessories to residential & commercial
clientele.

THE PLANTWORKS ....**(702) 795-3600**
    3930 Graphics Center Drive, Las Vegas   Fax: (702) 795-4643
    See Ad on Page: 452, 453
    <u>Principal/Owner:</u> Linda Lewis
    <u>Website:</u> www.plantworksnow.com <u>e-mail:</u> info@plantworks**now**.com
    <u>Additional Information:</u> Live & silk plants, custom designed trees & florals,
20,000 sq. ft accessory showroom open to the public. In-home consultation/
design available.

A distinctive element in home decor.

Majesty Of The Seas, $775

LLADRÓ CENTER
Las Vegas

The Grand Canal Shoppes at The Venetian
Las Vegas, Nevada 89109
Toll free: 866.724.8705

New York • toll free: 800.785.3490
Beverly Hills • toll free: 866.724.8704
Tampa • toll free: 866.744.6624

Silken Garden

5243 West Charleston Boulevard #4
Las Vegas, NV 89146
702-878-0944 • fax 702-878-7508

Noritake

FACTORY ☕ **STORE**

Setting Americas Tables since 1904

Save 25% - 70% everyday on

Bone china • Fine china
Everyday dinnerware • Stoneware
Crystal stemware • Crystal giftware

Noritake Factory Store
7400 Las Vegas Blvd. South • Suite 246
Las Vegas, NV • 702-897-7199

Hours: Mon. - Sat. 10 - 9, Sun. 10 - 6
Visit us on the web at www.noritakechina.com

Choose from over 200 patterns. All first quality. Shipping and gift wrap available. Phone orders welcome

LIFE LIKE BOTANICALS

"We Create Your Vision"

731 PILOT RD. • LAS VEGAS, NV • 89119
TEL 702.795.0010 • FAX 702.260.8888
www.lifelikebotanicals.com

New in the

GLASSIC ART
Glass Decorations:
Our new glass accents are custom-designed and made from durable, 1 in. thick glass. To match your decor, the glass can be infused with any color. We also offer a choice of edging styles.

THE PLANTWORKS
Holiday Looks: Our Holiday Décor Custom Package includes a custom-fabricated tree that is color coordinated to your home décor, as well as swags, garlands, centerpieces and wreaths. Plantworks' staff will handle installation and also dismantle these decorations after the holidays.

D. A. SEPPALA CO.
Children's Room Interactive Tree:
The design of an environmental sculpture may find its inspiration through pragmatic need, aesthetic desire or playful whimsy. All three aspects are reflected in the Children's Room Tree, a fiberglass sculpture that includes a hollow, lighted interior play space, trunk cutouts for puppetry, and a TV with VCR.

rEvolution
Concrete Furniture:
The Zen table is the most recent addition to rEvolution's Elements line of hand-crafted concrete home furnishings. This new line is available in custom sizes and colors, as well as several polish grades.

BILLIARD WORLD
Game Room Furniture:
Game room furniture and pool tables are now offered in solid exotic hardwoods, such as ash, oak, maple and cherry. A number of stain colors are also available, as well as custom color matching and up to 40 colors of felt.

Photo by **Opulence Studios**

DANIELS WEST
Pendant Lighting:
Light fixtures are no longer considered just "chandeliers." The hanging pendants in this dining room capture and enhance the Tuscan style, but could also provide an eclectic twist in a more transitional setting.

461

PACIFIC FITNESS EQUIPMENT
Elliptical Cross Training Machines: An elliptical cross training machine can replace all other cardio machines in your home. Available with electronic programming and heart rate control, these low impact machines provide great cardiovascular benefits and tone up your body all over.

MORTISE & TENON
The Dutchess Sofa: This design from the Carol Bolton collection celebrates luscious extravagance. Unique fabrics, bullions and fringe envelope the hand-carved mahogany frame. Supreme down cushions add to the intoxicating beauty and sumptuous comfort.

NORITAKE FACTORY STORE
New China Patterns:
Two new china collections have arrived at our store this season. The Venetian Scroll and Montebello collections feature a classic and formal design. The contrasting accent places have a scalloped edge to add versatility to the basic place setting.

HOUSE OF DRAPERIES
New Trim: Our vast array of passementerie adds a touch of inspiration to any custom designed window treatment, bedding ensemble, upholstery, slipcover or piece of furniture. The addition of crystal-beaded tassels will transform a basic drapery panel from blasé to brilliant. Suede fringe is just the right embellishment for a faux leather pillow. Whether casual country or serenely romantic, our new trims can harmonize or accent a design beautifully.

SHOWCASE SLOTS & ANTIQUITIES
Home Gaming: This five-in-one video poker machine is encased in a custom-built, oak Victorian cabinet with brass accents. Like all our popular casino slots, video poker and old fashioned antique slots, it comes with a full warranty.

CUSTOM BED SOURCE, INC.
Ultra King Size Beds: The 84 in. by 96 in. Ultra King and the 120 in. by 108 in. Super Ultra King mattresses are designed to enhance today's more spacious master bedrooms. Each handcrafted mattress features a patented, super dense pillow top for comfort, as well as a full line of perfectly sized luxury linens, upholstered headboards and comforters.

LLADRO
Art in Fine Porcelain:
A recent addition to the Lladró line, this 13.25 in. x 17.25 in. lovely porcelain sculpture is entitled, "Morning Dew."

BLINDS BY DEBBIE
Luminette Privacy Sheers:
Equally at home in traditional or contemporary interiors, Luminette Privacy Sheers combine the elegance of sheer draperies with the light control and privacy provided by blinds. The sheers can be opened to welcome in the outdoors during the day or closed for diffused light, and the vertical vanes can be tilted partially or completely for greater privacy.

463

ODYSSEY LIGHTING & DESIGN
The Medici Collection: The Medici Collection by Corbett is composed of hand-carved solid wood and sculpted by artisans. Each lantern is an illuminated sculpture, one which expresses the individuality of the craftsman while staying true to the design. The finishes are hand-applied in the time-honored methods of great Italian masters.

COTTURA
Biscotti Jars:
These biscotti jars are both functional and beautiful. Hand-painted on ceramic, the jars come in patterns that are bold in color and striking in design.

Lighting

ILA .... **(702) 893-8344**
5075 South Cameron Suite A, Las Vegas   Fax: (702) 893-8087
See Ad on Page: 456
Principal/Owner: Stephen Herman
e-mail: ila@mailink.net
Additional Information: A full service lighting company with over 20 years experience
in Las Vegas. Specializing in: landscape, cove, cabinet and integrated system lighting
for the residential and commercial client.

LIGHTING DESIGN CENTER .... **(702) 897-8866**
6415 Hinson Street, Las Vegas   Fax: (702) 897-8922
See Ad on Page: 466
Principal/Owner: Olga, Armand, & Ray Gregoryan
e-mail: contactus@l-lighting.com
Additional Information: We bring 16 years of experience to the Las Vegas market
(Southwest Electric Supply, Inc., Glendale California)

NORTHERN LIGHTS & FANS .... **(702) 396-6963**
8380 West Cheyenne, Las Vegas   Fax: (702) 396-6962
See Ad on Page: 467
Principal/Owner: Eric Peterson

NORTHERN LIGHTS & FANS .... **(702) 270-4145**
9302 South Eastern Ave, Las Vegas   Fax: (702) 270-9494
See Ad on Page: 467
Principal/Owner: Troy Simmons

ODYSSEY LIGHTING & DESIGN .... **(702) 855-0711**
6320 South Pecos Road #119, Las Vegas   Fax: (702) 855-0713
See Ad on Page: 468, 469
Principal/Owner: Paul Isensee

WIN SUPPLY CO. .... **(702) 795-4055**
3910 Graphics Center Drive, Las Vegas   Fax: (702) 795-4061
See Ad on Page: 470
Principal/Owner: Lou & Amy Winters
Additional Information: Supplying builders hardware & light fixtures to the
construction industry since 1969. Showroom Open from 8am–5pm Monday
through Friday.

Interior design by Nancy Love

- Cove Lighting
- Kitchen & Bath
- Landscape Lighting
- Specialty & Custom Applications
- Decorative Fixtures
- Home Theater Lighting
- Lighting Controls
- Ceiling Fans

Lighting...from the borders of your design
to the boundries of your imagination.

5075 S. Cameron Suite A
Las Vegas, NV 89118
Tel: 893-8344
Fax: 893-8087

a full service lighting company

Lighting Design Center

A comfortable environment for interior designers to resource all their lighting needs

Authorized Dealer for Vantage Home Automation and Contr

702/897/8866

Northern Lights is proud to carry Metropolitan Lighting, illuminating the finest interiors with antique reproduction lighting since 1939. Chandeliers, pendants, sconces and outdoor lanterns available in alabaster, brass, bronze, iron, wood and mouth blown Murano glass

northern lights

ILLUMINATING LAS VEGAS

9302 S. EASTERN AVE. LAS VEGAS, NV 89123 TEL: 702.270.4145
8380 W. CHEYENNE AVE. LAS VEGAS NV 89129 TEL: 702.396.6963

ODYSSEY
Lighting & Design

Escape from the Ordinary

◆ Chandeliers, sconces, and ceiling fans
   from traditional to contemporary
◆ Landscape Lighting and outdoor sculptures
◆ In-house custom lighting designs
◆ Unique home accessories

Admit It,
You Love Our Style.

sea gull lighting

Plantation by Sea Gull Lighting

Be taken back to a time of casual elegance, warm breezes, crisp-tailore white cotton shirts and a barefoot easiness. The Plantation series includes Home Décor products, beautiful lighting fixtures and portabl lamps featured in a dark, hand painted finish wrapped with natural rattan accents and shades.

Win Supply Company
3910 Graphics Center Drive
Las Vegas, Nevada
Phone: 702.795.4055

Window Coverings
Fabrics & Upholstery

BLINDS BY DEBBIE ....**(702) 643-6451**
9963 Ridge Hill Avenue, Las Vegas   Fax: (702) 364-0087
See Ad on Page: 474
Principal/Owner: Debbie Stalter
e-mail: blindsbydebbie@lvcm.com
Additional Information: At Blinds By Debbie, our number-one priority is high quality
customer service before, during, and after the sale.

HOUSE OF DRAPERIES ....**(702) 942-2244**
8626 South Eastern #108, Las Vegas   Fax: (702) 942-2248
See Ad on Page: 472
Principal/Owner: Carlos Picoy
Additional Information: Manufacturers of fine draperies, bedspreads, pillows,
and sofas direct to the public. Home consultations. Interior decoration available.

Blinds By Debbie

HunterDouglas
window fashions

Duette® Honeycomb Shades • Silhouette® Window Shadings
Luminette Privacy Sheers® • Country Woods® Plantation Shutters
Blinds • Serenette® SoftFold® Shadings • Vignette® Window Shadings

You'll never forget . . .

Blinds By Debbie

Phone • (702)643-6451   Fax • (702)364-0087

Specialty Painters
& Wall Finishes

CREATIVE FAUX FINISHES ....**(702) 595-4651**
3400 West Desert Inn Road #18, Las Vegas, NV   Fax: (702) 253-7734
See Ad on Page: 476
<u>Principal/Owner:</u> Roger Howard
<u>Additional Information:</u> Specialists in faux effects in Old World, Tuscan, and Venetian
finishes for your home or office. Interior/Exterior/Furniture.

ORIGINAL FINISHES ....**(702) 531-6000**
Las Vegas   Fax: (702) 313-6768
See Ad on Page: 477
<u>Principal/Owner:</u> Renee Ferrari

PHOENIX & COMPANY ....**(702) 396-9904**
5320 North Bonita Vista, Las Vegas   Fax: (702) 396-9905
See Ad on Page: 478
<u>Principal/Owner:</u> Phoenix Lloyd
<u>Website:</u> www.phoenixandco@earthlink.com   <u>e-mail:</u> phoenixandco@earthlink.com
<u>Additional Information:</u> Phoenix & Company specializes in faux finishes, murals
and skies. Work in both residential and commercial applications.

QUALITY PAINTING & DÉCOR ....**(702) 387-2468**
P.O. Box 97514, Las Vegas   Fax: (702) 898-9244
See Ad on Page: 479
<u>Principal/Owner:</u> Dean Allen
<u>Website:</u> www.paintqp.com
<u>Additional Information:</u> Custom painting, faux finishes, marbling crackle,
smooth wall, cabinet finishes and wall coverings.

475

D.A. SEPPALA CO. ....**(702) 858-2974**
4101 Roxanne Drive, Las Vegas
See Ad on Page: 480
<u>Principal/Owner:</u> Dwain Seppala
<u>Website:</u> www.decorativeaccents.com   <u>e-mail:</u> dwain@decorativeaccents.com
<u>Additional Information:</u> Seppala provides all types of specialty wall finishes including
murals, children's rooms, environmental sculpture, original border design stencils
and block printing; wood, stone and marble faux finishing; glazing, hand rubbing,
ragging, stripping & antiquing.

WHIMSICAL WALLS ....**(702) 363-3289**
2920 Peaceful Grove, Las Vegas   Fax: (702) 255-9867
See Ad on Page: 481
<u>Principal/Owner:</u> Gail Sachanko/Christopher Donohue

Photo Courtesy of Christopher Homes

Original Finishes

(702) 531-6000

"Express Your Creativity" became our bi-line to reflect people's need for self-expression in the new millennium.

The rules are out the window; but one thing is sure, walls are more important to set a mood, reflect a lifestyle, project a theme or complete

Phoenix & Compan

Custom Art
Faux Finishes • Trompe l'oeil • Skies • Mural
Tel (702) 396-9904 • Fax (702) 396-9905
www.phoenixandco.com

uality Painting & Decor

ecializing in home lifestyle enhancement

esidential & Commercial Painting Solutions

om faux finishing to home re-paints

om window treatments to custom concrete finishes

r name says it all-

Quality

Integity

and a new vision in the world of design and decor

Our mailing address is P.O. Box 97514

Las Vegas, NV 89193

(702)387-2468

License Number 41162

Visit us at www.paintqp.com

Seppala

Designer • Muralist • Artist

Decorative Accents, Specialty Wall Finishes,
Murals, Children's Rooms, Environmental Sculptures

702-858-2974

seppala@decorativeaccent.com

www.decorativeaccent.com

W
Whimsical Walls
decorative faux finishes

Home Office,
Closet & Garage

CLASSY CLOSETS..**(702) 739-0000**
4555 Procyon, Las Vegas
See Ad on Page: 483
<u>Principal/Owner:</u> Steven Mann
<u>Additional Information:</u> Custom designed storage for your home or office.
CLOSET MASTERS ....**(702) 876-5929**
3208 West Desert Inn, Las Vegas   Fax: (702) 876-1760
See Ad on Page: 484
<u>Principal/Owner:</u> Lee Levy
<u>Website:</u> www.closetmasters.com <u>e-mail:</u> info@closetmasters.com

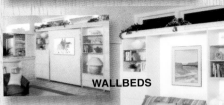

Call for a **FREE** in-home
design and estimate or
visit our new showroom

CLOSET MASTERS

Closets · Linens · Pantries · Laundry · Garages · Wall Units

"masters of organization"

3208 West Desert Inn Road, Las Vegas, NV 89102-8313
800-891-1836 **toll-free**   702-876-5929 **tel**   702-876-1760 **fax**
e-mail: info@closetmasters.com   **website:** www.closetmasters.com
Lic# 38791

Home Gyms &
Entertainment

BILLIARD WORLD...**(702) 259-6010**
5411 West Charleston Boulevard, Las Vegas
See Ad on Page: 488
Principal/Owner: Jim Roach
PACIFIC FITNESS ....**(702) 227-9850**
3850 West Desert Inn Road Suite 105, Las Vegas   Fax: (702) 227-9858
See Ad on Page: 486, 487
Principal/Owner: Peter Oh
e-mail: zateeny-angela@hotmail.com
Additional Information: We specialize in fitness room design and equipment, sauna
installation, rubber flooring, mirrors, and ballet bars. Delivery and install available by
qualified factory-trained service technicians.
SHOWCASE SLOTS & ANTIQUITIES..**(702) 740-5722**
4305 South Industrial Road Suite B-110, Las Vegas   Fax: (702) 740-5733
See Ad on Page: 489
Principal/Owner: Pete Castiglia
Website: www.showcaseslots.com e-mail: info@showcaseslots.com

Billiard World

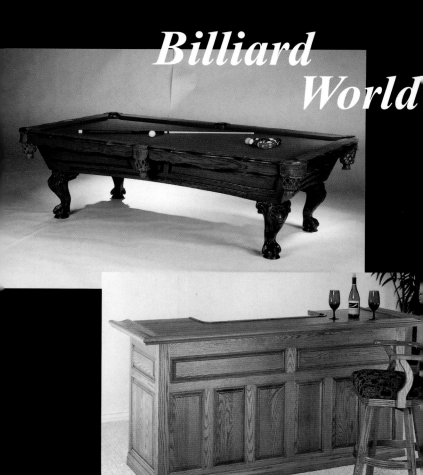

Family Owned & Operat

◆ Custom Pool Tables
◆ Game Room Furniture
◆ Billiard Accessories
◆ Dart Boards & Accessories
◆ Lighting & Wall Art
◆ Highest Quality
◆ Friendliest Service

702-259-6010
5411 West Charleston Blv
Las Vegas, NV 89146

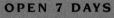

490

Photo by **John Alcon**

MORTISE & TENON
Maité Garcia:
"True to our name, Mortise & Tenon handcrafts
original designs using a traditional woodworking
method. We specialize in individually crafted pieces
for home office, dining rooms and bedrooms. We
also design, create and install individual television
cabinets and wall-to-wall home theater centers like
the Soho three-piece entertainment center shown.
Enjoy the excitement of designing your own piece
or let our designers do it for you."

Custom Furniture
Portfolio

PERSPECTIVES ENGRAVING, INC.

Edward and Patricia Hughes: "Our combined 55 years of talent and experience in glass and metal engraving has resulted in a new dimension in ornamental glass. Traditional sandblasting is influenced by the artistic techniques previously used in metal engraving. The work integrates the use of highly sculptured images, textures and light play to offer an alternative direction to enhance the interior design of any home or office. Years of working with graphic designers from all over the world have developed our insight and ability to reproduce whatever our customer has imagined. We pride ourselves in our ability to meet deadlines without compromising quality."

Las Vegas H

Your Guide to Your Dream Home

Tired of being lost? Feel that you don't know where you're going without a map? Can't find useful information regarding home improvement? The Las Vegas Home Book website, www.lvhomebook.com, provides you with a full color atlas of information to map out the home of your dreams.

eBook.com

OU WANT IT, WE'LL PROVIDE IT

Las Vegas Home Book website covers a full range of resources for building, remodel-
decorating, furnishing and landscaping projects. The site also provides you with a number
nique, functional features designed to help you locate all the necessary information
rding the design or enhancement of your luxury home. Just log on at
.lvhomebook.com, and we'll do the rest.

YOUR RESEARCH SOURCE

The site enables users to search for professionals by specific category: architects, interior
designers, kitchen and bath, and many more. Users can also search by keyword—
company name and/or profession—right off the home page.

THE PERFECT PAIR

The **Las Vegas Home Book** website, www.lvhomebook.com is best used when
complemented by a copy of the **Las Vegas Home Book**. The website picks up where
the book leaves off, allowing consumers to further research their home improvement
needs in depth. The two work in unison to provide consumers up-to-date and timely
information regarding their most prized investment—their home.

WE'RE ONLY A FEW CLICKS AWAY

If you are planning to design or renovate your home, please don't hesitate to consult
your local source to top design/build professionals, www.lvhomebook.com.
Allow us to be your road map, and we will gladly lead you to your final destination.
Thank you from everyone at the **Las Vegas Home Book,** and we all hope to see
you online!

There is only one premier resource provider for the luxury design and home enhancement market—the **Las Vegas Home Book!**

www.lvhomebook.com
www.homebook.com

The Ashley Group Luxury Home Resource Collect

If you're searching for luxury home improvement resources, **The Ashl[ey] Group (www.theashleygroup.com)** is pleased to offer, as your fi[rst] destination, the following **Home Books**: *Chicago, Washington DC, S[outh] Florida, Dallas/Fort Worth, Detroit, Atlanta, New York, Arizona, Philadelphia, Colorado* and the *Los Angeles* area. These comprehens[ive] hands-on guides to building, remodeling, decorating, furnishing, a[nd] landscaping a luxury home are required reading for the serious a[nd] selective homeowner. With more than 700 full-color, beautiful pag[es] per market, these hardcover volumes are the most complete and well-organized reference to the home industry. The **Home Books** c[over] all aspects of the building and remodeling process, include listings [of] hundreds of industry professionals, and are accompanied by informa[tive] and valuable editorial discussing the most recent trends. Ordering y[our] copy of any of the **Home Books** now can ensure that you have th[e] blueprints to your dream home, in your hand, today.

Order your copies today and make your dream come tru[e!]

ART&
ANTIQUES

SILVER LINING (CHANDELIER)

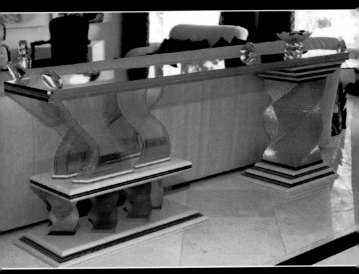

EXPRESSIONS

7' PROFILE

DIAMOND HEAD

TONY MILICI
SCULPTOR

MILICI STUDIOS
95 E. SHELBOURNE AVE.
LAS VEGAS, NV 89123
TEL. (702) 270-4414
FAX. (702) 270-6315
www.milicistudios.com
email: tm@milicistudios.com

ALSO SEE PAGE
WINDOWS & DOORS

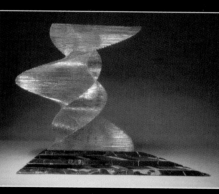

GRAND STAIRCASE

BEAR CLAW

THE EMPIRE

"**Art** does not reproduce the *visible;* it makes visible. "

Paul Klee

The Finesse of Fine Art

It's fun to imagine, but what might it actually cost to undertake a project described in this chapter? The example below describes a typical project and gives a general estimate of the costs involved.

Project Description

Analysis, research and procurement of six art pieces for a Mediterranean-style home.

Before the project began, the client established a budget based on the type of art desired (sculpture, drawings, paintings, tapestry), the quality of the art, scale (size of objects), and provenance (history and notoriety of the artist).

The art

A print for the hallway	$ 8,000
A classical bronze sculpture, 4 ft tall	$ 3,000
A still-life painting	$ 8,000
Two tapestries ($2,000 ea.)	$ 4,000
A Dufy painting	$32,000

Art total: **$55,000**

Additional expenses

Appraisal expenses	$750
Framing of pictures	$2,500
Installation and handling	$2,500
Insurance	$1,250/yr
Security system (motion detector)	$1,250
Consultation fees	
(Ten percent of art)	$5,500
(Hourly fee: $150/hr x 40 hrs)	$6,000

Includes analysis of art needs based on scale and style of house and artist preferences, research done on availability of art pieces and procurement of those pieces.

Additional expenses:.................................$19,750

Total:.. $74,750

502

Note: a project such as this one usually lasts 12 to 18 months.

know about so many different objects, time periods, and design, that it truly does take a lifetime to develop an expertise. The professionals at these establishments are first and foremost interested in finding you an antique that will impress and delight not only today, but also in the future. They usually prefer to have you invest in one or two good pieces, rather than in a handful of items that won't bring you as much pleasure in the long run.

VISITING ART GALLERIES

More than anything else, choosing to make beautiful, distinctive art objects a part of your home brings the joy of living with beautiful things into the daily life of yourself, your family and your guests.

The most important rule to know as you begin or continue to add art to your home is that there truly are no "rights or wrongs." Find what reaches you on an emotional level, and then begin to learn about it.

Use your eyes and react with your heart. Look at art magazines and books. There are many, many beautiful periodicals, and just as many books published on artists and art genres. Visit the museums in town, and those in other cities as you travel. Go to the galleries. Visit many of them for the widest exposure to different possibilities. Use the Internet to visit gallery and museum sites from all over the world. Let only your sense of beauty and aesthetics guide you at this point. Consider other constraints after you've identified the objects of your desire.

When you've found what really speaks to you on a personal level, start learning more about the artists who create art in that style, where it's available locally, and if it's within your budget. The more information you can take with you when you begin your shopping, the more help a gallery can be to you in your search.

EXPERT ADVICE

The most reputable art gallery owners and dealers have earned their reputation by establishing an expertise in their field, and serving their clients well.

Buying from these established, respected professionals offers many benefits. Their considerable knowledge of and exposure to art translates into opinions that mean a great deal. You trust the advice and education they offer you. They've done considerable research and evaluation before any item gets placed in their gallery, and determined that it's a good quality item, both in terms of artistic merit and market value. You can also rest assured they will stand behind the authenticity of what they present in their galleries. Most offer free consultations, trade-back arrangements, and installation, and will help you with selling your art at some point in the future as

THE FALL SEASON

Fall signals the beginning of the art season. Galleries will open exhibits and the excitement is contagious. Ask to get on gallery mailing lists to stay informed of fall openings.

SEE THE SHOWS

The Las Vegas Valley abounds with arts, antiques, and collectibles shows and festivals. These are great places to browse for and learn about thousands of items — from jewelry to pop culture collectibles. Local newspapers and magazines run announcements for these kinds of events, or ask your favorite gallery owner for information.

LEARN ABOUT ART & ANTIQUES

Part of the pleasure of collecting art or antiques is learning about them. Many homeowners buy a particular painting or sculpture they love, and find that following the art form or the artists becomes a lifetime passion.

The best place to start to familiarize yourself with art is at one of the many wonderful museums in the Las Vegas Valley. Wander through historic homes in the different historic neighbor-hoods of the city and get an idea of what the art feels like in a home environment. Go to auctions. Buy the catalog and attend the viewing. At the sale, you'll begin to get an idea of the values of different types of items. Finally, get to know a dealer. Most are pleased to help you learn and want to see more people develop a lifetime love affair with art, similar to their own. If a dealer seems too busy or isn't genuinely interested in helping you, then go to another dealer.

Haunt the local bookstores and newsstands. There are many publications dedicated to these fields.

THE WORLD OF ANTIQUES

Homeowners find their way to a love of antiques by many different paths. Some are adding to an inherited collection that connects them with past generations of family or with the location of their birth. Some are passionate about pottery or porcelain, clocks or dolls, and want to expand their knowledge while building a lifetime collection.

Antique furniture, artwork and collectibles also can be used to make a singular statement in an interior. Through a 19th Century English chest, an American Arts & Crafts table, or a beloved collection of Tiffany glass vases, homeowners put a personal signature on their interior design.

Making the right selection is as much a matter of taste and personal aesthetic as it is knowledge and experience. As top quality antique paintings, photographs and other desirable items become more and more difficult to find, getting expert guidance in identifying good and worthwhile investments is crucial. An interior designer or the knowledgeable professionals at the top galleries in the area are eager to provide just that. They can help you determine the value of pieces you are considering by assessing these four characteristics:

Rarity–In general, the more difficult it is to find similar pieces, the greater the value. Try to determine how many comparable pieces exist. However, it is possible to be too rare. If there are too few similar pieces in circulation, there may be limited demand.

Quality–The quality of the original materials and workmanship affects the Homeowners value significantly.

Provenance–The history of a piece, how many owners it has had, is its provenance. A piece with only a few owners has a better provenance.

Condition–The more that remains of the original finish, the more valuable the piece. However, in some cases, small imperfections can help to establish authenticity.

SELECTING ANTIQUES

When you visit an antique store or gallery, be prepared to seriously consider what type of investment you wish to make and how it will work in a given interior. In cases where someone other than yourself will also be involved in the final decision-making process, try to shop together.

If you are pursuing pieces to add to an existing collection, do your research to determine which dealers and galleries in the area cater to your interests. Or, check with a favorite gallery for information.

Be open to ideas and suggestions, especially when you're just beginning a collection, or a search for a special antique. The best galleries are gold mines of information and ideas. There is so much to

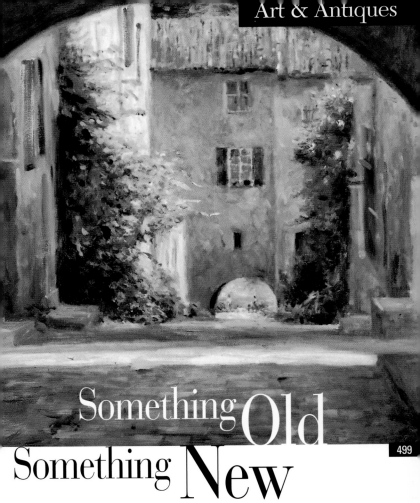

Something Old Something New

499

The fine art and antiques scene is as dynamic as ever. From cutting-edge modern galleries to showrooms of stately antiques, few places in the world offer more choice for bringing truly unique works of art into the home. Beloved one-of-a-kind items give a home personality in a way that other furnishings can't match. Fine art speaks to the soul of the owner. Antique furnishings tell their stories through the generations. Art and antiques, unlike so many other pieces purchased for the home, have the potential to become a family's heirlooms. Even an inexpensive "find" may someday become a most treasured item because of the warm memories it calls to mind. Truly, these choices are best made with the care and guidance of an experienced professional who understands the significance of these items in your home.

Photo courtesy of **Art At Your Door/Gallery II**

8' x 6'
Tapestry

Frame for
Dufy painting

your collection grows, you change residences, or your tastes change.

Don't expect these professionals to be experts in categories outside of those they specialize in.

VALUE JUDGMENTS

Buy for love, not money. This is the advice we heard time and again from the best art galleries. Not all art appreciates financially – often it fluctuates over the years according to the artist's career, consumer tastes, and the state of the overall economy. If you love what you own and have been advised well by a knowledgeable professional, you'll be happiest with your investment.

There is no upper limit on what you can spend on an art collection, or a single work of art, and there are no set standards for pricing. Gallery owners set prices according to their own standards, evaluations, and experience, to represent a fair market value.

Set a working budget (possibly a per-piece budget) and let the gallery know at the outset what the guidelines are. This saves both you and the gallery time and energy. You'll be able to focus on items that are comfortably within the range of your budget. Buy the best quality possible in whatever category you like. You will appreciate the quality for years. Don't hesitate to do some comparison shopping. Although each art object is unique in itself, you may find another piece in the same style that you enjoy equally as well.

The best dealers understand budgets, and respect your desire to get good quality at a fair price. They are happy to work with enthusiastic clients who want to incorporate beautiful art into their lives. Ask if the dealer offers terms, if you're interested in making your purchases on a payment plan.

GO TO AN AUCTION HOUSE

Attending an auction is an excellent way to learn about decorative arts, develop and add to a collection, and simply have a good time. Whether you attend as a buyer, seller, or observer, an auction is an experience that will enrich your understanding and enjoyment of the art and antiques world.

If you're a novice, it's important to choose a well-established auction house with a reputation for reliability. Try to be a patient observer and learn about the process as well as the value of items you may be interested in later on.

Buy a copy of the catalog and attend the viewing prior to the beginning of the auction itself. Each item, or "lot," that will be available for sale at the auction will be listed, and a professional estimate of selling price will be included. Professionals will be available during the viewing to answer questions and help you become familiar with the art objects as well as the

MATCHING ART TO ARCHITECTURE

If you're renovating an historic or old home of distinction, ask your favorite gallery owner or renovation specialist for guidance in choosing art that will fit your home.

504

ocess. Once bidding starts, it is done by "paddle,"
nall numbered placards used to signal a bid, which
e obtained before or during the auction.

HOOSING AN AUCTION

ind out about interesting auctions from the
proprietors of galleries you like, or ask to be
lded to the mailing list of a reputable auction house.
'ith these sources of information, you'll be informed
events that will feature quality items of interest to
u. Local newspapers and magazines also print
coming auction dates and locations. The
tablished auction houses that have earned a
putation for reliability and expertise generally have a
ngle location where they hold their auctions.
metimes an auction will be held at an estate site,
a seller's location.

Before attending the auction, spend some time
searching the art or antique you're interested in
dding on, so you'll be informed about its value and
n make an informed decision. Talk to people at the
lleries. Visit Internet sites to research your interests,
for information on upcoming auctions and recent
ction prices. There also are books available that
blish recent auction sales to help you get an idea of
ice and availability. Check your library or bookseller
r publications like Gordon's Price Annual.

There seems to be an air of mystery and
phistication that surrounds auctions, but don't let
at discourage you from discovering the auction
perience. They are enjoyable and educational for
yone who is interested in obtaining or learning
out art and antiques.

E REALISTIC

or many of us, an auction might seem an
opportunity to pick up an item at a bargain price.
ealize that there may be bargains to be found, but in
eneral, auctioned items are sold for a fair price.
here may be a "reserve price," which is a private
greement between the seller and the auctioneer on
e amount of a minimum bid.

If you educate yourself about the category you're
terested in, you'll be at an advantage at an auction.
's equally important to research the market value of
ny lot you may be considering. Remember that
ere is an auctioneer's commission of 10 to 15
ercent of the hammer price, to be paid in addition to
e purchase price, as well as applicable sales taxes.

Auctions are essentially competitive in nature,
ith potential buyers bidding against one another.
ait to become an active participant until you've
tended enough auctions to feel confident in your
wn knowledge, as well as in your understanding of
e auction process.

DESIGN

The following design books represent the premier works of selected designers, luxury homebuilders and architects.

This book is divided into 10 chapters, starting with design guidelines in regards to color, personality and collections. In these chapters, interior designer Perla Lichi presents beautiful, four-color photographs of the design commissions she has undertaken for clients accompanied by informative editorial on the investment value of professional interior design.

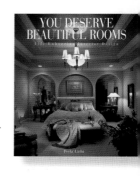

YOU DESERVE BEAUTIFUL ROOMS
120 pages, 9.75" x 14"
Home Design, Architecture
1-58862-016-6 $39.95   Hardcover

Orren Pickell is renowned as one of the nation's finest builders of custom homes. In this collection of more than 80 beautiful four-color photos and drawings, Pickell shows off some of his finest creations to give homeowners unique ideas on building a new home or adding to an existing one.

LUXURY HOMES & LIFESTYLES
120 pages, 9.75" x 14"
Architecture, Home Design
0-9642057-4-2 $39.95   Hardcover

Designer Susan Fredman has spent 25 years creating interiors, which, in one way or another, have been inspired by nature. In this book, she takes readers through rooms which reflect elements of our surroundings as they are displayed throughout the year.

AT HOME WITH NATURE
136 pages, 11.25" x 11.25"
Home Design, Architecture
1-58862-043-3 $39.95   Hardcover

The Ashley Group is proud to present these spe

CALL TO ORDE

BOOKS

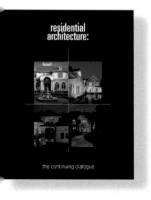

Michigan-based architect Dominick Tringali uses the skill and knowledge that has brought him over 20 industry awards to share strategies on building the ultimate dream house. By combining unique concepts with innovative techniques and materials, Dominick's portfolio displays an array of homes noted for their timeless appeal. This $45 million collection of elite, custom homes contains the residences of notable CEO's, lawyers, doctors and sports celebrities including Chuck O'Brien, Joe Dumars, Tom Wilson, Larry Wisne and Michael Andretti's estate in Pennsylvania.

**RESIDENTIAL
ARCHITECTURE:
THE CONTINUING DIALOGUE**
May 2002.
128 pages.
9" x 12"
Art & Architecture
1-58862-088-3
$39.95   Hardcover

Across the nation, homeowners often enlist the services of landscapers. Within this group lies an elite sector which specializes in breaking the mold on traditional landscaping. In this book, you will find truly groundbreaking approaches to the treatment of outdoor space.

**PORTFOLIO SERIES:
GARDEN DESIGN**
June 2002.
150 pages.
10" x 10"
Gardening,
Home Design
1-58862-087-5
$29.95   Hardcover

on luxury home style, design and architecture

Art Galleries

ART AT YOUR DOOR ....**(702) 256-7278**
8605 West Sahara, Las Vegas   Fax: (702) 255-5906
See Ad on Page: 509
<u>Principal/Owner:</u> Ken Zamani
<u>Additional Information:</u> Art & custom framing gallery presenting the works of internationally acclaimed artists, and offering the highest quality of custom framing.

INTERNATIONAL FINE ART & CUSTOM ....**(702) 990-2787**
10624 South Eastern Avenue, Suite E, Las Vegas   Fax: (702) 990-9005
See Ad on Page: 512
<u>Principal/Owner:</u> Steven Lebow, Gregg Ziegler
<u>e-mail:</u> touchstarsteve@yahoo.com

WIDMEN GALLERIES...**(702) 795-0003**
4795 Industrial Road, Las Vegas
See Ad on Page: 510, 511

ISCOVER BEAUTY AND EXCELLENCE IN ART & FRAMING

RUT

SHVAIKO

Providing the highest quality <u>custom framing</u> available. Thousands of exquisite designer frames.

WREN

A riveting display of fine art created by internationally acclaimed artists.

8605 West Sahara
(on the SW corner Sahara & Durango)

702.256.7278

Art and sculpture by VALENTI

Las Vegas' Newest Attraction......
overlooking the "strip"......
featuring ....

original fine art • Giclee' reproductions • bronze, stone, metal,
wood & glass sculpture • living art (custom water features)

<u>**NOW OPEN**</u> *- Our New (off-site) state-of-the- art facility provides*
digital printing and publishing services to suit the custom needs of
architects, builders, designers, artists, publishers and the general pub

M-F 10-6 SAT. 10-5 SUNDAY & EVENINGS BY APPOINTMENT
FINANCING AND ART CLASSES AVAILABLE
4795 Industrial Road, (1/2 block N. of Tropicana & 1-15)
(702) 795-0003

Widmen Galleries

▷ FINE ART

▷ PRINTING & PHOTO
REPRODUCTIONS

▷ PUBLISHING

Mirror, Mirror, on the Wall...

Unique Mirrors • Custom Mirrors • Custom Framing • Fine Art

International
Fine Art & Custom Framing

10624 South Eastern Avenue • Henderson, Nevada 89052
1 1/2 miles south of the 215 at Eastern and Horizon Ridge

702-990-ARTS (2787)

The Ashley Group Luxury Home Resource Collection

ou're searching for luxury home improvement resources, **The Ashley oup (www.theashleygroup.com)** is pleased to offer, as your final ination, the following **Home Books**: *Chicago, Washington DC, South Florida, Dallas/Fort Worth, Detroit, Atlanta, New York, Arizona, adelphia, Colorado* and the *Los Angeles* area. These comprehensive, nds-on guides to building, remodeling, decorating, furnishing, and ndscaping a luxury home are required reading for the serious and lective homeowner. With more than 700 full-color, beautiful pages per market, these hardcover volumes are the most complete and l-organized reference to the home industry. The **Home Books** cover aspects of the building and remodeling process, include listings of dreds of industry professionals, and are accompanied by informative l valuable editorial discussing the most recent trends. Ordering your opy of any of the **Home Books** now can ensure that you have the blueprints to your dream home, in your hand, today.

der your copies today and make your dream come true!

HE ASHLEY GROUP LUXURY HOME RESOURCE COLLECTION

Please send me the following Home Books! At $39.95 for each Home Book, plus $3.00 Shipping & Handling and Tax per book.

allas/Fort Worth Home Book *Premier Edition*	___ # of Copies	☐ Detroit Home Book *Premier Edition*	___ # of Copies
ew York Home Book *Premier Edition*	___ # of Copies	☐ Colorado Home Book *Premier Edition*	___ # of Copies
hicago Home Book *5th Edition*	___ # of Copies	☐ Los Angeles Home Book *Premier Edition*	___ # of Copies
ashington DC Home Book *Premier Edition*	___ # of Copies	☐ South Florida Home Book *Premier Edition*	___ # of Copies
rizona Home Book *Premier Edition*	___ # of Copies	☐ Philadelphia Home Book *Premier Edition*	___ # of Copies

red (# Of Books) _____ X $42.95 = $ _____ Total

Card: _____ Exp. Date:

: _____ Phone: _____

ss _____ Email: _____

_____ State: _____ Zip Code: _____

Send order to: Attn: Book Sales—Marketing, The Ashley Group—Cahners, 1350 E. Touhy Ave., Suite 1E, Des Plaines, Illinois 60018
Or Call Toll Free at: 1-888-458-1750 • Or E-mail ashleybooksales@cahners.com • Visit us on-line at www.theashleygroup.com

All orders must be accompanied by check, money order or credit card # for full amount.

Finally...
Las Vegas' Own
Home & Design
Sourcebook

The **Las Vegas Home Book** is your final destination when searching for home remodeling, building and decorating resource. This comprehensive, hands-on sourcebook to building, remodeling, decorating, furnishing, and landscaping a luxur home is required reading for the serious and discriminating homeowner. With more than 700 full-color, beautiful pages, t **Las Vegas Home Book** is the most complete and well-organiz reference to the home industry. This hardcover volume covers aspects of the process, includes listings of hundreds of indust professionals, and is accompanied by informative and valuab editorial discussing the most recent trends. Ordering your co of the **Las Vegas Home Book** now can ensure that you have t blueprints to your dream home, in your hand, today.

Order your copy now!

Published by
The Ashley Group
1740 Industrial Rd.,Las Vegas, NV 89118
702-614-4960 fax 702-263-6596
E-mail: ashleybooksales@cahners.com

HOME
THEATER

&

TECHNOLOGY

The Margison Residence at sunset, located in Mountain Trails Estates. Architect: South Coast Archite Builder: Bugby & Associates, Interior Design: David & Co., AV / Home Automation: Stereo Plus De

When Designing Your Dream Hom

Working closely with Architect, Builder, Interior Designer, the St Plus Design Team elega integrates High Perform Home Theater Sys seamlessly into any d Translating your H Entertainment Dreams in creative expression of personal taste and styl left, during the day o casual entertaining, a 36 provides the picture. Belo the evening or for spo events, a 100" screen d from a hidden recess in upper cabinet.

STEREO PLUS
DESIGN

Home Theater Rooms
▼
Multi-TV Media Rooms
▼
Beautiful Music Throughout
Your Home & Outdoor
Entertaining Areas
▼
Architectural Lighting
▼
Wireless Touchpanel
Automation Control

Call 876.4434

ind Out More About Stereo Plus Design On Page 528

To The Clean Lines Of Modern

The Tobian Residence at sunset, located in Spanish Hills Estates. Builder: Domanico Const., Interior Design: James Young of Jacqueline & Assoc., AV / Home Automation: Stereo Plus Design

Don't Forget The Popcorn...

agine, with the touch of the ntertaining Mood" button on Crestron wireless color chpanel, selected lights oughout your Home & tdoor entertaining areas gin to adjust to the perfect el, accenting your Homes' hitectural features and art as ll as creating mood, nosphere & drama. Next the ndow coverings begin to en, and as the fireplace ites, the House music stem begins to play your orite CD mix. Ph.D. in ctronics not required!

STEREO PLUS DESIGN

Home Theater Rooms
▼
Multi-TV Media Rooms
▼
Beautiful Music Throughout
Your Home & Outdoor
Entertaining Areas
▼
Architectural Lighting
▼
Wireless Touchpanel
Automation Control

Call 876.4434

Find Out More About Stereo Plus Design On Page 528

" There is *music* wherever there is

harmony, order and proportion. "

Sir Thomas Browne

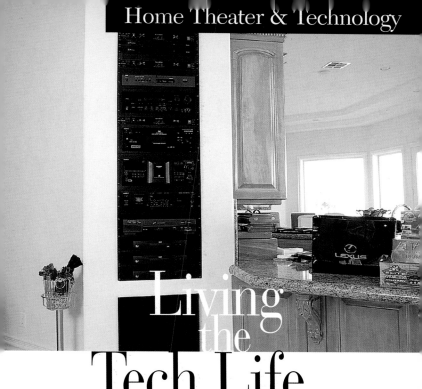

Home Theater & Technology

Living the Tech Life

519

Home technology just keeps getting better and better. Technology wizards continue to deliver bigger and better products less obtrusively, and more affordably, into our homes. What was once a rare home luxury has become a top priority item in new custom homes, and in home additions and renovations.

Sophisticated Las Vegas homeowners have had their level of appreciation for quality in sight and sound elevated through the years of experience in concert halls, movie theaters and sports arenas. As they gravitate toward making the home the focus of their lifestyle, and strive to incorporate that high level of performance into their leisure time at home, home technology becomes a more desirable and practical investment. Systems are used for viewing commercial movies, home videos, live concerts and sport events, playing games, and accessing interactive technology. Media or entertainment rooms, custom-sized and designed to deliver concert hall sound and a big, sharp picture, are frequently specified in new construction and remodeling projects. Interest in upscale prefabricated home theaters, which are far more luxurious than some of today's movie theaters, continues to increase. "Hey kids, let's go to the movies!"

Photo courtesy of **Absolute Audio-Video & Security Systems**

One Person's Project Estimate:

Your Personal Screening Room

It's fun to imagine, but what might it actually cost to undertake a project described in this chapter? The example below describes a typical project and gives a general estimate of the costs involved.

Project Description

Outfitting a room in the mid- to high-scale price range for a home theater

Initial consultation:	$0
Labor: $55/hour	$3,500
50-inch television	$4,000
DVD player	$900
VHS	$200
Amplifier with surround-sound decoder	$10,000
Six speakers with subwoofer	$10,000
Satellite dish (high definition)	$1,000
Delivery/installation	$2,500
Seating: Eight leather module seats	$15,000
Infrared sensors (Crestrom) to control lighting, motorized drapes, security system	$10,000
Total	**$57,000**

520

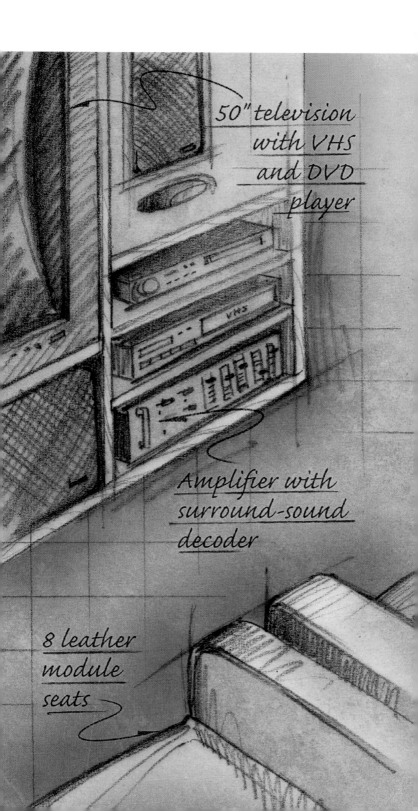

50" television
with VHS
and DVD
player

Amplifier with
surround-sound
decoder

8 leather
module
seats

THE IMPORTANCE OF A HOME THEATER DESIGN SPECIALIST

Home theater is widely specified as a custom home feature today. The sophisticated homeowner with a well-developed eye (and ear) for quality demands the latest technology in a home entertainment system that will provide pleasure for many years. Because of the fluid marketplace, the vast possibilities of the future, and the complexity of the products, it's crucial to employ an established professional to design and install your home theater.

The experts presented on the following pages can advise you on the best system for your home. They can find an appropriate cabinet (or direct you to expect custom cabinet makers), expertly install your system, and teach you to use it. Their expertise will make the difference.

THE HOME THEATER DESIGN PROCESS

Tell your builder or remodeling specialist early if you want a home theater, especially if built-in speakers, a large screen or a ceiling-mounted video projection unit are part of the plan.

Inform the interior designer so proper design elements can be incorporated. Window treatments to block out light and help boost sound quality, furnishings or fabrics to hide or drape speakers, and comfortable seating to enhance the media experience should be considered. If you plan to control the window treatments by remote control, these decisions will have to be coordinated.

Visit one of the following showrooms. Be ready to answer these questions:

• What is your budget? There is no upper limit on what you can spend.

• Do you want a television tube or projection video system? A DVD player or hi-fi VCR? Built-in or free-standing speakers?

• Do you want Internet access?

• What style of cabinetry and lighting do you want? Do you want lighting or a built-in bar? How much storage is needed?

• What are the seating requirements? Seating should be at least seven feet from the screen.

• Do you want whole-house control capability so you can distribute and control the system from different rooms of the house?

• How will you incorporate the system with the rest of the room? Must the home theater room meet other needs?

• Do you want extra luxuries, like multiple screens, or a remote control system that allows you to dim the lights and close the draperies? Ask your salesperson for ideas.

Will this room function in the future? As technology continues to change our lifestyle, plan for this room to grow and change as well. Ask your salesperson for advice.

Take your blueprints or pictures to a specialty store where an "experience room" is set up for firsthand testing of different components and knowledgeable consultants can answer your questions. Electronics is a complex subject, but a good consultant will educate, not mystify you.

An in-home consultation with the designer should take place early in the planning stages. You can discuss issues like speaker placement and location of wall control panels.

Before hiring a designer, make sure your service needs will be met in a timely and expert manner. Ask for the names of former and repeat clients for references.

Experienced audio-video or media consultants can astutely determine your needs. They can design and install an end product that is properly sized for your room, satisfies your desire for quality, and meets the terms of your budget. They respect cabinetry requirements and the decorating elements that must be addressed in the deliverance of a top quality home theater.

The media consultant should be willing to work with the architect, builder and interior designer to make sure your requirements will be met.

Home theaters are installed at the same time as the security and phone systems, before insulation and drywall. In new construction or remodeling, start making decisions at least two months before the drywall is hung. Allow four weeks for delivery and installation scheduling.

CREATING A HOME THEATER

For the best seat in the house, you'll need:

A large screen television and/or projection video system (from 32-inch direct view up to 200-inches, depending on the size of the room). New, compact products are available now.

A surround-sound receiver to direct sound to the appropriate speaker with proper channel separation.

A surround-sound speaker system, with front, rear, and center channel speakers and a sub-woofer for powerful bass response.

A hi-fi stereo VCR or DVD (digital video) player for ultimate audio and video quality.

Appropriate cabinetry, properly vented.

A comfortable environment, ideally a rectangular room with extra drywall to block out distractions. ■

PLAN AHEAD

Even if you aren't installing a home theater system right away, have a room designed to serve that purpose later. Get the wiring done and build the room an appropriate shape and size. Get the right antenna. Ask for double drywall for noise control.

THE FUTURE'S HERE

Smart homes, those with whole-house integrated control systems and computerized automation, even voice-activated automation, are a reality in the new century. Many professionals believe it will one day be as standard as central air conditioning. It will be commonplace for a system to start your morning coffee, crank up the furnace, close drapes during a downpour or send a fax.

BEST TIP:

Have phone lines pulled to every TV outlet in the house for Internet access and satellite reception.

Home Theater
Design

ABBOTT'S AUDIO AND VIDEO ....**(702) 871-7388**
  4601 West Sahara Avenue, Las Vegas Fax: (702) 871-5463
  See Ad on Page: 526, 527
  Principal/Owner: Chuck Abbott
  Website: www.abbotsav.com e-mail: info@abbottsav.com
  Additional Information: Custom design and installation of Home Audio, Video
  & Home Automation products.
ABSOLUTE AUDIO VIDEO & SECURITY ....**(702) 458-7233**
  3514 East Tropicana Ave #1C, Las Vegas Fax: (702) 458-8979
  See Ad on Page: 525
  Principal/Owner: Adam & Alex Bustios
  e-mail: absolute@sierranv.net
BANG & OLUFSEN ....**(702) 731-9200**
  3200 South Las Vegas Boulevard, Las Vegas Fax: (702) 731-9230
  See Ad on Page: 531
  Principal/Owner: Arthur Elliott
  Website: www.bang-olufsen.com
TECHNICOM SERVICES, INC. ....**(702) 639-8600**
  2530 Losee Road, North Las Vegas Fax: (702) 639-8620
  See Ad on Page: 529
  Principal/Owner: Jason Dunkerley
  e-mail: technicom@usa.com

ABSOLUTE
AUDIO-VIDEO & SECURITY

3514 E. Tropicana Ste.1-C Las Vegas, NV 89121
T 702.458.7233 F 702.458.8979

Home Theater So Real...
You Can Almost Smell The

Nine tastefully designed vignettes, each displaying different ideas as to how Home Theater might be presented in your home setting.

Whether your needs are Home Theater, Home Automation, Lighting or Computer Networking, we look forward to serving you in the way that is distinctly Abbott's Audio & Video.

Twenty years of exceeding our client's expectations.

STEREO PLUS DESIGN

Dedicated Multi-TV Media Rooms have quickly become a must have for the well appointed home. Located in Tournament Hills, a 100" HD Projection System is flanked by three 36" TV's!

Serving Our Clients Since 1987

The Home Of Your Dreams
Awaits Your Command...

Over the past 14 years Home Entertainment & Automation Control have come a lo way, and Stereo Plus Design has been there from the beginning. Stereo Plus Desi projects have been in long-term reliable service since 1987. A client list of updat testimonials is available upon request. Some of our past clients are available to call, a tell you first hand of their positive experience with our company over the years. N brother and I are directly responsible for each project from start to finish. We ha worked hard over many years to build a solid reputation for creative design, and person service, with on time delivery of equipment and accessories, at the guaranteed low price, while keeping open and accessible lines of communication with all part involved in the project. We cannot find employees who feel the same commitment excellence, so we can only take on a limited number of projects throughout the coun each year. In systems ranging from the affordable to the extreme, we guarantee perfect finish on each project without compromise on the finalized plan. M importantly, we treat each client with a level of professional, friendly service, rare today's fast paced and impersonal world. From the very first meeting, throughout t project and for the years that follow completion, we are here to help. Because of our o the top service, each of our clients, as well as the project architect, builder and inter designer have become friends, helping us build a rock solid word-of-mouth reputati one project at a time. Only the best from our family to yours! Dino & Darren Filardo

Ofc 702.876.4434 ▼ Stereo Plus Design ▼ Fax 702.255.992

Integrated
Home Systems

STEREO PLUS DESIGN ....**(702) 876-4434**
7473 West Lake Mead Road #100, Las Vegas   Fax: (702) 255-9922
See Ad on Page: 516, 517, 528
Principal/Owner: Dino A. Filardo
e-mail: stereoplus@lvcm.com
Additional Information: Specializing in custom design of home theater systems, beautiful music throughout your home, architectural lighting, home automation, telephone systems & more.

Go on, spoil yourself...
...with the ultimate in Home Theater entertainment

Pictures so sharp you feel you can reach in and touch the world beyond. Perfect sound from every direction wraps you in a total audio/video sensation.

The real world is put on hold as B&O puts you right in the center of the action.

We specialize in custom installations, light control and superb customer service wherever and whenever our customers need it.

To set up a free consultation in your home with one of our product specialists just call the store closest to you or better yet, stop by our store and experience Home Theater the way it was meant to be.

The BeoTheater Components
Available in 5 matching colors to coordinate with a wide range of decors.

BeoVision Avant 30"

30" State of the Art wide screen TV.

BeoSound 9000

Integrated 6 CD music system.

Beo4

Simple remote for easy operation.

Surround Sound speaker system with front, rear and center channel speakers.

BeoLab 1

Top of the line amplified loudspeaker.

BeoLab 6000

High performance amplified loudspeaker.

BeoLab 4000

Book shelf/wall mount amplified loudspeaker.

Location,
Location,
Location!

What better LOCATION for your
advertisement than the
LAS VEGAS HOME BOOK!

Just as our readers realize how important
location is when choosing a home, we realize
that it's just as important to you when
allocating your advertising dollars.
That's why we have successfully positioned the
LAS VEGAS HOME BOOK to reach
the high-end consumers you want as clients.

**Call 702-614-4960 to find out about our
unique marketing programs and
advertising opportunities.**

Published by
The Ashley Group
7140 Industrial Rd., Las Vegas, NV 89118
702-614-4960 fax 702-263-6598
E-mail: ashleybooksales@cahners.com

LOCATION

It's amazing what you can create when

Discover Summerlin's premier custom lot community.

Experience a lifestyle as beautiful as your surroundings. Perched high above the Las Vegas Valley, alongside the Red Rock Canyon National Conservation Area, The Ridges in Summerlin combines custom home lots with the natural landscape to create truly unique living environments with opportunities for breathtaking mountain and city views. Home to the world's first Nicklaus-designed Bear's Best golf course, The Ridges is poised to become the most exclusive golf mecca in the Southwest. Lot ownership comes with full privileges at Club Ridges, our private clubhouse. Discover an unparalleled lifestyle. Discover the incomparable location. Discover The Ridges today.

your lead architect is Mother Nature.

THE
Ridges

SUMMERLIN

Custom lot offerings from the $300,000s to the millions. Stop by Summerlin's Custom Homes & Lots Sales Office at the corner of West Sahara and Town Center Drive for a personal tour. Call 702.255.2500, 877.969.HOME or visit summerlin.com to learn more.

"Must I leave thee,

Paradise?

Thus leave thee,

native soil,

these happy walks

& shades. "

John Milton

Home Sweet Home

One of the most endearing charms of this area is the wide diversity and individuality of its neighborhoods. Whether your fantasy is to live in a stately, traditional home surrounded by lush sweeping lawns, or an ultra-modern, custom built home overlooking a golf course, you are sure to find a neighborhood to call home. To savvy homeowners, location is the most valuable of assets, and has long been their mantra. Today's state-of-the-art homebuilders have given life to new communities in masterfully planned environments. Visually delightful and diverse, yet cohesive in architectural style and landscape, these communities address with impeccable taste the needs of their residents: proximity to excellent schools, shops, restaurants, favored leisure pursuits, the workplace. Safe havens, often in country or golf course settings, these developments cater to the homeowners' active lifestyles. Artistically designed for ease, these gracious homes welcome family and guests; they are sanctuaries in which to entertain, relax and nourish the spirit.

Photo courtesy of **Christopher Homes**
Photo by **Greg Cava Photography**

THE ULTIMATE IN LUXURY LIVING

The builders and developers of custom homes in upscale locations throughout the city and the suburbs realize the value of simplicity and strive to deliver it.

Simplicity is one of the qualities we most desire in our lives. By offering a community designed and built on the philosophy that homeowners deserve a beautiful environment, peaceful surroundings and luxurious amenities to enhance their lives, locations like those featured in the following pages deliver simplicity on a luxury scale.

Homeowners who live in these kinds of communities and locations know what they want. They want an environment where architecture and nature exist in harmony. Where builders have proven dedication to protecting the natural surroundings. They want recreation, like golf, swimming, lakes, walk and biking paths, or tennis courts. They want to live where there's a sense of community, and the convenience of close-by shopping and transportation. Finally, they want the conveniences of a well-planned community — guidelines on buildings and landscaping, strong community identity, and commitment to quality.

FINDING THE PERFECT LOCATION

Think about what kind of location would enhance the lifestyle of yourself and your family:

• Do you need to be near transportation?

• Do you want the security of a gated community?

• What kind of recreational amenities do you want? Golf, tennis or pool? Paths, fishing lakes, or horse trails? Party facilities, restaurants?

• What kind of natural environment do you prefer? Wildlife sanctuary, urban elegance, club luxury?

• What kind of home do you want to build? Determine your dream house fits the overall essence of a particular community. Some planned communities allow only certain builders at their locations. Find out if these builders create homes that would satisfy your desires.

THE VALUE OF A LUXURY LOCATION

The availability of building sites diminishes with every passing year, and the builders and developers of our finest residential locations know that quality must be established to attract custom home owners. Their commitment to building top quality homes is apparent in the designs and materials used in their projects and in the reputations their locations enjoy.

The demand for homes built in these locations is growing. Their benefits, plus the unique opportunity to build a new custom home in a totally fresh, and new environment, are very enticing. ■

THE COMMUNITY SPIRIT

Enclave neighborhoods built in luxury locations have the benefit of being part of two communities. The neighborhood identity is strong and so is the larger community spirit. It's the best of both worlds.

THE MASTER PLAN

Homes and landscapes in "master plan" locations are as unique and customized as anywhere in the Las Vegas Valley. However, they are established according to a well-defined overall plan, which gives the homeowners the security of knowing that the high-quality look of their neighborhood will be rigorously upheld.

HE HOWARD HUGHES CORPORATION ....**(702) 791-4000**
10000 West Charleston Boulevard Suite 200, Las Vegas   Fax: (702) 791-4476
See Ad on Page: 534, 535, 540
<u>Principal/Owner:</u> Daniel Van Epp, President
<u>Website:</u> www.howardhughes.com <u>e-mail:</u> khaley@thhc.com
<u>Additional Information:</u> Real Estate developer - 22,500 acre master-planned
community of Summerlin as well as commercial and retail centers.
OUTHERN HIGHLANDS ESTATES ....**(702) 616-2500**
One Robert Trent Jones Lane, Las Vegas   Fax: (702) 616-2540
See Ad on Page: 164, 165, 541
<u>Website:</u> www.southernhighlandsestates.com

Your entry to extraordinary custom living.

Welcome to Willow Falls, a unique gated community in The Willows
village of Summerlin where you'll find spectacular 1/3-acre custom
home sites for sale in a truly magnificent setting. And with amenities
such as tennis, basketball, play area, park and beautiful paseo, Willow
Falls offers the best of both worlds – your dream home in Las Vegas'
most coveted community. For more information about Summerlin's
custom lots, visit our Custom
Homes & Lots Sales Center.
And start living the good life.

FIND YOURSELF HERE.

HE HOWARD HUGHES CORPORATION ....**(702) 791-4000**
10000 West Charleston Boulevard Suite 200, Las Vegas   Fax: (702) 791-4476
See Ad on Page: 534, 535, 540
Principal/Owner: Daniel Van Epp, President
Website: www.howardhughes.com e-mail: khaley@thhc.com
Additional Information: Real Estate developer - 22,500 acre master-planned
community of Summerlin as well as commercial and retail centers.

OUTHERN HIGHLANDS ESTATES ....**(702) 616-2500**
One Robert Trent Jones Lane, Las Vegas   Fax: (702) 616-2540
See Ad on Page: 164, 165, 541
Website: www.southernhighlandsestates.com

Your entry to extraordinary custom living.

Welcome to Willow Falls, a unique gated community in The Willows

village of Summerlin where you'll find spectacular 1/3-acre custom

home sites for sale in a truly magnificent setting. And with amenities

such as tennis, basketball, play area, park and beautiful paseo, Willow

Falls offers the best of both worlds – your dream home in Las Vegas'

most coveted community. For more information about Summerlin's

custom lots, visit our Custom

Homes & Lots Sales Center.

And start living the good life.

SUMMERLIN
FIND YOURSELF HERE.

www.summerlin.com | 877-969-HOME

Summerlin Custom Homes & Lots Sales Center
Take US 95 north to Summerlin Parkway, right on Town Center Drive. 702-255-2500

Finally...
Las Vegas' Own
Home & Design
Sourcebook

The **Las Vegas Home Book** is your final destination when searching for home remodeling, building and decorating resources. This comprehensive, hands-on sourcebook to building, remodeling, decorating, furnishing, and landscaping a luxury home is required reading for the serious and discriminating homeowner. With more than 700 full-color, beautiful pages, the **Las Vegas Home Book** is the most complete and well-organized reference to the home industry. This hardcover volume covers all aspects of the process, includes listings of hundreds of industry professionals, and is accompanied by informative and valuable editorial discussing the most recent trends. Ordering your copy of the **Las Vegas Home Book** now can ensure that you have the blueprints to your dream home, in your hand, today.

Order your copy now!

LAS VEGAS
HOME
BOOK

Published by
The Ashley Group
1740 Industrial Rd.,Las Vegas, NV 89118
702-614-4960 fax 702-263-6596
E-mail: ashleybooksales@cahners.com

INDEXES

INDEXES

design • feng shui

"If eyes were Made for seeing, Then Beauty is its own excuse."

Ralph Waldo Emerson

547

Alphabetical Index

Professional Index

Milton Homer Fine Home Furnishings 191
Quality Painting & Décor 479
rEvolution 400, 401

Home Theater & Sound

Audio/Video Retailers
Abbott's Audio 526, 527
Absolute Audio Video & Security 525
Bang & Olufsen .531
Furniture Showcase 221, 437
Stereo Plus Design 516, 517, 528
Technicom Services, Inc. 529

Design/Build
Technicom Services, Inc. 529

Entertainment Centers
Golan Cabinets 296, 297

Home Theater Design
Abbott's Audio 526, 527
Bang & Olufsen .531
Custom Cabinet Factory 349
Majestic Construction, Inc. 326, 327, 347
Stereo Plus Design 516, 517, 528

Integrated Home Systems
Abbott's Audio 526, 527
Absolute Audio Video & Security 525
ILA 456
Lighting Design Center 466
Stereo Plus Design 516, 517, 528
Technicom Services, Inc. 529

Lighting
ILA 456

Security System Contractors
Absolute Audio Video & Security 525
Technicom Services, Inc. 529

Telecom Systems
Absolute Audio Video & Security 525
Stereo Plus Design 516, 517, 528
Technicom Services, Inc. 529

Interior Designers

American Traditional
A Designing Woman 184
Coronado Consulting 443
Furniture Showcase 221, 437
Harmony Designs 186, 187
Herbert Gordon Press Design 188, 189
Joy Bell Design Associates, Inc 222
Milton Homer Fine Home Furnishings 191
Paula Corvin Interior Designers 194, 195
Rio Designs 217
Statement of Style 220
Sydni Jay Associates - Designers 218, 219
The Moffitt Partnership 89

Art Deco
De Atelier Design Group 183
Harmony Designs 186, 187
Joy Bell Design Associates, Inc 222
Panache Interior Design 192
Prism Interiors 182
Rio Décor Design & Fine Art 193, 544, 545
Rio Designs 217
Statement of Style 220

Asian
Joy Bell Design Associates, Inc 222
Nest Featherings 264, 434, 435
Paula Corvin Interior Designers 194, 195
Prism Interiors 182
Sydni Jay Associates – Designers 218, 219

Colonial
Coronado Consulting 443
Harmony Designs 186, 187
Herbert Gordon Press Design 188, 189
Magdalena's 412, 413, 429
Rio Designs 217
Sydni Jay Associates - Designers 218, 219

Contemporary
A Designing Woman 184
Coronado Consulting 443
De Atelier Design Group 183
Harmony Designs 186, 187
Interior Motives 170, 171, 185
Jan Stevens Design 190
Joy Bell Design Associates, Inc 222
Magdalena's 412, 413, 429
Nest Featherings 264, 434, 435
Panache Interior Design 192
Paula Corvin Interior Designers 194, 195
Prism Interiors 182
Rio Décor Design & Fine Art 193, 544, 545
Rio Designs 217
Stanley & Associates 196
Statement of Style 220
Sydni Jay Associates - Designers 218, 219
The Moffitt Partnership 89

Country
A Designing Woman 184
Diane Cabral Impressions 223
Harmony Designs 186, 187
Joy Bell Design Associates, Inc 222
Magdalena's 412, 413, 429
Statement of Style 220
Sydni Jay Associates - Designers 218, 219

Eclectic
A Designing Woman 184
Coronado Consulting 443
De Atelier Design Group 183
Diane Cabral Impressions 223
Interior Motives 170, 171, 185
Jan Stevens Design 190
Magdalena's 412, 413, 429
Nest Featherings 264, 434, 435
Panache Interior Design 192
Prism Interiors 182
Rio Décor Design & Fine Art 193, 544, 545
Rio Designs 217
Statement of Style 220
Sydni Jay Associates - Designers 218, 219

English
Harmony Designs 186, 187
Magdalena's 412, 413, 429
Milton Homer Fine Home Furnishings 191
Nest Featherings 264, 434, 435
Paula Corvin Interior Designers 194, 195
Rio Designs 217
Sydni Jay Associates - Designers 218, 219

Feng Shui
Coronado Consulting 443
De Atelier Design Group 183
Joy Bell Design Associates, Inc 222
Magdalena's 412, 413, 429
Panache Interior Design 192
Paula Corvin Interior Designers 194, 195
Prism Interiors 182
Rio Décor Design & Fine Art 193, 544, 545

French
A Designing Woman 184
Coronado Consulting 443
European Home Living Inc. 432, 433

553

Professional Index

555